FOR JEFFREY—
I HOPE YOU ENJOY THE
BOOK AND HAVE A CHANCE
TO SEE THE SHIPS UP
CLOSE.
Best Wishes,
Mark Thompson

Steamboats & Sailors
OF THE
Great Lakes

Steamboats & Sailors

OF THE
Great Lakes

MARK L. THOMPSON

WAYNE STATE UNIVERSITY PRESS   DETROIT

GREAT LAKES BOOKS

A complete listing of the books in this series can be found at the back of this volume

Philip P. Mason, Editor
Walter P. Reuther Library, Wayne State University

Dr. Charles K. Hyde, Associate Editor
Department of History, Wayne State University

Advisory Editors

Great Lakes Books edition copyright © 1991 by Wayne State University Press, Detroit, Michigan 48202. All rights are reserved. No part of this book may be reproduced without formal permission. Manufactured in the United States of America.

98 97 96 95 94   7 6 5 4 3

Library of Congress Cataloging-in-Publication Data

Thompson, Mark L., 1945–
    Steamboats and sailors of the Great Lakes / Mark L. Thompson.
        p.   cm.
    Includes bibliographical references and index.
    ISBN 0-8143-2359-6 (alk. paper).
    1. Inland water transportation—Great Lakes—History. 2. Steamboats—Great Lakes—History. I. Title.
    HE619.G73T46 1991
      386′.22436—dc20   91-12663
                                              CIP

Designer: Mary Primeau

For Scott and Meredith Thompson,
who bring such great joy to my life

Contents

Preface

Because I grew up in a small port community on the northern shores of Lake Huron, some of my earliest memories are of the lake freighters. From the bathing beach where I spent most of my summer days, I regularly saw the long ships passing across the horizon or steaming in and out of the Port of Calcite, which was just down the shore. To a small boy, the freighters were a source of fascination and mystery.

Being totally unfamiliar with Archimedes' Law, I was amazed that the massive ships could float. After all, steel doesn't float, nor does stone, so a steel ship full of stone shouldn't either! (Even understanding Archimedes' Law, I still find it miraculous that the huge freighters float.)

What went on aboard the freighters was also a complete mystery to me as a child. From my vantage point on the beach, the ships were nothing more than hulls and superstructures. I had no concept whatsoever of their inner complexities, or what crewmembers did aboard them. My friends and I were sure that crewmembers spent a lot of their time swimming during the hot summer months, as we did, and presumed that they also fished on nice days, trolling for whitefish or lake trout off the fantail. A constant point of debate was whether crewmembers waterskied behind the boats. We never saw anyone skiing along behind a freighter, but it just made sense that they would.

The time I have spent aboard freighters in the ensuing years has removed many of the mysteries about the ships, but none of my fascination with them. It is always a thrill to go aboard, and I will still drive miles out of my way merely to watch boats in the rivers or at ports around the lakes.

In my travels, I have come across hundreds of people from all walks of life who share my fascination with ships—people hungry for information about the boats and the maritime industry on the Great Lakes. Since I would rather talk boats than eat (and I am a prodigious eater), I have always enjoyed sharing my knowledge with other boatwatchers.

While working as an administrator at the Great Lakes Maritime Academy several years ago, I developed an introductory course about the industry for new cadets, each of whom had an insatiable appetite for information about the shipping industry on the lakes. In the course I tried to present a general overview of the industry, including information on the evolution of bulk freighters, crews, ports, cargoes, loading and unloading equipment, and so on. My lecture notes for that course eventually evolved into this book.

In writing *Steamboats and Sailors*, my goal has been to remove some of the mysteries about the ships and the industry, providing readers with the factual information necessary to arrive at a basic understanding of the Great Lakes shipping industry. It is not a definitive work on the industry, but I have tried to answer the questions that have been asked most often over the years by people who share, at least to some degree, my ongoing fascination with the boats.

There are many people around the lakes far more qualified to write a book about the industry than I am. On every topic I have covered, it has become clear to me how much I don't know. Nonetheless, I think readers will find that I have been able to deal adequately, if not always expertly, with each topic. After all, expertise is relative, and I know that there are many people with an interest in the industry who have far less knowledge about it than I do. It is for them, the boatwatchers and armchair captains, that this book is written.

For those who know more about the industry than I do, I hope they will accept *Steamboats and Sailors* in the spirit in which it was written: As a testimony to the sailors and ships that have played such pivotal roles in the development of North America, and in my life.

Most of all, I hope that readers enjoy the book, and that it contributes to their enjoyment and appreciation of the Great Lakes maritime industry.

Over the years, many people have contributed to the writing of this book, but none more than my family. My father, a former Great Lakes sailor and for many years a dock foreman at Presque Isle Corporation—the Port of Stoneport—loved the boats, and some of his fascination with the shipping industry rubbed off on me at an early age. My interest in writing was always encouraged by my mother, whose unwavering love and support has also helped steer me through some stormy seas. The rest of the Thompson clan—Gary, Liz, Gordon, Jenny Rose, and my own children, Meredith, Angela, and Scott—have each, in their own unique and important ways, contributed to this endeavor.

Betty and Jim Wilson have always run the best "motel" in Cleveland, and the vacancy sign was always lit when I needed a place to stay. Captain Wilson also contributed significantly to my knowledge of the boats, as did hundreds of Great Lakes sailors I have known over the years. While all of them cannot be listed here, I would specifically like to thank the crewmembers who served on the *Edward B. Greene, Benson Ford,* and *S. T. Crapo* while I was aboard those vessels. This book would have been impossible without their cooperation.

Captain Bob Massey has been a patient teacher and good friend for more than twenty years. He is an outstanding mariner and one of the few real "iron men" I've ever shipped with.

In doing research for this book, valuable assistance was provided by Captain Bud Zeber, John Greenwood, Gavin Sproul, Bob Wright, the staff at Bowling Green State University's Institute for Great Lakes Research, the staff of the Coast Guard's Marine Safety Evaluation Branch, George Miller of the Canadian Lake Carriers' Association, the staff of the Dominion Marine Association, personnel at the Lake Carriers' Association, the crew of the mailboat *J. W. Westcott,* and port officials of the International Association of Great Lakes Ports, who have been both good friends and sources of great insight into the shore side of the industry.

Finally, I need to thank Barbara Terry, although "thank you" doesn't begin to express my appreciation.

May Barbara and the many family members, friends, business associates, and shipmates who have contributed so thoughtfully and generously to the writing of *Steamboats and Sailors of the Great Lakes,* and to my life, accept this book as a small token of my heartfelt appreciation.

1

Blue Highways, Red Rivers, Long Ships, and Iron Men

Piercing the heart of the nation, reaching the rich prairies where grow the most bounteous crops, linking the rich iron ore of the West and the choicest fuel of the East, touching on every shore a verdure of forest growth of untold depths, it is little wonder that the lakes attracted a courageous and enterprising people, little wonder that cities and towns sprang up, and that white-winged ships appeared and multiplied to freight the commerce of this thrifty people.

—J. B. Mansfield,
History of the Great Lakes, 1899

November. Gales. Shipwrecks! The three words are almost synonymous to the sailors who crew the huge freighters that operate on the Great Lakes. During the fall, warm moist weather systems moving north and east out of the Great Plains clash with the colder air that hovers along the U.S.-Canadian border, spawning numerous gales and storms that unleash their awesome fury on the lakes. Throughout the fall these cyclonic low pressure systems regularly batter the lakes with winds that often exceed 50 miles an hour, piling the seas into towering black waves that tear at the long ships with unrelenting ferocity. Over the history of the Great Lakes shipping industry, the gales and storms of November have wrecked hundreds of ships and sent thousands of sailors to watery graves.

For a few days in November 1975, the attention of the entire nation was riveted on the Great Lakes following the sinking of the *Steamer (Str.) Edmund Fitzgerald* in a furious storm on Lake Superior. After being battered for a full day, the 729-foot freighter disappeared during the early evening hours of November 10, only 16 miles from the sheltered waters of Whitefish Bay and the entrance to the St. Marys River. Captain Ernest McSorley and the twenty-eight crew members who served under his command aboard the *Fitzgerald* disappeared with their ship.

As is usually the case with shipwrecks, the story of the *Fitzgerald*'s sinking was front page news across the U.S. and Canada for a few days following the disaster. Then, when reporters had covered the tragedy from every conceivable angle, the story rapidly faded from media prominence. In all likelihood, the *Fitzgerald* would soon have been forgotten by most people if the disaster had not been immortalized in a popular ballad by Canadian singer Gordon Lightfoot. "The Wreck of the *Edmund Fitzgerald*" soared to the top of the pop music charts and, even today, continues to be played regularly on radio stations across North America. The song romanticizes the wreck of the *Fitzgerald*, the gales of November, and "the big lake they call Gitchee Gumee" that never gives up its dead. Because of Lightfoot's song, the story of the "*Fitz*" has been indelibly imprinted on the minds of people across the continent.

Sailors on the Great Lakes have also been affected by the lore of the *Fitzgerald*, a constant reminder of the inherently hazardous nature of their occupation and the frailty of their ships in the face of nature's overpowering fury. With the approach of November, it is unlikely that there is a single sailor on the lakes who is not reminded of the loss of the *Fitz*. Most of them would prefer to spend November ashore.

As crewmembers aboard the *Str. Walter A. Sterling* enjoyed the balmy Indian summer breezes and tranquil seas in the early fall of 1984, they were acutely aware that the first storms of November lurked just over the western horizon. A few of them had saved up their vacation time so they could avoid being on the lakes in November. But most of the crewmembers on the 826-foot flagship of the Cleveland-Cliffs Iron Company fleet knew that they were destined to spend the treacherous month on the taconite run from the ore docks on Lake Superior to the unloading docks on the lower lakes. They watched as the days ticked off toward November, mindful that November 10, 1984, would mark the ninth anniversary of the sinking of the *Fitzgerald*. They watched the calendar and the barometer and they waited, wondering what November would hold for them and their ship.

The crewmen aboard the *Sterling* had no cause for worry, however. Before the first November storm beat its track across the lakes, the *Sterling* had laid up at a shipyard in Superior, Wisconsin. The sailors would be spared the hazards of November on the lakes, but it brought no joy to their hearts.

When they moored their ship at Superior in October, it didn't just mark an early end to the season, as occasionally happens in an industry whose fortunes fluctuate with the vicissitudes of the national economy. For the *Sterling* and its crew, it was just plain *the end*. After 130 years of operations on the lakes,

Cleveland-Cliffs was getting out of the marine transportation business.

Several crewmembers from the *Sterling* lived in the twin ports of Superior, Wisconsin, and Duluth, Minnesota. Through the winter months of 1984–85 they watched as shipyard workers removed the big red-orange *C* from the ship's massive black smokestack and replaced it with the familiar oval logo of the Ford Motor Company, new owners of the *Sterling* and its "sister ship," the *Str. Edward B. Greene*. It was a sad metamorphosis to watch, not just for the former Cliffs sailors, many of whom would never sail again, but also for thousands of Great Lakes sailors and maritime buffs who had grown familiar with the Cliffs's boats over the years.

Hundreds of fleets had come and gone during the long history of the industry, but Cliffs had been there from the very beginning. Cliffs was the oldest operating fleet on the lakes in 1985, and when their crews walked off the two ships for the last time, many people questioned whether the Great Lakes shipping industry itself might not be facing extinction.

Cliffs's departure from marine operations left only fifteen U.S. and fifteen Canadian bulk fleets on the Great Lakes; at one time there were more than three hundred. Of the fleets that survived in 1985, only seven U.S. fleets were involved in the iron ore trade, the mainstay of the industry for a century on the American side of the lakes. Only eighty-eight ships were left under U.S. Great Lakes registry, and only about half of them operated during the 1984 season, the worst on the lakes since the Great Depression of the 1930s. Things were not much better on the Canadian side of the industry, which was plagued by downturns in shipments of both iron ore and grain. The Great Lakes shipping industry had weathered slumps before, but nothing in its three-hundred-year history could compare to the dismal situation that existed in 1985.

The Great Lakes shipping industry can trace its lineage to the launching on Lake Erie in 1679 of the *Griffon*, a 60-foot galley of about 50 tons. The sailing vessel had been built by Robert Cavalier, better known as Sieur de la Salle, a French explorer who had been commissioned to search for a passage through North America to China. Before the launch of the *Griffon*, only Indian canoes had operated on the four lakes above Niagara Falls.

Some historians and writers have cavalierly, but

erroneously, traced the roots of the Great Lakes shipping industry to the birchbark canoes that had been in use on the lakes since long before the first Europeans ever set foot on North American shores. While canoes were clearly the first vessels on the lakes and the Indians did use them to engage in commerce with other tribes, they are not part of the genealogy of the bulk shipping industry that evolved on the lakes.

It was the *Griffon*, the first sailing ship to operate on the upper lakes, that signalled the dawning of the Great Lakes shipping industry that we know today. Ironically, the *Griffon* was also the first ship to succumb to a fall storm on the lakes, vanishing with all hands and a cargo of pelts during a four-day blow that struck while it was on the return leg of its maiden voyage—an augury of things to come for generations of ships and sailors on the great inland seas of North America.

Ships, however, are only one component of the Great Lakes bulk shipping industry. In order to understand the industry and how it developed and evolved, it is necessary to study the entire system, which includes ships, people, cargoes, and the waterway itself. Each of the four primary constituent parts of the system functions in a symbiotic relationship with the other parts. No part could have developed to its present state of sophistication without concurrent development of the other parts.

The story of the Great Lakes shipping industry is a story of change, and the catalyst for that change has always been *economics*. Economics justified construction of the *Griffon* in 1679, and economics forced Cleveland-Cliffs to abandon their shipping operations in 1984. In the interim, virtually every change that occurred in the system was fueled by economic considerations.

Blue Highways

Cleveland-Cliffs entered the shipping business in August 1855 when they chartered the brigantine *Columbia* to carry ore from the company's mining operations near Marquette, Michigan, to Cleveland for overland shipment by rail to iron smelters near Pittsburgh. The *Columbia* carried the first cargo of iron ore through the two locks on the mile-long ship canal that had just been completed at Sault Sainte Marie, Michigan. The canal and locks allowed ships, for the first time, to bypass the unnavigable rapids on the St. Marys River, which connects Lake Superior and Lake Huron. The Soo Locks, as they have come to be known, along with the locks of the original Welland Canal, which bypassed Niagara Falls and connected Lake Ontario with Lake Erie, made it possible for ships to travel from the St. Lawrence River at the east end of Lake Ontario to Chicago and Duluth in the west over a vast blue highway of commerce.

The five Great Lakes—Ontario, Erie, Huron, Michigan, and Superior—have a combined surface area of more than 95,000 square miles and constitute the greatest concentration of freshwater on planet Earth. They are a dominant feature on the topography of North America, 1,200 miles inland from the Atlantic Ocean. Geologists tell us that the Great Lakes were formed by the glaciers that covered the region on and off for a million years during the last ice age. The viscous blanket of ice, several miles thick, ground out the troughs that would eventually become the freshwater seas.

The five lakes began to evolve during the final recession of the glaciers, about eighteen thousand years ago. As the leading edge of the great ice sheet gradually withdrew northward, the southern portions of Lake Michigan and Lake Erie were the first to emerge, followed three to five thousand years later by the more northerly lakes—Huron, Ontario, and Superior. Fed by a steady flow of meltwater from the receding glacier, the lakes probably reached their present form about thirty-five hundred years ago. By geological standards, then, they are very young.

Evidence suggest that Indians may have arrived in the region even before the glaciers had fully retreated from the Great Lakes basin, between 8,000 B.C. and 2,500 B.C. Their origins are still a topic of debate, but the most widely held view is that they immigrated into North America from northeastern Asia between 12,000 B.C. and 9,000 B.C., probably crossing at what is now the Bering Strait between Siberia and Alaska.

By the sixteenth century, when Europeans first visited the lakes, the 7,900-mile shoreline bordering the Great Lakes was home to more than twenty

13

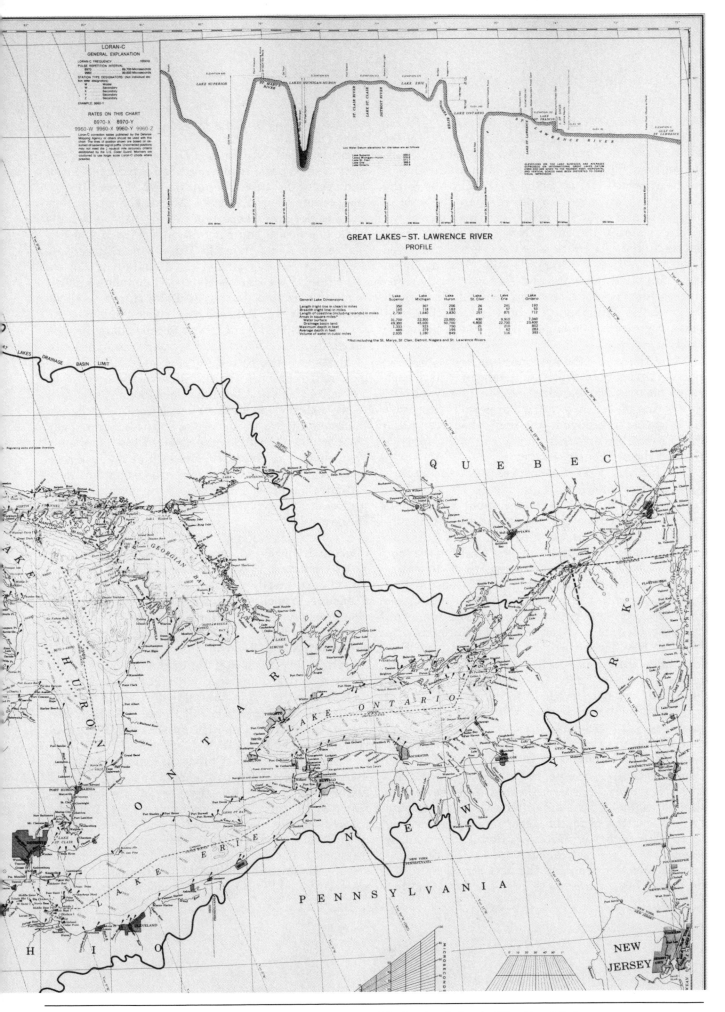

Navigational chart of the Great Lakes.

American Indian tribes, which belonged to three major language groups. In the north and west of the region were the Ottawa, Potawatomi, Fox, Illinois, Menominee, Sauk, and Ojibway (often referred to as the Chippewa)—all of whom spoke dialects of the Algonquian language. To the east, in the area of Lake Erie and Lake Ontario, were the tribes of the Iroquois family, including Neutrals, Huron, Erie, and the famous five nations of the Iroquois that lived in northern New York State—the Seneca, Onondaga, Mohawk, Oneida, and Cayuga. In the area that we now know as Green Bay, in northern Wisconsin, lived the Winnebago, the only tribe in the Great Lakes region that belonged to the Sioux linguistic family.[1]

While there is some evidence to suggest that the Indians' first contact with Europeans may have been with a party of Norsemen who made a foray into the area in the eleventh century, the period of continuous European presence in the region began with the first French settlements along the St. Lawrence River in the sixteenth century.

The Indians' first experiences with the French explorers were not always good ones. On one of his early trips to the St. Lawrence region, for example, Jacques Cartier reportedly kidnapped all of the important local chiefs and hauled them back to France for exhibition. The Indians all died while on the trip. The French later also aroused the ire of the entire Iroquois Nation by siding with the Hurons in their ongoing war with the Iroquois. The hostile Iroquois tribes blocked further French explorations westward along the lower St. Lawrence, and the Europeans did not have free access to Lake Ontario or Lake Erie until an accord was reached between the warring Indian factions in 1678. The westward explorations continued, however, as the French reverted to use of an ancient Indian trade route that connected the St. Lawrence with Georgian Bay on the east side of Lake Huron via the Ottawa River, Lake Nipissing, and the French River.

In 1610 or 1612, Samuel de Champlain, the Governor of New France, as Canada was then known, dispatched eighteen-year-old Etienne Brule to travel the route with a group of Hurons who were returning to their homes on Georgian Bay after a trading expedition to the settlements along the St. Lawrence. Brule was probably the first European to see the upper lakes, and there is some evidence that around 1615 he and his Huron guides also visited Lake Ontario.

Brule remained with the Hurons for most of the next two decades, exploring northern Lake Huron and eventually travelling up the St. Marys River to the present site of Sault Ste. Marie. His long career as an explorer and expert on the ways of the Indians came to a brutal end when he was clubbed to death and reportedly eaten by the Hurons in 1632, supposedly as the result of a dispute over an Indian woman.

Following in Brule's footsteps, Champlain himself made the arduous journey to Lake Huron in about 1615, and he was followed by a stream of explorers, missionaries, and traders who fanned out across the lakes. In 1634, Jean Nicolet made a reconnaissance of northern Lake Huron and northern Lake Michigan, still searching for the elusive trade route to China that had first brought Christopher Columbus to the Americas in 1492. When Nicolet's entourage landed on the western shore of Lake Michigan, near what is now Green Bay, he greeted the astonished Winnebagoes in an embroidered China damask robe he had carried with him in order to be appropriately attired when he was received by the merchants and princes of Cathay. Unfortunately, Green Bay was not Cathay.

With the cessation of hostilities between the Iroquois and Hurons in about 1678, the areas around Lake Ontario and Lake Erie, including Niagara Falls, were finally opened for exploration by the French. A Franciscan friar, Father Louis Hennepin, was probably the first European to see the breathtaking Niagara escarpment. Hennepin accompanied the Sieur de la Salle, who was continuing the futile search for a western route to China. La Salle established a shipyard above Niagara Falls, and in 1679 he launched the *Griffon* and sailed west and north to explore Lake Erie, the Detroit River, Lake St. Clair, the St. Clair River, Lake Huron, and the Green Bay region of Lake Michigan.

Although no route to China was found through the lakes, the region's rich bounty of fur-bearing animals attracted fur traders and trappers in growing numbers. Often they were accompanied by Catholic priests who also saw a rich bounty of Indians in need of conversion to Christianity. The sites of the early missions became the centers for fur trading, and small communities gradually grew up as settlers were attracted by the lure of economic opportunity.

Domination of the Great Lakes area by the French ended in 1763 with their defeat by the British in the Seven Years' War. The British maintained their supremacy throughout the vast region around the lakes until the end of the Revolutionary War. The Peace of Paris in 1793, which marked the end of hostilities between England and her former colonies along the Atlantic Coast, resulted in establishment of a boundary between British Canada and the fledgling United States of America to the south. The boundary line was drawn basically down the middle of Lakes Superior, Huron, Erie, and Ontario, with lands south and west of the lakes being ceded to the U.S., while England retained its claim to the vast wilderness areas north of the lakes.

Until the end of the War of 1812, most ships on the Great Lakes were either U.S. or British military vessels. But with the peace at the close of that war, a growing flood of settlers poured into the region. Passenger and cargo vessels soon outnumbered military ships. For a hundred years, until early in the twentieth century when first railroads and then highways finally crisscrossed the Great Lakes area, the lakes themselves were the principal means of transporting people and merchandise in the sparsely settled territories west of the St. Lawrence River and Lake Ontario. Passengers and merchandise would soon be eclipsed, however, by the bulk cargoes that are now the staple of the Great Lakes shipping industry.

Red Rivers

The history of the Cleveland-Cliffs Iron Company is rooted deeply in the mineral-rich landscape surrounding the Great Lakes. While Cleveland-Cliffs itself was not established until 1891, the company evolved from the earliest mining operations in the orefields of Michigan's Upper Peninsula, where the company is still one of the largest landowners.

Iron ore was discovered near Marquette, Michigan, in about 1844 by surveyors Douglas Houghton and William Burt, both of whom were involved in running section and township lines for the state of Michigan, which had been admitted to the Union in 1837. The reports by Houghton and Burt attracted prospectors to the rugged wilderness area, most accompanied by Indian guides.

In 1845, Philo Everett of Jackson, Michigan, found ore under the roots of a fallen pine tree near Negaunee, just west of Marquette. Everett began mining operations at what he named Jackson Mountain, incorporating his operation in 1846 as the Jackson Company. A few hundred pounds of ore from the Marquette Range were shipped down the lakes that first year, but most of the early ore went to forges set up near the mines.

The early shipments of ore on the lakes were primarily trial lots sent for testing in the iron furnaces of southern Ohio and Pennsylvania. Costs of transporting the cargoes were too high to make such operations profitable, however. The heavy ore had to be arduously loaded and unloaded by workers with wheelbarrows, and the unnavigable rapids at Sault Ste. Marie made it necessary to portage the cargoes around the rapids, a time-consuming and costly operation. Even the iron that was smelted at the Upper Peninsula forges could not be shipped to markets along the lower lakes at a profit.

It was the opening of the ship canal and locks at Sault Ste. Marie in 1855 that allowed the river of red ore to flow from the mines on Lake Superior to Cleveland for transshipment by rail to southern Ohio and western Pennsylvania. The first year the canal and locks were open to vessel traffic a total of 1,400 tons of ore was shipped. The following year, the total climbed to 11,500 tons, in addition to $2.25 million worth of copper that moved down the lakes with the iron ore, and $2.5 million in merchandise that moved up the lakes.

Demand for iron and steel during the Civil War stimulated mining operations on the Marquette Range and shipments grew dramatically. About 35,000 tons were shipped in 1857 at freight rates of about $3.00 per ton, but by 1860 rates had dropped to between $2.00 and $2.50 per ton, and the volume of cargo exceeded 124,000 tons. With the coming of the war, tonnages increased to 236,000 tons by 1865, and freight rates fluctuated from $2.50 to $5.00 per ton, with the demand for ore often exceeding the available supply of ships to carry it. The river of red was flowing.[2]

Iron ore was not the most important cargo on the lakes, however. From 1831 until 1888, wheat was

Crewmembers on the ore boats weren't the only "iron men" in the Great Lakes region in 1860. Here workers at the Jackson Mine near Marquette, Michigan, are shown laboriously loading horse-drawn carts with iron ore that has been blasted from the mine face. (State Archives of Michigan)

Three freighters and a passenger steamer entering the original Poe Lock at Sault Ste. Marie shortly after its completion in 1896. The white-hulled steamer being assisted into the lock by a tug is the 385-foot *North West,* then one of the most luxurious passenger vessels on the lakes. (State Archives of Michigan)

the primary bulk cargo moved aboard ships on the Great Lakes. In 1866, for example, 1.5 million tons of grain passed through the elevators at Buffalo, New York, while total iron ore shipments to Lake Erie ports totalled only 278,796 tons.[3]

In 1831, the brig *John Kenzie* hauled the first shipload of bagged wheat from Chicago to mills in Buffalo, where the wheat was processed into flour for shipment to the population centers along the Atlantic Coast via the Erie Canal. The first true bulk shipment of wheat, where the grain was loaded loose in a ship's hold, was 1,678 bushels of western grain that moved from Chicago to Buffalo in 1839 aboard the brig *Osceola.*[4] In a 1908 article in the *Marine Review*, Captain C. E. Sayre wrote about

that historic shipload of bulk grain: "We are told that five days were consumed in getting the cargo on board, fourteen days in making the run to Buffalo, and seven days in discharging the cargo."[5]

By 1841, the flourishing grain trade in the upper Mississippi valley led to the construction of the first grain warehouses in Chicago, which stored more than 100,000 bushels during the winter of 1841–42. By the winter of 1845–46, more than 700,000 bushels of grain were in storage at the Chicago docks, and the first grain elevators were built to provide improved storage and handling of the grain that was moving from the prairies west of the lakes to mills and markets in the East.

War and famine in Europe during the 1840s and

1850s pushed wheat prices upward from about sixty-five cents a bushel to more than two dollars a bushel. The demand for wheat from the Great Lakes region increased from a million bushels in 1840 to almost five million bushels in 1849 and a staggering twenty million bushels by 1858.[6]

Milwaukee, Duluth, and Thunder Bay, Ontario (then the twin cities of Port Arthur and Fort William), joined Chicago as major grain-shipping ports, while Buffalo continued as the primary grain-receiving port on the lower lakes, with other shipments going to Cleveland; Oswego, New York; and Kingston, Ontario. Ships discharging grain on Lake Erie and Lake Ontario would carry backhaul cargoes of coal, salt, and general merchandise. The trade was said to have been so lucrative that a ship could often pay for itself in a single season.

Copper also emerged as an important cargo during the 1840s, shipped from mines primarily located on Michigan's Keweenaw Peninsula on Lake Superior to ports on the lower lakes. Most of the copper moved in relatively small shipments aboard the packet freighters that were involved in the passenger and general cargo trades on the lakes. While the copper had a high value, it never moved in bulk quantities as grain and ore did.

By the middle of the 1850s, lumber was also a major cargo, as the vast virgin pine forests that bordered the northern lakes were harvested to supply building materials for the rapidly growing cities along the lower lakes. The industry reached its zenith on the lakes about 1888–89, but continued as a major factor in lake shipments until the early part of the twentieth century. By that time, the forests bordering the lakes had been largely exhausted, and railroads offered lumber barons a cost-effective alternative to ships for getting their cargoes to market.

By 1850, coal-mining regions south of the lakes were linked to ports on Lake Erie and Lake Ontario by a system of railroads and canals, and fuel coal began moving by ship in small quantities. In 1851, 167,500 tons of coal moved through Lake Erie ports, with another 3,600 tons shipped from ports on Lake Ontario. By 1898, however, total shipments on the lakes had increased to about ten million tons annually, virtually all of it moving through ports in Ohio. Freight rates from Lake Erie to cities on Lake Michigan and Lake Superior ranged from twenty-three to twenty-nine cents a ton in 1898, less than one-third of what they had been only ten years earlier.[7]

By 1888, iron ore shipments on the lakes surpassed all other cargoes in volume, a position that it has still not surrendered. The dawn of the industrial age in North America increased the demand for ore to feed the steel mills of the Midwest, and new discoveries of rich deposits of iron in Michigan's Upper Peninsula and northern Wisconsin and Minnesota seemed capable of providing a virtually unlimited supply of high quality ore. Until 1877, all of the iron ore shipped on the lakes came from the Marquette Range, but in that year the first ore moved off the Menominee Range, located along the Michigan-Wisconsin border near Iron Mountain, Michigan. The Menominee ore was loaded aboard ships at Escanaba, Michigan, on northern Lake Michigan. In 1884, the first ore was shipped from the Vermilion Range, about one hundred miles north of Duluth, Minnesota, through the port of Two Harbors, Minnesota, which was connected to the ore fields by the Duluth and Iron Range Railroad. By 1885, the mines of the Gogebic Range, near Ashland, Wisconsin, added their first ore to the tonnages moving down the lakes, which totalled more than two million tons that year.

By 1892, the Gogebic Range was shipping almost three million tons of ore each year, while the Marquette and Menominee Ranges each produced more than two million tons and the Vermilion Range generated just over one million tons, for total lake shipments in excess of nine million tons. Only a trickle of that total, just over 4,000 tons, originated at the mines of Minnesota's Mesabi Range, which would rapidly become the most productive in the world.

The Mesabi Range was discovered by Lewis Merritt and his sons, Napoleon, Cassius, and Leonidas. The soft hematite ore of the Mesabi assayed at about 64 percent pure iron, the highest quality deposits yet found, and, unlike the other ranges, the ore was contained in great beds located just under the covering of glacial drift. While underground tunneling operations, some going as deep as 3,000 feet, were needed to get at the ore in the other ranges, far less expensive open pit mining techniques could be used in the Mesabi Range.

The rich ore was moved from the Mesabi mines in northern Minnesota to the docks at Superior, Wisconsin, by the Duluth, Mesabi & Northern Railroad that had been built by the Merritts. In its second year, the Mesabi Range produced over 600,000 tons of ore, increasing to 1.7 million tons the following year and 2.8 million the fourth year, surpassing production from any of the other ranges. In 1897, its sixth year of operations, the Mesabi generated over 4 million tons of ore, 1.5 million tons more than the next largest range.[8] After the Mesabi went into production, tonnages increased so rapidly that Colonel Orlando Poe, superintendent of the Soo Locks for the Army Corps of Engineers, remarked, "The wildest expectations of one year seem absolutely tame the next."[9] In less than a decade, Duluth became the second busiest port in the world, surpassing London. James Oliver Curwood wrote: "Today you can ship a ton of ore from Duluth to Ashtabula, Conneaut, or Cleveland, a distance of nearly one thousand miles, for less than you can send by rail that same ton from one of these ports to Pittsburgh, a distance of only one hundred and thirty miles."[10]

The ability of the industry to move so much ore was due in part to improvements in mining and cargo handling technology. The ore was mined by hand until 1884, when steam shovels came into use, but hand loading of ore boats had ended in 1859 when the Cleveland Iron Mining Company, forerunner of Cleveland-Cliffs, built the first ore dock at Marquette. The dock consisted of a 25-foot high trestle with tracks on top for ore cars. The rail cars dumped their loads of ore into pockets, or bins, located under the tracks. Each pocket held about 50 tons of ore, which could be discharged into a waiting ship merely by opening a gate at the outer end of the pocket, which jutted out over the water. The Marquette dock was so large that three schooners and a steamer could be loaded simultaneously.

Unloading systems at the lower lake ports were much more primitive at the time, however, requiring a lot of backbreaking labor by dockworkers. Ore in the hold of a ship was shovelled into large wooden buckets, which were then hoisted out of the hold by a system of pulleys and lines attached to horses on the dock. The heavy buckets were tipped into wheelbarrows on scaffolding trestles that perched over the deck of the ship, and workers wheeled them along the trestles and dumped the ore into stockpiles on the shore.

During the 1880s, to keep pace with the growing quantities of ore that had to be unloaded, a variety of machines were developed to speed up unloading. One of the first mechanized systems was the Brown hoist, first used in Erie, Pennsylvania, in 1880. The hoist consisted of a number of buckets that could be raised and lowered by a crane operator at a central point on the dock. The buckets still had to be filled by hand, but unloading had been automated. A few ports also used whirly cranes that operated on railroad tracks alongside the dock, while other ports developed bridge cranes that extended out over the decks of ships. While crane operators were hampered by the fact that they could not see the crane bucket after it dropped through the hatch of the ship, it was still a vast improvement over manual labor.

Improved loading and unloading systems evolved rapidly to keep pace with the dramatic increases that took place in ore shipments during the latter part of the nineteenth century. Loading time dropped from 52.5 hours—over two full days—to only 5.6 hours, while unloading took 14 to 17 hours instead of several days.[11] The industry's most dramatic changes, however, involved the ships that moved the rivers of red down the lakes.

Long Ships

The *Columbia*, which carried the first load of ore through the Soo Locks, was a 91-foot-long, two-masted brigantine under charter to the Cleveland Iron Mining Company. That first cargo in 1855 amounted to just 132 tons. By 1867, when the Cleveland Iron Mining Company bought its first ship, the barque *George Sherman*, the vessel had a 550-ton capacity. Just five years later, in 1872, the company bought four wooden steamboats, each with a capacity of 1,000 tons. The company's first steel-hulled steamer, built in 1888, had a capacity of 2,800 tons, twenty-one times the amount that could be carried by the *Columbia* only three decades earlier. And when the *Str. Walter A. Sterling* made its last trip down the lakes in 1984, it carried in excess of 29,000 tons of ore for Cleveland-Cliffs, more than two hundred times the capacity of the *Columbia*. More significantly, even the *Sterling* had been dwarfed by the latest generation of ore boats, some of which could carry double its tonnage.

If there is a single overriding theme that has been consistent throughout the history of the Great Lakes bulk shipping industry, it has been the technological struggle to build ships capable of carrying more and more tonnage. As a result, the length and width of the ships have continually been pushed to the outer limits of the art and science of shipbuilding, and the transportation system on the lakes has been continually pressured to facilitate larger and larger vessels. Size, however, has not been the only aspect of the Great Lakes bulk freighters that has undergone change. The campaign for increased efficiency has touched virtually every aspect of the ships and the way in which they are operated, to the extent that the only similarities that exist between the *Columbia* and today's modern ships are that they have hulls and decks, are capable of moving over the water, and are operated by crews of people who are referred to as sailors. Everything else has changed.

Today's bulk freighters, referred to simply as *boats* by the people who crew them, are hybrid vessels that resulted from the merging of two separate streams of marine technology into a type of ship largely unique to the Great Lakes. The prototype for all Great Lakes bulk freighters was the *Str. R. J. Hackett*, which was launched at Cleveland in 1869.

Before the *Hackett*, the ships operating on the Great Lakes could be divided into two categories: Most of the bulk cargo at that time was carried aboard sailing vessels that had evolved from the *Griffon* and other European-style ships. While sailing vessels held a numerical edge on the lakes, they were rapidly being eclipsed by the growing number of steamboats, most of which were engaged in carrying passengers and merchandise between Great Lakes ports. The steamboats of the time had the advantage of not being subject to the vagaries of the wind and were, therefore, capable of making faster passages than sailboats, but they were not well-suited to carrying bulk cargo. The steamers that had emerged after the 1816 launch of the *Str. Frontenac*, the first steamship built on the lakes, generally had cabins running the entire length of their main decks, necessitating the loading of cargo through gangways in the side of the hull. That wasn't a major constraint when all cargo was being loaded by hand, but when the pocket-type ore docks emerged around 1860, the steamers lost ground in the bulk trade to the sailing ships that had long, unbroken decks with hatches that could line up with the pockets on the docks. The schooners, however, suffered from the disadvantage of being at the mercy of the wind and incapable of operating on any sort of a regular schedule.

The respective advantages of sailing ships and steamboats of the mid-1800s were first combined in the practice of using steam tugs to tow consorts of sailing ships, particularly in the winding river channels that connect the lakes. River tug service was inaugurated in 1845 by the sidewheel steamer *Romeo*, which operated out of Detroit. The shipping companies and shipbuilders soon realized, however, that the most economic operation could be achieved by a steamboat of large carrying capacity and low power, but with an uncluttered deck like those found on sailing vessels. It was in the design of the *Hackett* that the best of the two technologies was merged to create the modern self-propelled bulk freighter.

The *Hackett* was 211 feet long, with a beam of 33 feet. It had a clean deck, broken only by a series of hatches spaced on 24-foot centers that could match up with the spacing of the pockets on the ore docks. The steam engine was located at the stern, and there was a doghouse, or cabin, over the engine room that contained crew quarters. The *Hackett*'s pilothouse was located forward, on top of a second set of crew cabins. It was this "fore-and-aft" configuration that made the *Hackett* a unique type of ship, and the design is still associated almost solely with the bulk industry on the Great Lakes.

The design of the *Hackett* became the standard for the Great Lakes bulk shipping industry, and its launching triggered the evolutionary cycle that has led to the freighters of today. The *Hackett* was followed in 1882 by the construction of the *Str. Onoko*, the first iron-hulled freighter on the lakes, and in 1886 by construction of the *Str. Spokane*, the first steel-hulled ship in the system. Both the *Onoko* and *Spokane* were built in the unique fore-and-aft style pioneered by the *Hackett*.

Industry observers undoubtedly referred to the *Spokane* as the "most modern" freighter on the lakes when it was launched in 1886, as they had the *Onoko* and *Hackett* before, but progress in ship construction during the last two decades of the nine-

Drawing of the *Str. Ontario,* the first steam-powered vessel to operate on the Great Lakes in 1817, based on a sketch by Captain James Van Cleve. The Canadian steamer *Frontenac* had actually been launched before the *Ontario,* but the American boat beat it into service. (Great Lakes Historical Society)

One of the few surviving photos of the wood-hulled *Str. R. J. Hackett.* Launched in 1869, the *Hackett* was the prototype for the unique Great Lakes bulk freighters that are distinguished by having their pilothouse at the bow and engine at the stern. (Author's collection)

teenth century was so volatile that no ship could lay claim to that title for long. One writer of the time noted: "For ten years past it had been impossible to get a strictly modern boat on the lakes. Size and style changed between the laying of the keel and the launching of the ship. Nowhere in the world has progress in marine architecture been so pronounced as on the Great Lakes."[12]

More than five thousand ships were built on the lakes during the three decades between the launching of the *Hackett* and the onset of the twentieth century. In 1896, more tonnage was launched on the Great Lakes than in all the rest of the United States combined. At the same time, the ships had grown from the modest dimensions of the *Hackett* to the launching in 1900 of the first 500-foot ship on the lakes, with a cargo hold large enough to accommodate two entire ships the size of the *Hackett.* It was the dawn of the era of the long ships.

Driven by the skyrocketing demand for raw materials to feed the industrial appetite of the nation, the bulk industry on the Great Lakes frantically tried to keep pace by building more and bigger ships. By the turn of the century there were more than three thousand ships in operation on the lakes. While that was down from the high of 5,600 in 1874, the gross tonnage of the fleet in 1900 was almost double that of the 1874 fleet because of the growth in the dimensions of the ships in use. Even though the number of ships was actually declining, the lines of ships moving up and down the lakes at the turn of the century were similar to the bumper-to-bumper traffic experienced today on our urban freeways. During the 1896 shipping season, for example, 19,387 ships passed the vessel reporting station at Detroit, equating to one ship every twenty minutes for eight solid months.[13]

What a sight that must have been for the thousands of spectators who spread their picnic baskets along the river banks at Detroit on warm weekend afternoons during the summer of 1896. It was the Golden Age of the maritime industry on the lakes, and spectators would have been treated to the sight of steam passenger vessels, including some vintage sidewheelers; proud schooners, many of them being towed by steam tugs; bulk freighters of both wood and steel construction, many of them towing barge consorts; unique snout-nosed whalebacks; ferries crossing between Detroit and Windsor; and an almost indescribable flotilla of pleasure boats. The most majestic of them all, however, would have been the longs ships, the latest generation of bulk freighters moving down the river with their cavernous holds full of iron ore, stone, or grain, or heading back up the lakes laden with coal. The lakes had become a highway of commerce, and the people who ran companies like Cleveland-Cliffs had demonstrated a unique ability to meet the transportation needs of America's industrial and agricultural heartlands.

Iron Men

It is often said that the early days of the maritime industry were a time of wooden ships and iron men. The accuracy of the metaphor is certainly borne out by the historical record. The job of the early sailor was an arduous one. Deck crews loaded and unloaded their ships by hand, shovelling the heavy ore into wheelbarrows or buckets. They handled the heavy wooden hatch covers by hand and struggled to put heavy, unwieldy canvas tarps over the hatches in inclement weather. When they were off watch, the sailors passed the hours in cramped quarters that were too hot in summer and too cold in the spring and fall. Engine personnel on the early steamships fed the roaring fires of the boilers by hand in the scorching heat of the windowless engine rooms. And as they labored in the inferno of the ship's black hold, their constant companion was the threat of a boiler explosion or fire, both common occurrences in that day.

Even the captains of the wooden ships had to have iron wills. On the sailing vessels and early steamboats, they stood their watches not in a comfortably heated pilothouse, but atop the open air bridges where their visibility and hearing were unhampered. Their comfort took a back seat to concern for the safety of their vessels. In the often-congested passages of the lakes, the early captains did not have radios or radar to alert them to vessels ahead of them, but were totally dependent on their vision and hearing. The only weather forecasts they had were from their own barometers, the charts they used were rudimentary, and there were few navigational aids to mark the dangerous channels and shoals of the lakes and rivers. When a captain departed a dock, he (they were all males until 1986) did so with the clear knowledge that his vessel might well be involved in a collision or driven onto some rocky shore by a storm. Ships and their crews often disappeared without a trace, and the early captains had to have stout hearts to face the dangers that lurked on the lakes with every passage.

But the bulk shipping industry on the Great Lakes was not built only upon the strong backs and stout hearts of the men who crewed the early ships. The men who employed them, who organized and ran the early fleets, were also "iron men," although of a different genre. They were visionary businessmen who sensed the vital role that lake transportation of bulk materials would play in the industrial development of North America; aggressive businessmen who grasped every opportunity for economic gain. Yes, they too were iron men.

If there is a "first family" in the Great Lakes shipping industry, it is the Mathers. Samuel Mather, a Cleveland attorney, was the founder and central directing figure of the Cleveland Iron Mining Company. Under Mather's leadership, the company operated some of the earliest mines on the Marquette Range in Michigan's Upper Peninsula and chartered vessels to transport the ore to ports on the lower lakes. In 1867, the company established its own fleet, which it continued to operate for more than a century.

In 1883, Mather teamed up with Colonel James Pickands and Jay Morse to form Pickands-Mather, which also operated mines on the Marquette Range and later developed Interlake Steamship Company, today one of the fourteen remaining U.S. fleets on the lakes. In 1891, Mather's Cleveland Iron Mining Company merged with the Iron Cliffs Company of former presidential candidate Samuel Tilden to form the Cleveland-Cliffs Iron Company. William Mather succeeded his father at the company's helm, and he remained a key figure in the firm's operations until 1950.

Another early giant of the industry was Marcus Alonzo Hanna, whose M. A. Hanna Company was formed at about the same time as Pickands-Mather. Hanna Company began in the business of supplying coal to the steel mills and soon expanded into the wholesale grocery trade, serving retail outlets at communities around the lakes. Eventually, Hanna began chartering ships to carry groceries and other supplies to the orefields in the Upper Peninsula of Michigan and to bring back loads of ore. That involvement led Hanna to lease mining lands and purchase a fleet of ships, nicknamed "the Black Line" because they were the first ships on the lakes to have black hulls. Today, M. A. Hanna Company operates only one vessel, but the firm continues to manage extensive mining interests around the lakes.

Cleveland-Cliffs, Pickands-Mather, and Hanna dominated the early mining and bulk shipping industries. While it can be said that Sam Mather, Marcus Hanna, Colonel Pickands, and Jay Morse were present at the creation of the industry, they were soon eclipsed by a new generation of industrial giants whose names are still prominent in American history books: Carnegie, Rockefeller, and Morgan.

John D. Rockefeller made his early fortune in the oil fields, but got involved in iron mining operations in Michigan and Minnesota around 1893. Under his leadership, his Lake Superior Consolidated Iron Mines Company became the dominant force on the Mesabi Range. Rockefeller soon sensed the need to be able to control the transportation of ore from the mines to the mills in Ohio and Pennsylvania, and he arranged to have twelve new ships built for his Bessemer Steamship Company. By 1901, the fleet had grown to sixty ships; they were capable of carrying all the ore from his mining operations, plus all of the ore purchased by steel magnate Andrew Carnegie.

Carnegie soon became concerned about his dependence on fleets owned by others, so he formed the Pittsburgh Steamship Company and purchased six ships. While he was still largely reliant on other fleets, particularly Rockefeller's, to get his ore from the mines to the mills, his small fleet provided him with at least a partial safeguard against unfair freight rates.

In 1901, financier J. P. Morgan bought out Carnegie, Judge Elton Gary's Illinois Steel Company, and Rockefeller's interests in the Bessemer fleet and his Mesabi mining operations. Morgan formed U.S. Steel, with capital of almost $1.5 billion. U.S. Steel owned 65 percent of 104 mines, 5 railroads, and 112 lake freighters. The boats operated under the Pittsburgh Steamship Company name that Morgan acquired when he bought the Carnegie vessels, but they were widely known simply as the Pittsburgh Fleet or the Steel Trust Fleet. The ships had rust-red hulls and distinctive silver smokestacks, and they were soon tagged "the tin stackers," a nickname that endures yet today. The Pittsburgh Fleet was the largest U.S. fleet on the lakes from its creation in 1901 until 1987. Today, it operates as the USS Great Lakes Fleet and, with eleven ships, is still one of the largest of the U.S. fleets.

The early destinies of the mining and shipping industries rested on the shoulders of these pioneering industrialists, and they proved more than equal to the challenges. As the two industries whose destinies are so closely interwoven entered the twentieth century, they comprised the most efficient bulk mining and transportation operations in the world.

Mather, Rockefeller, Morgan, and the other industry pioneers oversaw the birth and early childhood of a mining industry that would eventually produce more than ninety million tons of ore each year and a bulk shipping industry capable of efficiently moving the ore to the steel mills of the great smokestack cities south of the lakes. During their tenure, the price of ore delivered at Lake Erie ports fell from as much as eighteen dollars a ton to about two dollars a ton at the turn of the century. While much of the reduction was due to improved mining techniques, a portion of it was also due to savings on transportation. During the fifty-year period ending in 1900, vessel rates for shipping ore from Marquette to the lower lakes fell from a high of more than six dollars a ton to about fifty cents a ton, a reduction of more than 90 percent.

The twenty-two ore docks on the upper lakes were handling more than 12.5 million tons of ore a year in 1899, representing 70 percent of the total iron ore production of the United States. The sophisticated and efficient bulk freighters that moved the ore down the lakes also carried more than 200 million bushels of grain and over 12.1 million tons of coal each year. Lumber shipments had declined dramatically by the turn of the century, but the industry still transported close to ninety million board feet of lumber in 1898.[14]

Cleveland-Cliffs and the other fleets that comprised the Great Lakes bulk shipping industry entered the twentieth century as the most efficient bulk shipping industry in the world. The capability of the industry to move bulk materials inexpensively played a significant role in the development of both the U.S. and Canada. In doing so, the industry has directly or indirectly touched the lives of every person in North America—putting bread on our tables, cars in our garages, and coal in our furnaces.

Thrill of *Victory*

As the twentieth century began to unfold, the fortunes of Cleveland-Cliffs and the other mining and shipping firms in the Great Lakes region rose and fell from one year to the next in response to fluctuations in the national economy, but the trend was a dynamic upward spiral. No one who had been involved with the industry during its first faltering steps in the 1850s could have foreseen the dramatic growth that was taking place. With the nation demonstrating what seemed to be an insatiable appetite for iron and steel, iron ore shipments rose from about 15 million tons at the turn of the century to a staggering 73 million tons by 1929. It was a period of unequalled prosperity for the mining companies and the fleets. The biggest problem facing the industry in 1929 was finding enough seaworthy vessels to haul all the cargo that was under contract to be moved.

Shock waves caused by the financial crash that struck the stock markets of Wall Street in the fall of 1929 rolled through the offices of the ore mining and shipping firms during the winter months of 1929–30. Orders for millions of tons of ore were summarily cancelled. Mining operations on the iron ranges ground to a halt and by the time winter's ice cover gave up its grasp on the shipping lanes of the lakes, the shipping companies found that they had only enough orders to operate a few of their ships during the 1930 season.

By the 1932 season, the impact of the Great Depression had decimated the shipping industry. Only about 4 million tons of iron ore moved that year and shipments of all bulk cargoes amounted to less than 42 million tons, almost 100 million tons less than was shipped during the watershed 1929 season. Shipping company officials who only three years earlier had struggled to find enough ships to meet the skyrocketing demand for cargo movements now faced a new problem—finding sufficient dockage around the lakes to accommodate all their idle vessels.

In 1933, tonnages began to rebound, growing modestly at first, then rising steeply as relative prosperity returned to the nation toward the end of the decade. More than 21 million tons of iron ore was shipped during the 1938 season, out of total bulk shipments of 75 million tons. Most of the 308 freighters owned by the twenty-one U.S. shipping companies that had survived the depression were still laid up, but shipping executives were encouraged by the gradually strengthening economy and growing rumors of an impending war in Europe. With a fleet of twenty-four ships, the third largest on the lakes, Cleveland-Cliffs was poised to lay claim to a healthy share of the growing tonnages.

Shipments of all bulk cargoes climbed to record levels during World War II. In 1945, the last year of the war, iron ore shipments alone exceeded 75 million tons and total cargo moved surpassed the 175 million ton mark. To keep pace with the exceptional wartime demand, sixteen Maritime-class freighters were added to the U.S. fleet on the lakes, including Cleveland-Cliffs's *Champlain* and *Cadillac*.

The 1950s brought another surge in demand for iron ore as the U.S. became embroiled in the Korean War. Cleveland-Cliffs had contracted for the construction of a new 647-foot freighter, which would become the *Str. Edward B. Greene*, but the ship would not be delivered until 1952. Cliffs saw an immediate need for additional tonnage, but the order books of all the Great Lakes shipyards were already filled as shipping companies scrambled to keep pace with demand. In an innovative move, Cliffs officials contracted with the U.S. Maritime Administration for purchase of the *Str. Notre Dame Victory*, one of the famous Victory-class cargo ships built for the government during World War II. The *Notre Dame Victory* had been launched near the end of the war and had spent its brief career under charter to various saltwater shipping companies or mothballed as part of the U.S. reserve fleet.

The *Notre Dame Victory* was towed from its berth near Newport News, Virginia, to the Bethlehem Shipbuilding Company in Baltimore, where it was lengthened from its original 439 feet to 620 feet in less than ninety days. After conversion, it was towed more than 3,000 miles around Florida and up the Mississippi, entering the lakes through the Illinois River and the Chicago Ship and Sanitary Canal. For the trip, the ship's superstructures were removed and placed down inside the cargo hold so that it could squeak its way under a number of low bridges that would be encountered on the trip to the Great Lakes. When the ship arrived on the lakes, shipyard workers replaced the pilothouse, aft cabins, and smokestack. The latest addition to the Great Lakes fleet was rechristened *Cliffs Victory*, the first large ocean vessel put into service on the lakes. For many years it had the reputation as the fastest ship in the fleet, capable of speeds of more than 20 miles an hour. In 1957, *Victory* was lengthened by another 96 feet, bringing her overall length to 716 feet. During refitting on the East Coast, *Victory*'s pilothouse was moved to the bow, but the engine room, after cabins, and smokestack were left amidships. As a result, it

had the most unique profile of any ship in the Great Lakes fleet and was always a favorite with boat-watchers around the lakes.

Cliffs converted a second ocean vessel for lakes service during the early 1960s, adding a converted Navy tanker to the fleet as the *Str. Walter A. Sterling*. As the demand for ore again climbed during the 1970s, both the *Sterling* and the *Greene* were lengthened and converted to self-unloaders to make them more versatile and efficient. In 1972, Cliffs was awarded the lucrative contract to supply ore to Republic Steel's mills on the Cuyahoga River at Cleveland, the largest iron ore delivery contract in the history of the lakes. In addition to lengthening the *Sterling* and *Greene*, Cliffs acquired six 600-foot lakers, bringing their total fleet to fourteen ships and making them one of the largest bulk operators on the lakes. Cliffs was also involved in the growing movement of western coal to utility plants on the lakes, and company officials were working with naval architects on the design for a 1,000-foot collier for that trade.

Cliffs's success during the 1970s came as no surprise to its competitors. The fleet had gained a strong reputation for innovation over the years and was clearly established in a leadership position on the lakes.

When the giant Republic contract came up for renewal in 1980, however, Cliffs's fortunes rapidly changed. A dramatic and precipitous decline in the demand for iron ore had left most fleets on the lakes with excess vessels, increasing competition between the fleets and driving rates downward. In a fierce bidding war with several other fleets, Cliffs lost the lucrative contract that had supported the majority of its fleet to Pickands-Mather's Interlake Steamship Company.

The proud Cleveland-Cliffs fleet entered the 1980s with most of its ships tied up at docks around the lakes. By the summer of 1983, fleet officials were only able to find enough cargoes to sustain the operations of two ships, and the *Sterling* and *Greene* were the only Cliffs vessels to be seen on the lakes. Virtually all of the mates serving on the two ships had previously commanded vessels themselves, while most of the assistant engineers had been chief engineers when Cliffs operated their fourteen-boat fleet. Hundreds of Cliffs sailors were without work and many would never sail again.

The *Str. Cliffs Victory* being pushed up the Mississippi River by a tug on its way to the Great Lakes in the spring of 1951. Both of the ship's superstructures had to be removed and stowed in its cargo hold so that it could clear a number of low bridges encountered along the route. (Great Lakes Historical Society)

Despite the dogged efforts of Cliffs management to secure additional contracts, only the *Sterling* and *Greene* would ever fly the Cliffs fleet flag again. The bulk trade on the lakes continued to worsen and in the face of the industry's most severe depression since the 1930s, company officials made the difficult decision to abandon their 130-year tradition in the Great Lakes bulk industry, selling the *Sterling* and *Greene* to Ford Motor Company. Most of the other Cleveland-Cliffs vessels were sold for scrap, but the distinctive *Victory* was given another lease on life. In 1985, the ship was sold to a Liberian shipping company and transferred to Panamanian registry as the *Str. SAVIC*. The unusual name was easily arrived at by painting out most of the former name and inserting an *A* between the remaining *S* from CLIFFS and the *VIC* from VICTORY. After forty years on the lakes, the ship, still painted in the black hull and pea green superstructure colors of Cliffs, took on a load of scrap for delivery to Taiwan. It was reported that the ship ultimately would participate in the bulk trade in the Pacific, but in mid-1987, word filtered back to the lakes that it was being put under the shipbreaker's torch in Taiwan.

The departure of the *Victory* and the demise of the oldest of the Great Lakes bulk fleets testified to the dramatic change that the industry was undergoing. Between 1976 and 1986, the surviving U.S. fleets scrapped sixty-two ships for which there were no cargoes. Tonnages moved on the lakes plummeted

Vessels of the Hanna Mining fleet lying idle at Detroit during the 1983 season. Included in the photo is the *Str. Joseph H. Thompson,* a converted saltwater ship that was the first 700-footer and the longest ship on the lakes when it entered service in 1952. (Author's collection)

from a high of 214 million tons in 1979 to just over 140 million tons in 1985. Only fifty-two of the surviving eighty-eight U.S. freighters on the lakes were in operation during the peak of the season that year, the smallest fleet to trade on the lakes during the twentieth century.

Cliffs, of course, wasn't the only fleet that had fallen on hard times. The USS Great Lakes Fleet, the largest of the U.S. fleets and successor to the Pittsburgh Steamship Company, which had once operated over a hundred vessels, was able to put only about ten ships into service out of a total fleet of twenty-six. Hanna Mining Company, which had been operating ships on the lakes for almost a hundred years, decided to follow Cliffs's example and abandon its vessel operations. Hanna eventually ended up continuing to run one ship in the ore trade when they were unable to find a buyer for their almost-new thousand-footer, the *M/V George A. Stinson*, even though they offered the vessel for sale at a bargain-basement price.

Canadian companies, too, were adversely affected by reductions in the demand for iron ore, as well as by a downturn in grain shipments on the lakes that resulted from reduced world demand for North American grain. Fleets on both sides of the border struggled to adjust to the protracted shipping market and the reduced freight rates that prevailed on the lakes. Many observers eyed the shrinking fleets and concluded that they were watching an industry in its death throes.

Notes

1. Jonathon Ela, *The Faces of the Great Lakes* (San Francisco: Sierra Club Books, 1977), 1–27.
2. J. B. Mansfield, ed., *History of the Great Lakes*, vol. I (Chicago: J. H. Beers & Co., 1899; reprint, Cleveland: Freshwater Press, 1972), 566.
3. Ibid., 532.
4. Ibid., 529.
5. Quoted in Norman Beasley, *Freighters of Fortune* (New York: Harper & Brothers, 1930), 49.
6. Mansfield, 526–44.
7. Ibid., 550–53.
8. Harlan Hatcher, *Century of Iron and Men* (Indianapolis: Bobbs-Merrill, 1950), 43–61.
9. Walter Havighurst, *The Long Ships Passing* (New York: Macmillan, 1975), 222.
10. James Oliver Curwood, *The Great Lakes* (1909; reprint, The Archives of James Pugliese, 1967), 8.
11. Hatcher, 165.
12. Mansfield, 358.
13. Ibid., 509.
14. Ibid., 120–22.

2

Birth of the Great Lakes Steamboat, 1869–1919

Every ship has a story. Men wrap their lives about it, and women their loves, and in so doing it makes fiction appear dull in comparison.
—Dana Thomas Bowen,
Lore of the Lakes, 1940

The people who work aboard Great Lakes bulk freighters refer to them simply as *boats*. That's a clear violation of the conventions of nautical terminology used throughout the world maritime community. Mariners always differentiate between *boats* and *ships*, although the distinctions between the two basic categories of vessels are not at all precise. Some contend that a boat is what you take to get to a ship or that boats are carried aboard ships, as in the case of lifeboats. Others argue that ships are capable of going to sea, while boats are not. Even though the terms are not precise, there is a consensus that ships are somehow superior to boats, whether it is in their size or their seaworthiness. Saltwater captains are seriously offended if you refer to their ships as boats. Not so, however, on the Great Lakes.

It is also interesting to note that crewmembers aboard lake freighters refer to themselves as *sailors*, a term that is today more commonly associated with people involved in recreational sailboating. The people who work on the freighters would be referred to more accurately as *seafarers* or *merchant seamen*, although they seldom use that terminology. Use of the terms *boats* and *sailors* is a throwback to the period when the Great Lakes bulk freighter first emerged. *Boats* derives from *steamboats*, while *sailor* is a carryover from the era when commercial sailing vessels were the backbone of the marine transportation industry.

The Great Lakes bulk freighters, also referred to as steamboats, lake freighters, ore boats, or lakers, represent a unique class of vessels that was developed more than 120 years ago. The first laker was a hybrid, combining characteristics of both the steamboats and sailing vessels that were in operation on the lakes at that time. In 1869, there were 2,388 ships and about 100 unpowered barges operating on the lakes. The fleets were dominated by sailing vessels, which accounted for 73 percent of the total, and shipyards would continue to turn out primarily sailing ships until about 1875.[1]

Most of the bulk cargo being moved on the lakes in 1869 was carried by sailing vessels. Their decks were comparatively uncluttered, and their holds could be loaded and unloaded through easily accessible deck hatches. The early vintage steamboats evolved as passenger vessels serving the most lucrative trade on the lakes at that time. Few roads or railroads existed in the region, so passenger travel relied almost totally on ships. The 636 steamboats that plied the lakes in 1869 were capable of making faster passages between ports and could usually keep to a schedule far better than sailing vessels. Given their advantages, it was only natural that steamboats rapidly eclipsed sailing ships in the passenger trade.

To accommodate as many passengers as possible, most of the early steamboats were constructed with one or two decks of cabins extending their full lengths. This arrangement necessitated the loading and unloading of cargo through gangways in the side of the ship's hull, making it difficult to use any mechanical loading or unloading apparatus. If a steamboat carried bulk cargo, it had to be loaded and unloaded by crewmembers and dockworkers using wheelbarrows, a system that was both time consuming and expensive. With the advent of the gravity loading dock in 1859 and the subsequent development of mechanized unloading equipment, sailing ships were better suited to the carriage of bulk cargoes than steamboats were. However, the sailing vessels were slower than the steamboats and subject to being becalmed or blown off course by the variable winds on the Great Lakes. Their ability to operate on any sort of a regular schedule was, in fact, totally contingent on wind conditions.

In an effort to take advantage of the benefits of steam propulsion, many operators of sailing vessels began using steam tugs to tow their ships. This practice was first used in harbors and in the St. Marys, St. Clair, and Detroit Rivers, where the narrow, winding waterways and strong currents made navigation of sailing vessels extremely difficult. The use of tugs eventually spread beyond the rivers and

harbors, and steam tugs often towed consorts of up to four or five sailing ships across the lakes.

While the practice of towing prolonged the economic life of sailing ships in the Great Lakes bulk trade, the construction in 1869 of the first steam-powered ship designed specifically for bulk commerce sounded the death knell of the majestic schooners and brigs. In less than twenty years, steamers outnumbered sailing vessels, and while sailboats continued in operation on the lakes well into the twentieth century, they rapidly dropped out of the mainstream of commercial shipping activity.

Most crewmembers on the early steamboats had begun their careers aboard sailing ships, and they continued to refer to themselves as *sailors* even after they made the transition to service on steamboats. *Sailor* became a generic term that applied to any merchant seaman on the lakes, regardless of the type of vessel he worked on, and it is still widely used today.

The use of the term *steamboat*, as opposed to the more accurate *steamship*, undoubtedly came into general use because most of the early steam vessels were small; they were designed for use on the rivers and canals where they had a decided advantage over the cumbersome sailing ships. They were *boats* because of their size and because they weren't designed for ocean use. The term *steamboat* was used on the lakes until diesel propulsion came into widespread use in the 1960s and 1970s, and it is still heard frequently today.

The steamboats on the lakes grew in both length and carrying capacity until they were among the largest vessels in the world, but use of the term *boat* has persisted. Even though the vessels clearly deserve to be referred to as ships, Great Lakes sailors and shipbuilders seem to resist use of the more formal terminology. Theirs is an unpretentious industry, and they find it totally unnecessary to use any fancy nautical jargon.

When the National Maritime Hall of Fame opened at the U.S. Merchant Marine Academy in 1982, the first inductee from the Great Lakes shipping industry was the late Captain Alexander McDougall. His shipyard at Superior, Wisconsin, had built more than forty cigar-shaped *whaleback* barges and steamers during the late 1800s. With their rounded decks and snoutlike bows, McDougall's whalebacks were comparatively inexpensive to build and their stream-

The three-masted schooner *Emma L. Nielsen,* with all of her canvas set, works her way up the St. Clair River. Built at Manitowac, Wisconsin, in 1883, it is typical of the thousands of wooden sailing ships that once flourished on the Great Lakes. Their numbers declined rapidly after steam-powered freighters like the *Hackett* cornered the bulk trades on the lakes. The *Nielsen* eked out a living until 1911, when it sank after colliding with the *Str. Wyandotte.* (State Archives of Michigan)

The powerful steam tug *Joseph Goldsmith* towing six schooners with their sails fully set. The *Goldsmith* operated on the Detroit and St. Clair Rivers from 1882 until 1903. River tug service was developed at Detroit in 1845 to help sailing vessels compete with steamboats that were not dependent on the wind. (Great Lakes Historical Society)

lined hulls sliced cleanly through even the heaviest seas. While the innovative whalebacks represent a colorful chapter in the history of shipping on the lakes, they were never very functional, and the unconventional design was abandoned after only eight years in favor of the standard type of lake freighter that had been developed in 1869. The choice of Captain McDougall to be the first inductee from the Great Lakes into the Maritime Hall of Fame was, in fact, analogous to inducting the designer of the Edsel into the Automotive Hall of Fame, but overlooking Henry Ford.

The "Henry Ford" of ship design on the Great Lakes was Eli Peck, a shipbuilder from Cleveland who was once described as being brusque and not easily approachable, "but a man of kindly instincts and a charitable disposition."[2] Although not nearly as well known as McDougall, it was Captain Peck who designed and built the *Str. R. J. Hackett*, the prototype for a unique class of bulk freighters that has been the hallmark of the shipping industry on the lakes for more than a century. Launched at Cleveland in 1869, the *Hackett* was specifically designed for the iron ore trade, and it combined the best features of both the steamboats and sailing ships of the period into an entirely new type of vessel.

The *Hackett* was 211 feet long, with a beam of 33 feet, and a carrying capacity of about 1,200 tons, similar in size to the schooners, brigs, and barkentines that were its contemporaries on the lakes. The wood-hulled boat had, in fact, three masts from which sails could be set for auxiliary power, a common practice on most of the early steamboats. Like the sailing ships, the *Hackett* also had a boxy hull with flat sides and a flat deck that was lined with hatches spaced 24 feet apart. From the steamboats of the day, the *Hackett* got its boxy stern and perpendicular stem, in addition to its propulsion system. While the steamboats of that era usually had their engines located amidships, where they had originally driven paddlewheels, the *Hackett*'s engine was located below the main deck at the stern of the vessel. Cabins for crewmembers, the galley, and a tall smokestack were located directly above the engine room. The pilothouse was located all the way forward, perched atop a second set of cabins.

Why the *Hackett*'s pilothouse was placed forward is subject to some speculation. One reasonable explanation is that every steamboat of that period had its pilothouse located at the bow, sitting atop the tier of cabins that spanned the length of the deck. If the pilothouse had been placed aft, the captain's view would have been blocked by the cabins. Masters of steam vessels, then, were used to navigating from the bow of the ship, whereas captains of sailing vessels always navigated from the stern where they could easily see the trim of the ship's sails. A second possible explanation for placing the pilothouse forward was that it improved the captain's view when docking, making locks, or maneuvering in restricted waters. The forward pilothouse put the captain closer to the action, where he could better gauge distances and speeds when maneuvering.

The *Hackett* was well designed to haul bulk cargoes. Its boxy hull maximized its carrying capacity, and the deck-mounted hatches were spaced on 24-foot centers so that they would match up with the 12-foot spacing of the chutes on the gravity ore docks on the upper lakes. When loading, every other chute on the dock could be lowered, discharging their cargo into the hold of the ship. Then, by moving the vessel forward or aft only 12 feet, the remaining chutes could empty their ore, and the loaded ship could be on its way down the lakes.

Referred to initially as a *steam barge*, the *Hackett* was the prototype for all subsequent bulk freighters on the lakes. So effective was Peck's design that no substantive changes were made to it for more than one hundred years, a design longevity that may be unparalleled in the history of the transportation industry. By comparison, if the body styling of the first Model-T automobiles had been as durable as the design embodied in the *Hackett,* either we would still be driving cars with Model-T bodies or the first Model-T would have looked like a late model Mustang or Thunderbird.

In the introduction to a paper presented at a 1956 meeting of the Great Lakes Section of the Society of Naval Architects and Marine Engineers, Professor Harry Benford of the University of Michigan Department of Naval Architecture and Marine Engineering noted that "all naval architects and marine engineers are historians, at least to the extent that they base their design decisions on experiences learned in the past. The history of ships is one of evolution and the design lineage of every ship afloat can be traced back for countless 'generations.' "[3] In this respect, Eli Peck was an astute student of history, combining

Samuel Ward Stanton's drawing of the passenger steamer *Walk-in-the-Water,* the first steam vessel to operate on the upper lakes. Supposedly named after an Indian chief from Detroit, the paddlewheeler operated primarily between Detroit and Black Rock, New York, on the Niagara River. (Author's collection)

An 1838 lithograph of the *Great Western*, the first passenger steamer on the Great Lakes to have two decks of cabins. A sidewheeler, its ornately decorated pilothouse is located at the forward end of the top deck of cabins. (Institute for Great Lakes Research, Bowling Green State University)

design features borrowed from both steamboats and sailboats to create a new class of vessels that would soon dominate an entire industry.

One side of the *Hackett*'s ancestral family consisted of the sailing ships that evolved from the *Griffon* and other European-style vessels brought to North America by the early explorers and commercial interests. From the time of the *Griffon*, launched in 1679, until the emergence of the *Hackett* 190 years later, sailing vessels increased dramatically both in size and the amount of sail they could carry. The other side of the *Hackett*'s family had a much shorter history. It went back only to about 1807 and Robert Fulton's launching on the Hudson River of the *North River Steamboat*, better known as the *Clermont*, the first successful steam-propelled vessel

in North America. Fulton's successes led to the launching a few years later of the first steamship on the Great Lakes, the *Frontenac*.

The *Frontenac* went into the water near Kingston, Ontario, in the fall of 1816 and was put into service on Lake Ontario the following spring, hauling passengers between Kingston, York (now Toronto), and Niagara. The first U.S. steamboat on the lakes was the *Ontario*, launched in the spring of 1817 at Sackett's Harbor, New York. While it was launched after the *Frontenac*, the *Ontario* actually went into service about two months before the Canadian steamer. The *Ontario* was built under license from Fulton and ran between Oswego, New York, and York and Niagara in Canada.

The first steamboat above Niagara was the fa-

35

mous *Walk-in-the-Water*, launched at Buffalo in 1818 and supposedly named after a Wyandot chief who lived on the Detroit River. Like the earlier steamboats, the 135-foot *Walk-in-the-Water* was a paddlewheeler with its paddles jutting out from each side of the hull about midway between bow and stern. Like sailing vessels and the other early steamers, it was steered from the stern from a raised quarterdeck that stood about 5 feet above the main deck. The quarterdeck housed cabins for passengers. In addition to its steam engine, *Walk-in-the-Water* was rigged as a two-masted schooner to provide auxiliary power in fair winds or in the event the engine broke down. Most of the hull of the ship below the main deck was taken up by the steam boilers and stacks of wood needed for fuel.

The *Great Western*, launched in 1839, was the first steamer on the lakes to have upper cabins that ran the full length of the main deck, allowing it to carry more passengers. That required moving the steering position to a pilothouse or *steering room* located atop the cabin deck at the bow. Because the master and the wheelsman were located so far forward on the ship, they could no longer sight along the deck to aid them in steering a straight course toward some landmark on the shore. To compensate for that, vessels with pilothouses forward soon began using a *steering pole* sticking out from the bow of the ship to give them some reference point to use in steering.

A far more dramatic change occurred in 1841 with the launching of the *Str. Vandalia*, the first propeller-driven ship on the Great Lakes and the first commercial ship in the world to be driven by a propeller. The propeller had been developed by Captain John Ericsson, a Swedish inventor, and its introduction revolutionized the shipping industry. Propeller-driven ships used less fuel than paddlewheelers. They were also far safer in heavy seas because the rolling of the ship didn't cause the propeller to come out of the water, which often happened with paddlewheelers, causing engine damage. Propellers were initially slow to be accepted, though, because they required shipowners to make a hole in the stern of the ship below the waterline for the shaft that connected the engine to the propeller. Shipowners and sailors were reluctant to violate the watertight integrity of the hulls of their ships, which makes a certain amount of sense. The development of stern tubes and packing to prevent water from entering the ship from

around the shaft reduced opposition and led to widespread use of propellers and the eventual abandonment of paddlewheels.

The *Hackett* evolved from both the *Griffon* and the early steamboats and took advantage of the many improvements that had been made in each over the years, including the use of a propeller. In the same way, other shipbuilders soon began to improve on Peck's revolutionary design. In 1882, the first iron-hulled laker was launched at Cleveland. Built for the Nicholas Transit Company, the *Str. Onoko* was 282 feet long and set a new cargo record by carrying 2,164 tons of iron ore on its maiden voyage. Insurance underwriters were skeptical of the new material, however, fearing that the iron plates would shatter if the vessel ever ran aground. Because of the high risk factor that the insurance companies assigned to the iron hulls, shipbuilders built a number of vessels with composite hulls consisting of oak planking sheathed with iron from the waterline to the main deck. The cautious views of the underwriters were at least partially justified when the *Onoko* sank in Lake Superior in 1915, probably as the result of losing one of its iron hull plates.

While the *Onoko* and the other early steamers all carried auxiliary sails, steamboats were rapidly replacing sailing vessels on the lakes. By 1884, steamers accounted for 75 percent of all new vessels constructed at shipyards around the lakes. Of the 2,498 vessels operating on the lakes, 1,165, or 46 percent, were steam, and 2 or 3 steamboats were being built for every sailing ship that went down the ways.[4] The growing dominance of steam propulsion was further accelerated by the withdrawal from service of many older sailing ships that could no longer be operated economically in competition with the steamboats.

During the 1886 navigational season, the number of steam vessels on the lakes finally surpassed the number of sailing ships.[5] The bulk shipping industry was changing so rapidly that shipyards would often begin construction of a schooner, only to have the owners decide in the middle of construction that they wanted the vessel to be steam powered. A revolution was also taking place in construction materials, which would have a long-term impact on the industry.

In 1886, the Globe Iron Works, which had built the *Onoko*, launched the *Str. Spokane*, the first steel-hulled freighter. Steel rapidly became the preferred

A Sprague painting of the *Str. Onoko,* the first iron-hulled freighter and the longest ship on the Great Lakes in 1882. Referred to by some as a "floating boot box," the *Onoko* is shown here with its auxiliary sails set. (Institute for Great Lakes Research, Bowling Green State University)

The *Str. Spokane,* the first steel-hulled freighter on the Great Lakes, just moments before launching at Cleveland in 1886. The people crowding the decks and the tops of the cabins got a short, but wild ride when the giant vessel plummeted sideways down the greased ways and entered the water for the first time. (Institute for Great Lakes Research, Bowling Green State University)

building material for lakers, and shipyards soon discontinued the use of iron or composite hulls. Wood continued to be used into the early 1900s, but primarily for smaller vessels where minimizing construction costs was a major consideration for the owners. Operated by Thomas Wilson of Cleveland, the durable *Spokane* was lengthened to 311 feet in 1892. Converted to an auto carrier in the 1920s, it was eventually scrapped in 1935 after sitting idle during most of the depression years.

During the 1880–1910 period, the term *modern freighter* had virtually no meaning on the lakes. The bulk carriers evolved so rapidly that no sooner would the newest, largest, most-sophisticated ship slide off the ways than it would be followed by a vessel that was even more sophisticated and capable of carrying greater tonnages. A number of factors accounted for the spurt in creative shipbuilding. First was the growth in shipments of iron ore from the northern lakes. In 1884, just over two million tons were shipped. By 1890, shipments had quadrupled to more than eight million tons, and by 1898 well over thirteen million tons of red ore were moving down the lakes each year.[6] In 1888, ore shipments surpassed grain as the dominant cargo on the Great Lakes, a distinction that it has never relinquished. The geometric growth in iron ore shipments, combined with continued increases in shipments of grain, coal, and stone, taxed the ability of the industry to move all of the available cargo and provided an economic incentive for the construction of newer and larger ships.

Ship size on the Great Lakes had always been limited by ship design and construction technology, the size of the locks at Sault Ste. Marie and on the Welland and Lachine Canals, and by the depth of the river channels and harbors. Until 1895, channel depths and the dimensions of the Weizel Lock at the Soo limited vessels in the ore trade to a draft of 14 to 16 feet, lengths of less than 400 feet, and maximum beams of 35 to 40 feet. Vessels built to those dimensions were capable of carrying about 4,000 tons of ore, a staggering quantity compared to the 132 tons carried by the *Columbia* only a few decades earlier, but not adequate to placate vessel owners who saw higher profits in the economies of scale that would result from still larger ships.

Not only were the locks at Sault Ste. Marie too small to suit fleet officials, but they were proving incapable of efficiently handling the amount of vessel traffic on the lakes. By 1895, the delay at the Soo waiting for an open lock averaged nearly five hours per ship. A record number of transits was recorded on July 17, 1895, when 119 vessels were locked through in a twenty-four-hour period.[7]

Constant pressure from shippers and vessel owners led to the deepening of channels to 20 feet and the construction at Sault Ste. Marie of the first Poe Lock. Opened in late 1895, the new lock was 800 feet long, 100 feet wide, and could accommodate ships with drafts up to 22 feet. Designed to handle four vessels at once, the Poe Lock removed the size limits that had frustrated vessel designers. Both the size and carrying capacity of bulk freighters immediately ballooned. Before the Poe was put into operation, the newest ships on the lakes were so large that only two could transit the lock simultaneously.

One of the first ships to use the new Poe Lock was the *Str. Victory*, the first of the 400-footers, launched in 1895. With a 48-foot beam and 18-foot draft, it was capable of carrying payloads of 5,200 tons. But the *Victory* was just an intermediate stop in the challenge to build ships capable of carrying ever larger cargoes. By 1900, bulk freighters had been stretched to 500 feet, and in 1906 they reached the 600-foot plateau, with carrying capacities in excess of 11,000 tons. By then, only one of the new goliaths could lock through the Poe at a time. Officials at Sault Ste. Marie went back to the drawing boards to begin planning an even larger lock.

The 1880–1910 period was one of superlatives for shipbuilders and vessel owners. Adjectives like longest, widest, deepest, fastest, biggest, and newest became an important part of the lexicon of the lakes, as did less flattering terms like oddest, strangest, and most unusual. As vessel designers tried continually to improve on the basic design of the Great Lakes bulk freighter, it was inevitable that some would produce boats so dramatically different that they essentially constituted a new type of vessel, rather than just another step in the evolutionary process. Such was the case with Captain Alexander McDougall's now-famous *whalebacks*.

McDougall, an experienced ship captain on the lakes, established a shipyard at West Superior, Wisconsin, and launched his first cigar-shaped barge in 1888. Known simply as *No. 101*, the barge had a flat bottom with a rounded top and snoutlike bow. It was the most streamlined bulk vessel ever to operate on the lakes, but its unusual design elicited few favorable comments from onlookers, many of whom began to refer to it derisively as a "pigboat." McDougall's goal had been to develop a steel barge that was less expensive to build than the wood-hulled consorts towed by many of the steamers of the period, while also improving vessel strength and stability. The curved deck and turret-shaped pilothouse, which was located at the stern, were intended to reduce resistance to waves, thereby making them more seaworthy and easier to tow.

The idea for McDougall's whalebacks may actually have derived from a series of four ships built between 1858 and 1866 by the Winan brothers, a pair of well-to-do railway engineers. Unlike the Winans's, however, McDougall's design, while ridiculed by many of his contemporaries, proved to be reasonably functional. A total of about forty-three whalebacks were built between 1888 and 1896. In 1893 alone, McDougall's American Steel Barge Company had ten ships under construction at one time, with one whaleback launched every Saturday for eight consecutive weeks and two whalebacks and a tug launched on the ninth Saturday. While the first whalebacks were barges, McDougall added steam engines to his uniquely designed vessels in 1890 with the launching of the *Str. Colgate Hoyt*. The whaleback steamers became a familiar sight on the lakes, often towing whaleback barges behind them.

The whaleback design had some advantages, but it also had a number of distinct problems. The rounded deck was difficult for crewmembers to work on, particularly if waves were washing across it, which was often the case. The ships also had little reserve bouyancy due to the rounded deck and low freeboard; that made them more dangerous in cases where flooding occurred. The biggest drawback, however, and the one that eventually led to their demise in the dry bulk trade, resulted from their narrow hatches and cargo hold stanchions, which were necessary because of the tubular design of the whalebacks.

Because of the difficulty of working on the steeply sloping decks of the whalebacks, use of conventional wooden hatches with tarpaulin covers for foul weather was not feasible. McDougall addressed that problem by designing the industry's first one-piece steel hatch covers. Since only manual labor was available to handle the hatch covers, however, the hatch openings had to be much smaller than those used on most lakers of that era, only 8 feet by 10 feet. The small hatches proved unsuitable for use with mechanized unloading systems that developed around the turn of the century, particularly the Hulett unloaders, which rapidly became the standard for the industry. It was difficult to get the huge clamshell buckets of the unloading rigs through the small hatches, and the hold stanchions supporting the deck made it impossible to open the buckets to their full width, 24 feet for a Hulett, once inside the cargo hold.

The last two whalebacks were built in 1896: the *Str. John Ericsson*, named for the inventor of the propeller, and the *Str. Frank Rockefeller*. The *Ericsson*, at 430 feet in length and with a beam of 50 feet, was one of the largest freighters on the lakes at the time and the only whaleback built with its pilothouse forward in the style of conventional lakers. The *Ericsson* was also unique in being the first vessel on the lakes to have arc lights on deck to assist the crew when loading or unloading at night.

Although the popularity of the whalebacks declined, a number of them remained in the iron ore trade until as late as 1942. With their hulls and machinery still in good condition, many of them were converted ultimately into specialty vessels, serving out their remaining years as tankers, autocarriers, or even self-unloaders. The *Str. Rockefeller* became part of the famous Pittsburgh Steamship fleet in 1901. In 1928 it was converted to an auto carrier and continued in the auto and grain trade until 1942 as the *South Park*. In 1943 it was acquired by the Cleveland Tankers fleet, converted to a liquid bulk freighter, and renamed *Meteor*. The stalwart old whaleback continued to operate on the lakes until 1969, putting in seventy-three years of reliable service. The last surviving example of McDougall's unique ships, the *Meteor* was donated to the City of Superior, Wisconsin, where it had been built, and it began yet another career as a museum ship in 1973.

Interestingly, while McDougall's innovative ships were scorned by many in the Great Lakes industry, the vessels did achieve many of the builder's initial goals and carved out a distinctive niche for themselves in the maritime history of the lakes. McDougall, in fact, was chosen to be the first of the Great Lakes industry's "great people" to be honored by induction into the U.S. Merchant Marine Academy's National Maritime Hall of Fame in 1982. The

The whaleback steamer *South Park* entering Cleveland harbor with a load of new cars in 1934. Launched in 1896 as the bulk freighter *Frank Rockefeller*, it was modified for the sand trade in 1925 and converted to an auto carrier and renamed *South Park* in 1928. In 1943 it was rebuilt as a tanker and renamed *Meteor*. Now a maritime museum at Superior, Wisconsin, it is the only surviving whaleback vessel. (Institute for Great Lakes Research, Bowling Green State University)

tribute was paid to McDougall in honor of the innovative and efficient whalebacks he designed.

The unique design was mimicked by some other ship designers and led to construction of monitors, turtlebacks, and turret ships for service on the lakes. The most popular of these modified whalebacks were the turret ships built in England by William Doxford and Sons between 1892 and 1911. The ships were essentially typical ocean freighters, with their pilothouses and crew accommodations located amidships, except that they had rounded decks. Five of them were brought to the lakes by Canadian owners and at least one of them continued in operation until after World War II.

A number of designers also began experimenting with the location of engine rooms and pilothouses during this period. The *Str. Maryland*, built in 1890, had its pilothouse and engine room located amidships in the fashion of saltwater ships, as did the *Str. Curry*. Because of the high seas encountered on the oceans, a pilothouse located at the bow would be subject to wave damage, a problem less likely to occur on the lakes. The *Curry* was the largest ship on the lakes when launched in 1893, 360 feet long and 45 feet wide. When it was lengthened during the winter of 1904–5, the pilothouse was moved forward and the engine room aft so that it finally looked like a conventional laker.

In 1892, Cleveland-Cliffs had a bulk freighter, the *Choctaw*, built with its pilothouse at the stern, atop the engine room and cabins. The *Str. Yuma*, built in 1893 for the Owen Transportation Company, had the same arrangement. Both ships were built at Cleveland Shipbuilding, but there is no record of why the designers of the two ships chose to move the pilothouse from its traditional location at the bow, or why the practice was subsequently abandoned.

Another very unusual vessel on the lakes during the 1890–1910 period was the *Str. Helena*, built in 1888 for the Armour Grain Company. The ship had a five-story-high grain drying and processing house built on its deck just forward of the after cabins. The towering structure was used to dry grain while underway, an innovative idea, but one that did not catch on.

With the growth in the size of lake freighters, many fleets began ordering guest accommodations to be included on their ships for use by company officials or passengers, who were generally impor-

tant customers of the shipping company. These accommodations were usually located in the forward cabin area and ranged from spartan to luxurious in their size and decor. After making a trip in the guest quarters aboard the *Str. Thomas F. Cole*, author James Oliver Curwood wrote that "behind their uninviting exterior there is a luxury of marine travel that is equalled nowhere else in the world except on the largest and finest of private yachts." [8] One of the most unusual arrangements for guest quarters was aboard the *Str. Frank H. Goodyear*, a 450-by-50-foot freighter built in 1902 for John Mitchell, an owner of the Buffalo & Susquehanna Railway. The quarters consisted of a luxuriously outfitted passenger car from the railroad that Mitchell had installed amidships on the *Goodyear*'s deck.

Not all of the innovations in ship design during the important 1880–1910 period resulted in vessels that can retrospectively be viewed as oddities, however. The most significant new development during the period was the conversion in 1902 of the *Str. Hennepin* to a self-unloader at the Sturgeon Bay, Wisconsin, shipyard of Leathem D. Smith. The *Hennepin*, a 220-foot wood-hulled bulk freighter, launched in 1888 as the *Str. George H. Dyer*, was retrofitted with a crude conveying system that carried cargo out of the cargo hold to a conveyor boom located on the deck. The long boom was suspended from a four-legged derrick located amidships and could be swung over the ship's side to deposit cargo on the shore without assistance from shoreside unloading equipment. The tiny self-unloader, rated at only 990 gross tons after its conversion, was owned by the Lake Shore Stone Company of Milwaukee and was used primarily in the stone trade.

Indications are that the new type of vessel was not well received by people in the industry, even though the self-unloading system allowed the little ship to discharge its cargo at virtually any port on the lakes, including hundreds of ports that lacked shoreside unloading equipment. There are several possible explanations for why the seemingly versatile self-unloaders did not immediately catch on with vessel owners. Perhaps the most common argument against the innovative vessels was that they represented a dramatic departure from a system that was already deeply entrenched on the lakes. The role of the ships in the system consisted of hauling as much cargo as they could on every trip, and the alterations

The ice-laden *Str. Yuma* at Sault Ste. Marie around 1900. One of the first ships on the lakes to be built with its pilothouse and all accommodations on the stern, the *Yuma* was sold to a saltwater shipping firm during World War I and it operated in the coastal trade on the North Atlantic until 1949, spending its last sixteen years as a barge. (Institute for Great Lakes Research, Bowling Green State University)

The wood-hulled *Str. Hennepin* shown discharging a cargo of stone at Chicago on July 26, 1924. Launched in 1888 as a bulk freighter, the little vessel became the first self-unloading ship on the Great Lakes when it was converted in 1902. Ridiculed at first, the self-unloaders eventually came to dominate shipping on the lakes. (Institute for Great Lakes Research, Bowling Green State University)

necessary to the cargo hold of the self-unloader decreased the amount of cargo the vessel could carry. Not only did the self-unloaders seem like a retreat from the goal of increasing carrying capacities, but the self-unloading equipment also added to the cost of constructing a ship. Loading and unloading systems were in place at all of the key ports at both ends of the lakes and were beyond the concern of shipowners, whose only interest was in cargo tonnages. There was little incentive to incur additional construction costs when the growth in the Great Lakes bulk market was providing substantial profits to anyone who owned a ship capable of moving cargo from the upper lakes to the lower lakes. Those profits, the owners knew, were based on tonnages hauled, so there was a strong tendency for them to stick with the status quo operating system.

The *Hennepin* continued to operate on the lakes until it sank in a 1927 storm off South Haven, Michigan. But before the pioneering vessel met its violent end, it had been joined by a number of other, more-

sophisticated self unloading ships. The *Str. Wyandotte*, a 364-foot, steel-hulled self-unloader was launched at the Great Lakes Engineering Works at Ecorse, Michigan, in 1908. It is viewed by many as the prototype for the modern self-unloading ship. The *Wyandotte* was designed by George B. Palmer, chief engineer for the vessel's owner, the Wyandotte Chemical Company, and by engineers of the Stephens-Adamson company, an Aurora, Illinois, firm that specialized in the design and manufacture of conveying equipment for a variety of applications. Wyandotte chemical's interest in self-unloaders grew out of its desire to speed the delivery of bulk raw materials, primarily limestone, to its plant on the Detroit River without incurring the expense of installing shore-based unloading equipment.

The *Wyandotte*, which operated on the lakes until 1966, had a cargo hold with sides that angled inward, sloping toward the center of the vessel's keel. Where the two sides came together, a system of steel gates contained the cargo above two steel pan con-

The *Str. Wyandotte,* the first large self-unloader on the lakes and the first ship actually built as a self-unloader. By using self-unloading ships, its owners, the Wyandotte Chemical Company, avoided the expense of installing shoreside unloading equipment at their manufacturing facility on the Detroit River. The *Wyandotte*'s skeleton-like self-unloading boom is suspended from an A-frame located just behind its forward cabins. (Institute for Great Lakes Research, Bowling Green State University)

veyors located in tunnels running the full length of the hold. The gates could be opened and closed by crewmembers, called gatemen, who controlled the amount of cargo allowed to spill into the conveyor tunnels. Cargo in the tunnels was moved to the forward end of the ship by a system of scrapers. The heavy, crescent-shaped scoops were pulled through the tunnel by chains, pushing cargo along ahead of them on the smooth steel floor of the conveyor. At the forward end of the hold, the cargo was pushed up a slight incline, at the end of which it fell into a hopper. The scrapers would then lift to the top of the tunnel and return to the aft end of the cargo hold to begin another cycle.

Cargo dumped into the forward hopper spilled through it onto a rubberized conveyor belt that carried it up and out of the cargo hold to a second hopper located just aft of the superstructure at the forward end of the ship. Flowing through the second hopper, the cargo dropped onto another endless conveyor belt mounted in the ship's 50-foot long unloading boom. The forward end of the long, skeleton-like boom was mounted on a king post located just behind the superstructure, and the boom extended aft just above the deck. A system of cables ran from the boom to the top of the A-frame that towered above the king post, then down to a winch. The system allowed the boom to be raised and swung over the side of the ship in much the same way the boom on a crane can be moved. Cargo flowing along the conveyor belt that ran the length of the boom could then be deposited on the dock.

The *Wyandotte* had a total carrying capacity of only 2,095 tons when it was launched. At the close of its second season operating on the lakes, it was lengthened by 60 feet, which raised its capacity to 2,450 tons. With its conveying system, the little vessel could discharge its cargo at about 500 tons per hour.

Another wood-hulled bulk freighter, the *Maggie Marshall*, was converted to a self-unloader in 1908 for the Douglass Transit Company, the same year the *Wyandotte* was launched. A second steel-hulled self-unloader, the *Str. Alpena*, was launched in 1909 by Wyandotte Chemical. Like the *Wyandotte*, both the *Marshall* and the *Alpena* were small ships. The *Marshall* was a diminutive 157 feet long, while the *Alpena* measured 376 feet overall. All three were dwarfed by the latest generation of bulk freighters that were then being launched for the iron ore trade, most of which measured 600 feet in length and had carrying capacities of 10,000 tons or more, three times that of the biggest of the self-unloaders.

The first large ship to be equipped with a self-unloading system was the *Str. W. F. White*, built in 1915 for the Bradley Transportation Lines. With a carrying capacity of 10,000 tons, the *White* was equal in stature to any ship operating on the lakes at that time, and larger than most. The unloading system on the *White*, also developed by Stephens-Adamson, was similar to that used on the *Wyandotte*, except that the steel pan conveyors were replaced by two rubberized belt conveyors, and a bucket elevator system was used to lift the cargo from the tunnels under the hold to the level of the self-unloading boom. The rectangular buckets on the elevator system could lift the cargo much more vertically than the conveyor belt elevator used on the *Wyandotte*, reducing the amount of cargo hold area that had to be allocated for the elevator system and thereby maximizing the carrying capacity of the ship. Both the bucket elevator and the conveyor belts in the cargo hold were capable of operating at a much higher speed than the system on prior vessels. The *White* could unload at the impressive rate of 2,800 tons an hour.

The early self-unloaders were considered specialized vessels, operating outside the mainstream of the Great Lakes bulk industry. They clearly served a useful purpose, however, and one that could not be served by conventional freighters without self-unloading equipment. The self-unloaders appear to have slowly gained in popularity until the 1920s, when their numbers increased significantly. Until the 1970s, they were primarily engaged in hauling stone and coal, while iron ore continued to move almost totally in the traditional-style bulk freighters, which began to be referred to as *straight-deckers* to differentiate them from the self-unloaders. The limited number of iron ore unloading ports, located in proximity to the steel mills south of the lakes, handled sufficient volumes of cargo to justify the expense of building and operating shoreside unloading systems. Much limestone and coal, however, was bound for small ports that did not have unloading equipment and could be served most efficiently by self-unloaders.

Around 1890, another new type of vessel emerged on the lakes: small steel steamers designed to transit the diminutive locks in the St. Lawrence and Welland Canals. The *canallers*, as they were known, operated almost solely under Canadian flag as both bulk freighters and packet freighters. Many of the canallers, which were only about 250 feet long, were built by shipyards in England, as were some larger Canadian freighters.

The larger foreign-built ships, those too long to negotiate the locks in the Welland or St. Lawrence, were also too large to transit the canals on their way into the lakes. Upon their arrival in the St. Lawrence, the ships had their midbodies removed, and the remaining bow and stern sections were welded together. With the midbody sections stowed in their cargo holds, the downsized ships made their way through the locks of the St. Lawrence and Welland Canals and onto the Great Lakes. Once above the Welland, the vessels would again be cut in half and the midbody sections reinstalled before the ships were put into service. This procedure allowed fleets in Canada, which was then a British possession, to augment its modest shipbuilding capability by obtaining vessels from the many established yards in Great Britain. On the U.S. side of the lakes, however, shipyards sprang up in scores of port cities as shipbuilders and would-be shipbuilders tried to keep pace with the growing demand for both bulk and passenger vessels.

During the early years of the twentieth century, there were major shipyards at Wyandotte, Port Huron, Marine City, West Bay City, Gibraltar, Grand Haven, Alpena, Mount Clemens, East Saginaw, and Detroit in Michigan; Lorain, Toledo, Cleveland,

Saugatuck, Milan, and Ashtabula in Ohio; Milwaukee, Superior, Manitowac, Sheboygan, Sturgeon Bay, and Twin River in Wisconsin; South Chicago, Illinois; and Buffalo, New York. Major Canadian yards existed at Lauzon, Quebec, and Midland, Collingwood, and Port Arthur in Ontario.

In addition to the construction of new ships, the shipyards also began to be involved in lengthening existing steel freighters. One of the earliest recorded lengthenings involved the *Str. Lewiston* and took place in 1897. The practice subsequently became common on the lakes. Because most lakers operate solely in freshwater, they are not subject to the corrosive action of saltwater that is experienced with ocean vessels. As a result, the hulls of Great Lakes ships can remain serviceable for fifty to seventy years, although most of them become economically obsolete because of their size long before their hulls deteriorate. Lengthening, or stretching, provides vessel owners with a way to extend the economic life of a boat by increasing its carrying capacity at a rather minimal cost, particularly compared to the cost of new vessel construction. Most generations of vessels on the lakes were built to the maximum dimensions that could be accommodated by the Soo Locks at the time of their construction. Each time a new, larger lock has been added at the Soo, it has generally touched off a flurry of lengthenings around the lakes, with older, smaller ships being stretched to the new limits of the locks.

Between 1901 and 1910, shipyards on the Great Lakes built 297 new ships, more than presently exist in the combined U.S. and Canadian bulk fleets. It was perhaps the single most important decade in the history of Great Lakes shipping, not just because of the numbers of ships added to the fleet, but because of the advancements that took place in vessel design during those ten years. Except for the fact that ships were longer, wider, and deeper, the changes made during this period did not substantially alter the external appearance of the bulk carriers. Typical of ships launched during the first decade of the twentieth century was the *Str. Augustus B. Wolvin*, built for the Acme Steamship Company in 1904. When the *Wolvin* was launched it was the largest ship on the lakes, 540 feet in length and with a beam of 56 feet. The *Wolvin*, which operated on the lakes until 1967, was best known during its early years for its unusual hull color. While most vessels operating on the Great Lakes have their hulls painted black or rust color, the *Wolvin*'s was a brilliant yellow, almost orange, and it was soon nicknamed "The Yellow Kid."

The most significant aspects of the *Wolvin*'s construction would not have been so readily obvious to observers, however. It was the first ship on the Great Lakes built without main deck beams or hold stanchions, which had been standard on lakers until then. Girder arches provided support for the *Wolvin*'s deck and eliminated the need for any additional structural supports within the cargo hold. Prior to the *Wolvin*, the construction techniques used for steel ships basically had imitated the methods used for centuries in building wooden vessels. The deck rested on deck beams, which were suspended at each side of the hull on supports similar to the knees used in wooden ships. A second set of beams ran transversely across the inside of the hold, about half way between the deck and the keel, and those beams also rested on the steel equivalent of knees. The centers of the beams on both levels were supported by vertical stanchions that rested on the keel at the ship's centerline. The cargo hold looked like the inside of an immense barn, with posts and beams cluttering the cavernous space. Through the use of girder arches, the cargo hold of the *Wolvin* became a great, open expanse. The elimination of all supporting members within the hold facilitated both loading and unloading, but proved to be particularly important in unloading by mechanized systems like the Huletts.

Most of the ships built during the period had ballast tanks between the bottom of the hull and the floor of the cargo hold, an area known as the *double bottom*. On the *Wolvin*, vertical side tanks were also added for additional ballast, extending the length of the cargo hold and sandwiched between the exterior of the hull and the walls of the cargo hold along both sides of the ship. The ability to carry additional ballast water increased the seaworthiness of vessels operating in heavy seas and made it easier for the larger ships to get under the loading spouts at ore docks on the upper lakes.

The *Wolvin* was also one of the early ships built with 12-foot spacing on its hatches, instead of the 24-foot spacing that had been standard on the lakes. The 12-foot spacing made it possible for the hatches of the ship to line up with every loading spout on the ore docks, instead of every other spout. This elimi-

Acme Steamship's *Str. Augustus B. Wolvin,* launched in 1904, was the first ship built with arch girders supporting its decks, instead of the hold stanchions that had been used previously. The *Wolvin*'s unusual yellow-orange hull made it popular with boatwatchers around the lakes. (Institute for Great Lakes Research, Bowling Green State University)

nated the need to reposition the ship during loading, thereby reducing loading time. The *Str. James H. Hoyt*, another Acme vessel and the first ever built with 12-foot hatch centers, could load 5,250 tons of iron ore in just 30.5 minutes; the average loading time for lake freighters was then about 5.6 hours.

The *Wolvin* was also the first ship on the Great Lakes to have telescoping, or leaf-type, steel hatch covers, instead of wooden ones. Manual removal of the wooden hatch cover sections before loading and unloading, and their replacement afterward, was a time-consuming and labor intensive process, adding greatly to vessel turnaround time in port. The telescoping hatches were designed in overlapping sections that could slide back to the outboard edge of the hatch opening, automatically stacking on top of each other. Substantially less manual labor was involved; deckhands merely ran cables from the hatch covers to steam winches on the deck, and the winches provided the power to open or close the leaves. Telescoping steel hatch covers became the standard for the next two decades, although a few ships continued to be equipped with wooden hatch covers through at least 1936.[9]

The innovative construction techniques employed on the *Wolvin* were instantly accepted by shipbuilders around the lakes, and all subsequent bulk freighters incorporated the arched girders and side tanks, although both have been further refined. Many ships built before the *Wolvin* were later reconstructed, with their deck beams and centerline stanchions removed to clear away structural members that interfered with unloading equipment.

The *Str. William G. Mather*, launched in 1905 for Cleveland Cliffs, was one of the first bulk freighters with a 60-foot beam, which became the standard for the industry until 1938. The *Mather* was also equipped with steam mooring winches, and while manila mooring lines were then in use, they were soon replaced by steel cables that were substantially stronger and more durable.

The 1905 shipping season also saw vessel carrying capacities reach the 11,000-ton mark with the launching for the Pittsburgh fleet of the steamers *William E. Corey*, *Henry C. Frick*, *Elbert H. Gary*, and *George W. Perkins*. The four ships were each 549 feet long, with beams of 56 feet. They were the first new ships built specifically for the famous "steel trust" fleet created in 1901 with the purchase by J. P.

Morgan and Judge E. H. Gary of John D. Rockefeller's Bessemer Steamship Company, Andrew Carnegie's Pittsburgh Steamship Company, and the Minnesota Steamship Company, thus creating the giant United States Steel Corporation fleet. The *Gary* class, as they were known, were variations on the design of the *Wolvin*, and they introduced the modern style of forward cabin arrangements. The ships were designed with their pilothouses set atop a Texas deckhouse on the forecastle. The *Corey*, built to serve as the new flagship for the Pittsburgh fleet, had a larger Texas house than the others to accommodate guest quarters.[10]

In the following year, 1906, six ships were launched that were even larger than the *Gary*-class ships. They were the first of the famous *standard 600-footers*, which were to play a central role for the industry for the next seventy years. The six steamers, the *J. Pierpont Morgan*, *Peter A. B. Widener*, *Henry H. Rogers*, *Norman B. Ream*, *Edward Y. Townsend*, and *Daniel J. Morrell*, were actually 604 feet long, while later additions to the 600-foot class would range up to 612 feet in actual length. The six original ships had beams of 58 feet and drafts of 19 feet. They were powered by triple expansion steam engines that generated about 1,800 horsepower. The early 600-footers had carrying capacities of just over 11,000 tons and were constructed at a cost of about $440,000 apiece. A ship of similar size would cost more than $40 million today. Improved shipbuilding techniques allowed the shipyards to turn out a 600-footer in an average of four to five months, although one ship was reportedly built in only fifty-three days. As many as 700 to 800 shipyard workers were employed on each hull, and many components were prefabricated prior to installation in the hulls to save time.

The first of the 600-footers had interesting careers. One of the ships, the *Ream*, was in service until 1990, spending its final years as a storage barge and dock extension at Port Huron, Michigan. The *Morrell* sank in a fierce Lake Huron storm in 1965 (see chapter 7). The *Townsend* broke in half and sank while being towed to Spain for scrapping in 1968, and the other four ships were all scrapped between 1974 and 1986 after long years of service on the lakes.

The "modern era" of Great Lakes bulk shipping had essentially emerged by 1910. Although many sailing vessels and wood-hulled ships were still operating on the lakes, they were vestiges of a bygone era. Wood was being used only in the construction of the very smallest vessels on the lakes, all of which operated outside the mainstream of the bulk industry. The last true schooner had been launched in 1889, and while sailing vessels survived on the lakes until 1929, their size limitations doomed them to eventual extinction.

Consorts, too, were rapidly disappearing from the lakes. The unpowered barges commonly had been towed by steam freighters ever since the launching of the *Hackett* and its consort, the *Forest City*, in 1869 and 1870, respectively. As ships grew larger, however, operators found that the greatest economy was reached through use of a single steamer with a large carrying capacity and relatively low horsepower engine, rather than a steamer with the larger engine required if the vessel was also to tow a consort. The last consort, the *Alexander Maitland*, was built in 1902.

By 1910, all of the major unloading ports on the Great Lakes had installed sophisticated unloading systems, primarily Huletts. Smaller ports that were not receiving large quantities of bulk materials had to begin relying on service by ships that were equipped to unload themselves. The market that existed for self-unloading ships was partially filled by continuous self-unloaders, like the *Wyandotte* and *Alpena*, but by 1912 a second type of self-unloading ship emerged to serve that growing market. The alternative to the continuous self-unloader, which used either a scraper or conveyor belt system, was the crane ship or crane boat. While early information about the crane boats is sketchy, we know that the *Str. John Lambert*, a 250-foot freighter built in 1903, had unloading cranes installed in 1912. The *Lambert*, operated by the Great Lakes & St. Lawrence Transportation Company, may have been the first of what became a common sight on the lakes.

Like the continuous self-unloaders, the crane boats were generally smaller vessels that had their lives extended by the installation of cranes. This allowed them to unload at the many ports around the lakes that did not have shore-based unloading systems. They generally carried salt, coal, or limestone. In addition to the traditional bulk cargoes, however, many of them were also used to transport breakbulk cargoes such as steel or pig iron, which they unloaded through the use of electromagnets, instead of the clamshell buckets used to handle bulk products. While many fleets, including Bethlehem, Columbia, and U.S. Steel's Great Lakes Fleet, continued to operate crane boats during the 1950s and 1960s, decreases in interlake shipments of steel and pig iron, combined with the growing efficiency of continuous self-unloaders, led to the demise of the crane boats. By 1986, only one crane boat, the *Buckeye*, was still handling bulk cargoes on the lakes, and it was being operated as a towed barge, rather than under its own power. The barge *Buckeye* had begun life on the lakes in 1910 as the *Str. Leonard B. Miller*, but its name was changed to the *Charles W. Galloway* in 1937. In 1958, the ship was again renamed, becoming the *Robert C. Norton*, and it was converted to a crane boat with two revolving cranes on its deck. The *Norton*, operated by Columbia Transportation, differed from other crane boats in that the two cranes fed cargo to a 200-foot boom, similar to those used on the continuous self-unloaders. In 1979, the ship was acquired by the Upper Lakes Towing Company and converted to a barge. Since then, the again-renamed *Buckeye* has been a frequent visitor to ports around the lakes, being towed by the powerful tug *Olive L. Moore*.

While great strides had been made in ship construction techniques and both deck and engine equipment had been improved dramatically in the period since the launching of the *Hackett* in 1869, few changes had been made in navigational equipment. As the storm clouds that would erupt into World War I gathered over Europe, the sole piece of navigational equipment aboard most ships was a simple magnetic compass. The men who commanded the ships on the inland seas relied more on their knowledge of the lakes and rivers than they did on their compasses, which were subject to great error at times. On most ships, the captain or a mate stood watch "on top of the pilothouse," out in the open air where his hearing and vision were best. It was always a lonely vigil, and during inclement weather, particularly in the early spring and late fall, it was often a brutal post to stand. The chief mate on the *Schooner Milwaukee* actually froze to death at the wheel during a severe storm in the fall of 1842.[11] Communications between vessels, or between a ship and the shore was by whistle signals or use of a megaphone, like the ones cheerleaders use at football games. For the most part, the ships were incom-

At 576 feet, the *Str. Elbert H. Gary* was the longest ship on the lakes when it was launched in 1905. Shown here passing Mackinac Island on its maiden voyage, the venerable ship was scrapped in 1973 after being in service for more than six decades. (Institute for Great Lakes Research, Bowling Green State University)

municado from the time they left one dock until they arrived at the next.

With the coming of World War I in 1914, a large number of ships from the lakes, primarily smaller packet freighters from the Canadian fleets, were pressed into ocean service in support of the war effort. Vessels that were too large to transit the locks of the Welland and St. Lawrence were cut in two to make the passage from the lakes to the ocean, reversing the procedure that had been used to get many foreign-built ships into the lakes. Quite a number of former Great Lakes ships were lost to enemy fire and U-boats during the war years.

For the ships left on the lakes, the wartime demand for iron ore brought another boom period. Every ship in the fleet was pressed into service, and although they often had to operate shorthanded, they carried on valiantly throughout the war years, supplying American heavy industry with the raw materials needed to manufacture weapons and other equipment for the Armed Forces of the U.S. and its allies.

When the "war to end all wars" ended in 1919, fifty years had passed since the launching of the *Str. R. J. Hackett* in 1869. In those fifty years, ships had almost tripled in length and carrying capacities had increased tenfold. The latest generation of lake freighters were nothing short of leviathans, great smoke-belching steamboats unmatched throughout the world in their efficiency. Yet it was just the beginning. The Great Lakes steamboats that dominated the waterways had barely reached adulthood. The most productive years, the years of the greatest growth, still lay ahead for the industry, though it is unlikely that many people who had seen the great strides made during those first fifty years could have foreseen the staggering changes that waited just over the horizon.

While the 1869 to 1919 period saw the beginnings of the Great Lakes steamboat and the modern bulk industry, it was also a time of endings: the "Golden Age" had passed for the maritime industry. Highways and railroads were crisscrossing the states and provinces bordering the lakes, and people were turn-

The *Str. J. Pierpont Morgan,* the first of the standard 600-footers launched in 1906 for U.S. Steel's Pittsburgh Steamship fleet. (Institute for Great Lakes Research, Bowling Green State University)

Huletts unloading U.S. Steel's Maritime Class freighter, the *Str. Robert C. Stanley*. The worker operating the Hulett is visible in the cab located just above the clamshell bucket. (Author's collection)

The 434-foot crane ship *Clifford F. Hood* on Lake St. Clair in 1968. The *Hood,* operated by U.S. Steel's Great Lakes Fleet, was one of the last crane ships on the lakes. (Author's collection)

ing away from boats and ships as a primary means of travel in favor of automobiles and trains. Goods that had been shipped for centuries on the lakes were diverted to trucks and trains. At hundreds of communities that dotted the shorelines of the lakes, once bustling harbors began to see less and less vessel traffic.

The majestic sailing ships that were a part of our cultural heritage began to disappear under the pall of economic inefficiency, unable to compete with the larger and faster steamboats. Passenger steamers, which had brought hundreds of thousands of immigrants to the fertile farmlands and industrial meccas that bordered the lakes, sat idle at docks in Detroit, Cleveland, and Buffalo, too slow to compete with steam locomotives and automobiles.

Gone, too, was Captain Eli Peck, the obscure shipbuilder from Cleveland who revolutionized the bulk freight industry when he launched the little *R. J. Hackett.* After building more than one hundred steam and sailing vessels, Peck had left shipbuilding in the early 1870s and organized his own steamship line, the Northwestern Transportation Company, which operated in the passenger and freight trades. Although trained as a ship's carpenter in his youth, Peck was a competent navigator and commanded one of his own ships, the *Fountain City,* for a number of years. He died in 1896 after a short illness. His body was carried from Detroit to Cleveland aboard the tug *E. M. Peck,* which he had built and which bore his name. He was interred in Lakeview Cemetery, within sight of the shipping lanes navigated by the unique breed of Great Lakes steamboats that he had created.

Notes

1. J. B. Mansfield, ed., *History of the Great Lakes*, vol. I (Chicago: J. H. Beers & Co., 1899; reprint, Cleveland: Freshwater Press, 1972), 45.
2. Ibid., vol. II, 281.
3. Harry Benford, "Sixty Years of Shipbuilding," paper presented at the meeting of the Great Lakes Section of

the Society of Naval Architects & Marine Engineers, October 5, 1956, 1.

4. Mansfield, vol. I, 439.

5. Ibid.

6. Ibid, 566.

7. John W. Larson, *Essayons: A History of the Detroit District, U.S. Army Corps of Engineers* (Detroit: U.S. Army Corps of Engineers, 1981), 93.

8. James Oliver Curwood, *The Great Lakes* (1909), 138–39.

9. Harry F. Myers, "Remembering the 504's," *Inland Seas* 44 no. 2 (Summer 1988): 91.

10. Gary S. Dewar, "A Forgotten Class," *Telescope* (Mar.–Apr. 1989): 31–39.

11. Larson, 40.

3

The "Super Steamboats," 1919–1969

They are not beautiful. Freighted low down, their steel sides scraped and marred like the hands of a labourer, their huge funnels emitting clouds of bituminous smoke, their barren steel decks glaring in the heat of the summer sun, there seems to be but little about them to attract the pleasure seeker.
—James Oliver Curwood,
The Great Lakes, 1909

In the years immediately following World War I, the maritime industry benefitted from technology developed during the war by the military. In 1922, the *Str. Daniel J. Morrell* became the first ship on the lakes to be equipped with a gyrocompass, which soon replaced the magnetic compass as the standard navigational tool. The gyrocompass is a mechanical compass that utilizes the forces of gravity and inertia, rather than magnetism, to determine true north, or what we would refer to as the North Pole. Unlike magnetic compasses, gyrocompasses are not affected by the earth's magnetism or ferrous metals in proximity to them.

Magnetic compasses, on the other hand, are simply sensitive magnets that will react to any iron objects that disturb their magnetic field. Magnetic compasses, in fact, do not point to polar north; they vary from polar north because of magnetic disturbances within the crust of the earth. In the Great Lakes region, compasses will show variation from true north as the result of iron ore deposits that attract the slender magnet that serves as the needle of the compass. The usual amount of these deflections are known and are shown on navigational charts so that mariners using magnetic compasses can correct for the amount of variation. However, magnetic compasses are also subject to deviation as a result of magnetic forces in the immediate vicinity of the compass. The steel hull of the ship itself affects the compass, as will magnetic fields resulting from the operation of electric motors near the compass. In fact, a crewmember standing close to a magnetic compass with a wrench in his pocket can cause the compass to deviate dramatically.

While transient deviations are a problem that mariners are sensitive to, but have to live with, those more constant deviations caused by the normal magnetic forces that exist aboard a ship can be "compensated" to eliminate most of the deviation. This is done by placing magnetic objects on each side of the compass and adjusting their position until deviations caused by the magnetic field of the vessel are substantially eliminated. Most magnetic compasses used aboard commercial vessels have a large metal ball mounted on each side of the compass for use in compensating for deviation.

Gyrocompasses, however, because they do not operate on magnetism, are capable of being adjusted so that they do point to true north. While their accuracy is somewhat dependent on the location and speed of the vessel, they are much more accurate than magnetic compasses. Commercial vessels on the lakes still have magnetic compasses aboard, but crewmembers rely almost totally on gyrocompasses for navigation.

The year 1922 also saw the beginning of marine radio communications on the Great Lakes. Using a 500-watt Navy surplus transmitter, radio station WCAF began broadcasting messages in Morse code to a limited number of ships on the lakes equipped with radio receivers. WCAF was owned by the Michigan Limestone and Chemical Company of Rogers City, Michigan, operators of a massive limestone quarry—the Calcite Plant—along the northern shore of Lake Huron. The first broadcasts were to vessels of the Bradley Transportation Company, a subsidiary of Michigan Limestone. Bradley was subsequently purchased along with the quarry by U. S. Steel and is today operated as part of the USS Great Lakes Fleet. A few ships of Boland and Cornelius Shipping, which has since become American Steamship, were also equipped to receive the early broadcasts from WCAF. Before the opening of the 1923 shipping season, the radio station was licensed as a public station that could serve any fleets on the lakes. The station's call sign was changed to WHT and a stronger transmitter, capable of broadcasts in both Morse and voice, was installed.

A Bradley freighter, the *Carl D. Bradley*, which was subsequently renamed and operates today as the *Irvin L. Clymer*, was the first ship equipped to receive and transmit messages in both Morse and voice. By 1924, there were about twenty vessels on the lakes

that had been equipped with Morse and voice equipment, despite outspoken objections from most of the captains who commanded the freighters. The captains feared that ship-to-shore communications, particularly in voice, would lead to the fleet offices attempting to control the daily operations of their ships. They were willing to accept the use of Morse communications, which tended to be shorter and more formal because the messages had to be transmitted by a radio operator. But they feared voice communications would allow office personnel to merely sit down at a microphone and dictate orders to their captains. After all, what did those landlubbers know about the hard realities of running a ship on the lakes? That had always been the captain's bailiwick. After a two-year test of the voice communications system, which included broadcasts of news, religious services, and an occasional live talent show, the captains won out. WHT reverted to the use of only Morse transmissions at the end of the 1924 shipping season.

In late 1924, the little station at Rogers City changed its call sign again, to WLC, concurrent with acquisition of a powerful 10,000-watt transmitter from Navy surplus. WLC continued to serve the fleets on the lakes with Morse, or radiotelegraph, communications until the early 1940s, when voice broadcasts were again instituted. Despite continued opposition from many captains, voice rapidly became the sole mode of both ship-to-shore and ship-to-ship communications.[1] WLC continues to serve the industry today, along with many other marine radio stations scattered around the lakes. While voice communications still predominate, using VHF or single-sideband radios, a number of fleets are now relying on sophisticated telex and satellite transmissions to send messages between the ships and fleet offices.

Communication costs are high for the fleets on the Great Lakes. On the U.S. side of the system, most fleets relied for many years on the Great Lakes Maritel Network to handle their communications between company offices and their ships. The Maritel Network, a VHF voice system operated by Lorain Electronics of Lorain, Ohio, consists of a network of stations around the lakes that are automatically tied in to the firm's central radio facility in Lorain by telephone lines. All calls from ships are handled from Lorain, regardless of the ship's location. Because of the limited range of VHF transmissions, a ship operating on the upper lakes cannot contact

Lorain directly. Instead, the call is made to one of many unmanned relay stations around the lakes. Through the relay station, the ship is connected with the Lorain facility and tied in to the regular telephone system. Because the system is almost completely automated, it is possible for shipboard personnel to make direct dial calls to any shoreside telephone.

The Maritel Network is an expensive operation, however. During the 1984 season, fleets subscribing to the service were billed a total of $1.3 million, most of which represented overhead costs for maintaining and operating the system. Each fleet's share of the total was apportioned based on the fleet's share of the total gross vessel tonnage operated by the companies subscribing to the service. As the number of ships in operation on the lakes declined and the shares apportioned among fewer ships, the high costs of operating the Maritel Network became increasingly difficult for the fleets to justify. As a result, most of the fleets withdrew from the network at the end of the 1985 season, although many still use the system occasionally, paying on a per call basis.

To reduce their need to rely on the Lorain system and in an effort to reduce their communications costs, a number of fleets installed cellular telephone systems aboard their ships. Cellular phones, the latest generation of mobile radiotelephones, are primarily designed for business use in urban areas. Much of the lower lakes, in the Cleveland-Detroit-Chicago corridor, is served presently by cellular systems, but it will be a number of years before the service can be extended to the northern lakes.

Where cellular service is not available, the fleets either use the Lorain VHF system or single-sideband transmissions through WLC. To further cut costs, several companies using single-sideband have also installed SITOR telex equipment. Messages to be broadcast via SITOR are first prepared on a microcomputer using standard word-processing software. The messages can then be transmitted over the radio link at a very high rate of speed, which reduces the transmission costs.

Two of the U.S. fleets and several Canadian fleets have also installed satellite communications (SATCOM) systems aboard some of their vessels. SATCOM messages, which can be either voice or data, are bounced off communications satellites circling the earth and relayed by a land station via regular telephone lines. The SATCOM systems are highly effective, but expensive to install and operate.

A study of communication costs conducted in 1985–86 by Columbia Transportation showed that satellite charges were among the highest of any of the alternative modes, about $10 per minute of air time. By comparison, the Lorain VHF system then cost about $10 for the first minute and $3.35 for each additional minute; single-sideband cost $3.50 a minute; and cellular transmissions cost $1.00 to $1.25 per minute.

As the cellular system is expanded to serve the less-populated areas on the northern lakes, it is likely that more and more companies will rely on cellular phones for their primary ship-to-shore and ship-to-ship communications. In the interim, the fleets will use a mix of systems, while continuing to use VHF for ship-to-ship transmissions that do not need to go through a shore station.

Another piece of equipment that was put into use for marine navigation after World War I was the radio direction-finder (RDF). Since there were few radio stations operating around the lakes at the time, the Navy installed a system of radio beacons for use specifically in direction finding. The beacon transmitters broadcast a continuous radio signal, usually a letter of the alphabet repeated continuously in Morse code. Locations of the beacons and other commercial broadcast stations around the lakes were printed on the navigational charts carried aboard ships.

RDF is nothing more than a radio with a sensitive directional antenna. When the radio is tuned to a radio transmitter in a known location, the operator is able to determine the line bearing from the ship to that transmitter. By taking bearings on two or more transmitters, the navigator can plot a reasonably accurate location of the ship through triangulation. RDF was an important navigational tool on the lakes until the use of radar became widespread after World War II. A few ships still have RDF equipment installed in their pilothouses, though it is no longer used.

By the end of World War I, major strides had also been made in perfecting internal combustion engines, both gasoline and diesel, and in 1924 the 611-foot *Henry Ford II* became the first large vessel on the lakes to be powered by a diesel engine. The *Henry II*, as it is commonly referred to, was desig-

The *M/V Henry Ford II,* the first large ship with a diesel engine on the Great Lakes. Launched in 1924 as the flagship of Henry Ford's fleet, it originally carried a portable elevator on its deck for use by the famous automaker and his guests. (Author's collection)

nated as a Motorship (M/S) or Motor Vessel (M/V) to differentiate it from the steamers that dominated the fleet on the Great Lakes. Today, the M/V designation is most often used.

The 3,000-horsepower diesel engine installed aboard the *Henry II* was both smaller and lighter than comparable steam engines, and it required fewer crewmembers to operate it. On the other hand, diesels were considered less reliable than the time-tested steam engines that powered most lakers. While other diesel-powered ships followed in the wake of the Ford boat, they did not come into wide-spread use until the 1970s.

Another innovation on the *Henry II* was the first use of electric winches on the lakes. The winches are located on deck and are used to moor the vessel and open and close hatch covers. Until the construction of the *Henry II,* all ships on the Great Lakes used steam winches that operated off steam generated by their engine room boilers.

The launching of the *M/V Henry Ford II* in 1924 marked Ford Motor Company's entry into Great Lakes shipping. Henry Ford, founder of the Ford Motor Company, personally presided over the gala launching of the ship, the first to fly the fleet flag of the giant automaker. Ford named the boat after his then seven-year-old grandson, who eventually went on to become president and chairman of the board of the Detroit auto company.

Most of the freighters on the Great Lakes have been named for executives in the shipping, mining, or steel industries, or for members of the owner's family. Three of the ships in the Ford fleet were named for grandsons of Henry Ford—the *M/V Henry Ford II,* the *Str. Benson Ford,* and the *Str. William Clay Ford.* Other ships that have flown the Ford flag

Cleveland Tanker's tankship *Saturn* unloading at a terminal on the Rouge River near Detroit. The 384-foot *Saturn* can carry 48,000 gallons of petroleum products. (Author's collection)

have honored top executives of the auto company—Ernest R. Breech, John Dykstra, and Robert S. McNamara, perhaps better known as secretary of defense under President John F. Kennedy. While the namesakes of most of the Ford boats were familiar to people outside the shipping industry, those of most Great Lakes ships are largely unknown to people outside of the industry. It is even quite common for crewmembers aboard lakers to be unaware of the person for whom their ship has been named.

Most of the boats bear men's names, since the shipping, steel, and mining industries have historically been dominated by men, even though ships have for centuries been referred to using the feminine gender. "What boat is that," a crewmember might ask one of his shipmates, pointing at a pass-

ing freighter. "Why, *she's* the *George A. Sloan*," would come the seemingly contradictory reply. The feminine pronoun is always used, even though the ship is named after a man.

While Great Lakes ships are generally named for industry leaders, there have also been many ships with more imaginative names. The same year that the *Henry Ford II* made its debut, the Minnesota-Atlantic Transit Company began putting together the famous "poker fleet" of the lakes. All of the ships in the fleet were named after playing cards: *Lake Ace*, *Lake King*, *Lake Queen*, *Lake Jack*, and so on. Ships in the Cleveland Tankers fleet have always been named after celestial bodies, such as *Meteor*, *Jupiter*, and *Saturn*. Canada Steamship Lines has had classes of ships named for rivers, forts, and bays, while the company's self-unloaders have all had Indian names. Cleveland-Cliffs named many of its ships after explorers and pioneers who played important roles in the early development of the Great Lakes region, such as the *Str. Frontenac*, named for the French explorer, and the *Str. Pontiac*, which bore the name of the famous Ottawa chief. Columbia Transportation named a number of its ships for steel companies or steel mills that have been major customers for the fleet, including *Armco, Ashland, Middletown*, and *Reserve*. Tankers in the Halco fleet have taken their names from bodies of water, such as the *Bay Transport* and *Cape Transport*, while the names of self-unloaders in the fleet have all used the suffix "fax," including the *Hallfax, Orefax*, and *Stonefax*.

Some of the more unusual names that have been given to vessels on the lakes include the *Str. Maunaloa*, which was named after a volcano on the island of Hawaii; the *Chicago Tribune* and *New York News*, operated by Group DesGagnes and named after newspapers that were major consumers of the rolls of newsprint carried by the two ships; the *Str. Red Wing*, named after the Detroit hockey club in honor of Bruce Norris, who was owner of the Red Wings and also a major shareholder in Upper Lakes Shipping, which owned the vessel; and the *Highway 16*, a car carrier that operated across Lake Michigan and served as the link between terminuses of U.S. Highway 16, which ended at the water's edge in Milwaukee, Wisconsin, and Muskegon, Michigan. A few ships on the lakes have also been named for women, including the steamers *R. W. Webster, Helen Evans, Martha Hindman, Hilda Marjanne*, and *Kaye E. Barker*. Most of the ships bearing women's names honor the mothers, wives, grandmothers, daughters, or daughters-in-law of fleet executives.

Name changes are very common, and it is not unusual for a ship to operate under two or more names during its career on the lakes. The most common reason for renaming is change of ownership. Some names have also been used for a number of different ships over time, for example, the *Benson Ford*. The first *Benson Ford*, like the *Henry Ford II*, was launched in 1924. In 1982, the fleet decided to scrap the aging ship, but the name was preserved by giving it to a newer ship in the fleet, which had been operating as the *Str. John Dykstra*. In 1985, Ford acquired two large self-unloaders from Cleveland-Cliffs and one of them, the *Edward B. Greene*, was then renamed the *Benson Ford*. The name was in continuous use on the lakes from 1924 until 1989, but on three different ships.

The year 1925 brought three "firsts" to the lakes, including the first one-piece, or patent, hatch covers on a regular bulk freighter, the first ship with twin engines and twin propellers, and the first large vessel built with a steam turbine engine. Single piece steel hatch covers had been used on the small hatches of the whalebacks built before the turn of the century, but the first ship with normal-sized hatches to be equipped with single-piece, steel hatch covers was the *Str. William C. Atwater*. The advantage of the single-piece hatches was that they were capable of better sealing off the hatch openings and did not have to be tarped during inclement weather to keep water out of the cargo hold, as did telescoping and wooden hatches.

While the small hatch covers used on the whalebacks could be handled manually by deckhands, the full-sized hatch covers on the *Atwater* required the use of a hatch crane. The hatch crane, or "iron deckhand," as it is often called, straddles the hatches and moves up and down the deck on tracks. Most of the hatch cranes are powered by electric motors hooked into the ship's electrical generating equipment by a heavy-duty extension cord, which runs the full length of the deck. Some ships have also been equipped with hatch cranes operated by small diesel engines.

The cranes can be operated by one person; three or more crewmembers were needed to remove and replace telescoping or wooden hatch covers. The operator positions the hatch crane over the hatch and lowers two hooks into steel eyes welded to the top of the hatch cover. Motors on the crane then lift the cover and it can be stacked on the deck between the hatch openings. The *Atwater* was built with 11-foot wide hatches on 24-foot centers, leaving 13 feet between hatches for the stacking of hatch covers.

The single-piece hatch covers speeded up the opening and closing of hatches, reducing turnaround time in port. All straight-deckers built after 1938 were equipped with the single piece hatch covers and iron deckhands. Telescoping hatches continued to be used on self-unloaders, because they had boom supports that interfered with the operation of a hatch crane. Modifications were subsequently made to the self-unloading booms that allowed the use of hatch cranes, and today virtually every ship on the lakes has single-piece steel hatch covers.

The hatch covers are secured in place on the rubber-gasketed hatch coaming by hatch clamps spaced approximately every two feet around the hatch. The clamps are attached to the hatch coaming and can be positioned over the hatch cover and secured. Many types of clamps have been used on both telescoping and single-piece hatch covers, but most contemporary ships use Kestner clamps, which operate on a cam, or double pivot, principle and can be snapped into place by deckhands using a special tool so that the cover is locked securely to the coaming.

The first ship on the Great Lakes built with twin engines and twin propellers, or screws, was the *Str. Charles C. West*, a self-unloader built for the Reiss Steamship Company. It was designed for use in small ports and channels around the lakes, mainly in the coal trade. The installation of twin screws improved the 470-foot freighter's maneuverability because the screws made it possible to pivot the ship through turns by backing with one screw while the other pushed the vessel forward. Power was supplied by two 1,000-horsepower triple expansion steam engines. When it was put into service, the *West* carried a crew of 38. Most ships on the lakes continued to operate with single propellers, however, until the 1970s and '80s, when a number of vessels were built with two or four diesel engines and twin screws to assist them in maneuvering in confined harbors and channels.

Advancements in steam propulsion were reflected on the lakes in 1925 with the launching of the *Str. T. W. Robinson* for the Bradley Transportation Line. The *Robinson* was equipped with a turbo-electric engine and was the first major turbine-powered vessel on the lakes, whereas all of the previous steamboats had reciprocating triple or quadruple-expansion engines. In steam turbine engines, the steam produced by the boilers is used to drive a large turbine. On the *Robinson*, the turbine supplied power to a generator motor that turned the vessel's propeller shaft. On later steam turbine ships, the turbines were connected to a reduction gear that powered the shaft. Similar to an automobile transmission, the reduction gear is needed because the turbines spin at too high a speed to supply power directly to the shaft. The reduction gear reduces the rotation of the propeller shaft to about 100 revolutions per minute at full power. On reciprocating steam engines, steam pressure is used to drive large cylinders, from 20 inches to more than 60 inches in diameter, which are mounted on a crankshaft similar to what is found in a gasoline engine. The crankshaft supplies power to the propeller shaft. Turbine engines are capable of producing greater power than reciprocating steam engines can.

The *Robinson* was rated at 3,600 horsepower and was among the most powerful ships on the lakes when it was put into service. The vessel's boilers were fueled by coal, which had replaced the wood used as fuel by the early steamboats on the lakes. In addition to having the first steam turbine, the *Robinson* was also one of the first ships equipped with mechanical stokers to feed coal to its boilers. On other steamboats, the boilers were hand-fired by coalpassers, part of the "black gang" that manned the dark holds deep in the bowels of the ship where the boilers and coal bunkers were located.

The *Robinson*, like the other ships in the Bradley fleet, had a grey hull. The color was chosen because the Bradley boats were primarily engaged in transporting limestone, a dusty, grey rock. Painting the hulls of the stone boats grey helped to mask the dust that settled on the hulls when the boats were loading or unloading. Throughout the Great Lakes industry, ships in the cement and stone trades have generally had grey hulls, while ships in the iron ore trade have had rust-colored hulls, and ships in the coal trade have had black hulls. The colors used aren't the most aesthetic, but they are functional and help to keep lakers looking good even when they are coated with a layer of dust.

By the 1920s, cement had come into wide use in construction of buildings and highways. A number of freighters were converted for use in carrying the dry, powdery bulk material, and in 1923 the *Str. Lewis G. Harriman* became the first vessel built specifically for the cement trade. The *Harriman* was followed in 1927 by the *Str. S. T. Crapo*, both operated by the Huron Portland Cement Company of Alpena, Michigan. The cement boats differ quite significantly from other bulk freighters. To reduce the possibility of water getting into the cargo hold and hardening the cement, the ships have small, circular scuttle hatches for loading, instead of the large, rectangular hatches found on other bulk freighters. When loading, the loading spouts on the cement storage silos are connected directly to the scuttle hatches so that the cement that flows into the hold is totally protected from exposure to any moisture that might be in the air.

All of the cement boats are self-unloaders, but their equipment is very different from that used for unloading ore, stone, or coal. On the *Crapo*, air is injected into the cargo hold to lighten up the cement so that it will flow down through gates at the bottom of the hold and into a trough that runs the length of the cargo hold. The cement is then carried to the forward end of the cargo hold by a long auger, or screw, that rotates inside the trough. At the bow, the cement is pumped up and out of the ship by a 2,000-horsepower turbine, which can unload the ship at the rate of about 390 tons per hour. Piping on the cement boat is mated to shoreside piping by a length of large-diameter reinforced rubber hose, and the cement is pumped to the top of the storage silos at the terminals by the ship's powerful pumping system.

The *Robinson*, a self-unloader, continued in service until laid up by its owners in the spring of 1982. In 1987, it was sold to a Canadian salvage firm to be cut up for scrap. The *Harriman* and *Crapo* continue to operate in the cement trade even though both have put in more than sixty seasons on the lakes. In 1987, when the *Crapo* celebrated the sixtieth anniversary of its launching, it was one of only four coal-fired steamboats left on the Great Lakes. With coal bunkers getting increasingly difficult to find at ports around the lakes, its owners were considering having the three boilers converted to burn fuel oil.

Shipbuilding virtually ground to a stop on the lakes from 1930–38 as a result of the Great Depression, which greatly reduced the demand for bulk commodities, particularly iron ore. Tonnages plummeted and the majority of the ships in the U.S. and Canadian fleets remained laid up throughout the period. In the midst of the depression, the Coast Guard acted to put loadline regulations into effect for vessels operating on the lakes. The regulations were intended to reduce the number of founderings that occurred as a result of ships being overloaded with cargo. With shipowners constantly trying to maximize the amount of cargo their ships hauled, there was a natural tendency for the ships to be overloaded. The secret to optimum loading is to take on as much cargo as possible, while still retaining sufficient freeboard to insure that the vessel is sea-worthy. Freeboard, the distance between a ship's waterline and its main deck, represents reserve buoyancy, a margin of safety in case the vessel takes on water.

Overloading was a particular problem in the iron ore trade. Because iron ore is such a heavy mineral, it is impossible to entirely fill a ship's hold with ore without having the deck awash with water. It was against the nature of many shipowners to send a ship down the lakes with a hold only partially full of ore, however, and it was very common for ships to be overloaded to the point where they were no longer seaworthy.

The loadline regulations promulgated by the Coast Guard in 1936 were based on similar restrictions on loading that had been put into effect in England a full sixty years earlier. The landmark British rules were largely the result of lobbying by Samuel Plimsoll, a member of the British Parliament who was concerned about the safety of seamen. During the 1860s, the number of British-flag vessels being lost each year as the result of overloading had reached scandalous proportions. Plimsoll, in an effort to encourage public support for needed ship safety legislation, wrote a book entitled *Our Seamen, An Appeal*. In it he proposed specific action to deal with nine different causes of vessel casualties. He recommended legislation to prohibit the undermanning of ships, improve transverse stability, regulate vessel construction and repair, and set loading limits. To deal with the problem of overloading, Plimsoll presented the following recommendation:

> Let provision be made for painting on the ship's side what the Newcastle Chamber of Commerce calls the "maximum load line," and that no ship under any circumstances be allowed to leave port unless that line be distinctly visible at or above the waterline; and let this fact be ascertained and communicated to the Board of Trade by a photograph of the vessel's side as she leaves the port or dock. It will not cost more than a few shillings, and would save a great deal of false swearing afterwards.[2]

Plimsoll's standards for safety were enacted into law in England in 1876 and rapidly spread to other maritime nations. The loadlines painted on the sides of ships came to be known as Plimsoll marks, in recognition of Samuel Plimsoll's leadership in improving vessel safety.

The Plimsoll mark is painted on each side of a ship's hull at amidships. On the lakes, the Plimsoll mark actually consists of four horizontal lines, one above the other, indicating the maximum draft to which the vessel can be loaded during each of four seasons of the year: midsummer, summer, intermediate, and winter. For most vessels, approximately one additional foot of freeboard is required during the winter period than during the midsummer period when the lakes are generally calm. The winter period, during which the least amount of cargo can be carried, goes into effect on the lakes on November 1 each year.

Loadlines are assigned to U.S. vessels by the American Bureau of Shipping and a number of other "classification societies," based on their evaluation of a ship's seaworthiness. The loadline for a given vessel can change over time, generally as the result of modifications made to the ship that enhance its seaworthiness. Many ships, for example, used to have wooden doors on their fore and aft superstructures on the main deck level. Those doors were particularly vulnerable to being damaged if the ship was taking waves across its deck, which could lead to flooding of the fore or aft sections of the hull. When the wooden doors were eventually replaced by stronger steel doors, reducing the likelihood of their damage and the possibility of flooding, the classification societies often determined that loadlines could be raised slightly without diminishing the vessel's seaworthiness.

Since each inch of cargo that can be added results in an overall increase in carrying capacity of 100 to 300 tons per trip, there is an obvious economic return on a vessel owner's investments to improve seaworthiness and operate with the least amount of allowable freeboard. With each ship making fifty to sixty round trips each year, a one-inch reduction in freeboard means that a ship could carry 5,000 to 18,000 more tons per year, a net increase that means more profit in the shipowner's pocket.

As the recession began to wind down during the late 1930s, Great Lakes shipping companies again began to place orders with the shipyards for new tonnage. Among the first vessels launched at the end of the depression were four new 600-footers for the giant Pittsburgh Steamship Company. Two of the ships, the *Str. John Hulst* and *Str. Ralph H. Watson* were built at the Great Lakes Engineering Works in Detroit, while the *Str. Governor Miller* and *Str. William A. Irvin* came out of American Ship Building's Lorain, Ohio, yard. The *Hulst* and *Watson* were actually 611 feet long, while the *Miller* and *Irvin* were a few inches over 609 feet. All four ships had 60-foot beams and carrying capacities of slightly over 14,000 tons.

The new ships embodied a number of innovations that made them unique on the lakes at that time. All four had steam turbine engines that provided power directly to their propeller shafts through a reduction gear, unlike the previous turbines that drove electric motors, such as on the *Str. T. W. Robinson*. The directly-linked turbines, simpler and less expensive than the previous turbo-electric systems, soon became the preferred propulsion system for fleets operating on the Great Lakes. Officially, the *Str. Hulst*, the first of the four ships to actually go into operation, was the first vessel in the inland bulk fleet to have a direct steam turbine.

The vessels were also the first built with enclosed passageways running from bow to stern just below the main deck level and above the ballast tanks located between the cargo hold and the sides of the hull. The port and starboard "tunnels," as they are now called, allowed crewmembers to move fore and aft during inclement weather without having to go out on deck. Before that innovation in design, a safety line was strung down the center of the deck from bow to stern cabin areas to aid crewmembers in moving fore and aft when the ship was taking waves across its deck. In some instances, crewmembers would also climb across the top of the cargo in the ship's hold, a drier and safer alternative to using the safety line, but an option that wasn't available if the hold was completely filled.

Before the installation of tunnels, it was not uncommon for deck personnel who lived in the forward cabins to be cut off from the stern for a day or two at a time when particularly severe storms made venturing out on the exposed deck dangerous. The seriousness of that situation is underscored by the fact that galleys on lake freighters are generally located at the stern, so when deck personnel were stranded forward they had to go without meals. The enclosed passageways were rapidly adopted as a standard feature on lakers!

The four new "tin stackers" were also the first ships on the lakes with hulls that were partially welded. Up until that time, all steel fabrication on the ships was done with rivets, which added significantly to a vessel's weight and reduced its carrying capacity by a like amount. As welding techniques improved, the use of rivets declined.

The *Str. Irvin* was designed to be the flagship for the Pittsburgh fleet. It had an extra deck of cabins forward, called the "Texas deck," which contained accommodations for company VIP's and guests. The luxurious staterooms on the Texas deck were richly panelled in walnut, trimmed with gleaming brass, and rivaled the accommodations found on the grandest passenger ships of the period. The passenger quarters also featured an observation lounge with a spectacular view and a private galley and dining room. When passengers were aboard, the normal working crew of thirty-six was augmented by a guest cook, guest waiter, and guest porter, who were responsible for tending to every need of the VIP's during their voyage aboard the *Irvin*. Diversion from the normal monotony of a trip on the lakes was provided for guests by shuffleboard games on the deck and the construction of kites. Many trips included kite competitions, with prizes for the most kites on a single line and for the longest flight.

On the *Irvin*'s maiden voyage, the passenger quarters aboard the "Pride of the Silver Stackers" were occupied by the ship's namesake, U.S. Steel President William A. Irvin and his wife, Gertrude. Irvin and his wife made many subsequent trips on the vessel, often entertaining important customers and other dignitaries.

The *Irvin* and the three other ships launched in 1938 joined a U.S. fleet that totalled 308 ships, operated by twenty-one shipping companies. The Pittsburgh fleet, with 79 ships, was the largest. The total single-trip carrying capacity for all of the U.S. boats on the lakes was 2,640,000 tons, and that figure rose steadily as new ships were added to replace smaller vessels that were no longer economical to operate.

When the U.S. was drawn into World War II in December 1941, Great Lakes shipyards retooled to support the war effort, building hundreds of vessels for the government. Wartime production at yards on the lakes included thirty-five N-3 cargo ships; eighty-two of the larger, diesel powered, C-1 cargo ships; twenty-eight 310-foot submarines; plus an assortment of frigates, landing craft, motor torpedo boats, and minesweepers. In an effort to assist the

Great Lakes shipping companies in meeting the wartime demand for iron ore and other bulk products, the U.S. Maritime Commission also contracted for the construction of sixteen new bulk freighters. The "Maritime boats," as they came to be known, were each 620 feet long, with 60-foot beams, and were capable of carrying about 16,000 tons on a 24-foot draft. Because of the wartime shortage of both turbines and gears, the ships were powered by older model steam reciprocating engines, rated at about 2,500 horsepower.

Six of the ships were built with cruiser sterns instead of the bulkier elliptical sterns normally used on lake freighters. The fantails of the ships extended far enough beyond the end of the keel to protect the rudder and propellers from damage if the ship should happen to back into a dock. The streamlined cruiser sterns also reduced resistance and improved flow conditions at the stern, which enhanced propulsion efficiency. They also reduced the tendency of the stern to squat, or drop down in the water, an important consideration because lake vessels operate in shallow channels much of the time.

While the Maritime boats were not exactly state-of-the-art in either size or propulsion, they were an improvement over many of the older ships operating on the lakes at the time. Great Lakes shipping companies were allowed to trade their older vessels with low carrying capacities to the Maritime Commission in exchange for the new Maritime boats on a ton-for-ton basis.

The Maritime ships served their owners well in the decades following the war. Although ships in the class set few records during their lifetimes, they were familiar sights around the lakes until the 1980s when the downsizing of the U.S. fleet sent many of them to the shipbreakers. Several are still around the lakes, primarily in reserve status in the event that cargo tonnages increase. One Maritime boat, the *George A. Sloan*, was converted to diesel propulsion during the 1984–85 winter lay-up period and is the only ship of its class still in active service on the lakes.

While the Maritime boats were larger than many of the boats operating on the lakes during the World War II years, they were overshadowed by the launching of the first of what became known as the "supers." The first of the big ships, the steamers *Leon Fraser*, *Enders M. Voorhees*, and *A. H. Ferbert*, were built in

The *Str. Leon Fraser,* one of the 640-foot "supers" launched in 1942 for the USS Great Lakes Fleet, sat idle at the former American Ship Building yard in Lorain, Ohio from 1982 to 1989. In 1990 she was moved to Superior, Wisconsin, to be shortened 120 feet and converted into a cement carrier for Inland Lakes Transportation. The *Fraser's* bow-thruster tunnel is clearly visible just above the waterline. (Author's collection)

1942 for the Pittsburgh fleet. The supers were 640 feet long, with beams of 67 feet and carrying capacities of 17,700 tons, making them by far the largest ships operating on the Great Lakes. Equipped with steam turbine engines that were in short supply because of the war effort, the ships were rated at 4,000 horsepower. That pushed them along at 14 miles an hour, 2 miles an hour faster than the smaller Maritime boats and ships like the *Irvin*. Throughout the war years, the supers established new cargo and speed records for the lakes. Together with the Maritime boats, they were the workhorses of World War II, helping the industry keep pace with the record demand for bulk products needed to support the war efforts of the U.S. and its allies.

In the aftermath of the war, navigation again took a major leap forward as a result of military development of radar equipment. The first vessel on the lakes equipped with radar was the Coast Guard Icebreaker *Mackinaw*, the largest and most powerful breaker on the lakes (see chapter 8). The "*Mac*" was built during the war years to assist in keeping harbors and navigational channels open during the early spring and early winter sailing periods. In 1946, Inland Steel's *E. J. Block* was the first commercial freighter to have radar installed as standard equipment rather than on an experimental basis, signalling the dawn of a new era for navigation on the lakes. Radar rapidly became standard equipment on all lakers. It dramatically reduced vessel collisions and resulted in an extension of the shipping season by about a month and a half, because ships were able to operate in spite of the inclement weather conditions that commonly exist on the lakes during early spring and early winter.

It should be noted that the *Block* holds one other first for the fleet on the lakes. Originally built in 1908, it was almost completely rebuilt in 1946, when it underwent conversion from steam to diesel electric propulsion. It was the first, and one of the only, diesel electric ships ever to sail on the lakes. Its diesel engine actually served as an electrical generator, providing electricity to operate the large electric motors that drove the ship.

The first new ships built after World War II were the *Str. Hochelaga*, owned by Canada Steamship Lines, and Inland Steel's *Str. Wilfred Sykes*. The *Hochelaga* was launched in 1949, while the *Sykes* came out of American Ship Building's Lorain yard in

1950. The *Hochelaga* was 640 feet long, with a beam of 67 feet, virtually identical in size to the supers launched during the war for the American fleets. On its first voyage, it broke a cargo record that had stood for twenty years by carrying 589,290 bushels of wheat. Its total carrying capacity was around 18,000 tons.

At 678 feet in length and with a beam of 70 feet, the *Sykes* became the largest ship on the Great Lakes. With a capacity of 21,700 tons, it established a new cargo record on its maiden voyage of the 1950 season. The *Sykes* also had the most powerful engines of any ship on the lakes, with steam turbines capable of producing 7,000 horsepower. Capable of operating at 16 miles an hour, it was the fastest ore carrier of the time, and the first steamship to use oil, instead of coal, for fuel.

Both the art and science of shipbuilding were pushed to new levels in the design and construction of the *Str. Sykes*. In the postwar period, it distinctly represented a new generation of bulk freighters and gave new definition to the label "super." The evolutionary process that began with the *Hackett* seemed to finally have reached perfection in the *Sykes*. At the same time, its improvements over previous vessels were so significant that it was in a class alone. The *Sykes* was hailed as the prototype for the vessels of the future on the lakes, and wherever it went the flagship of the Inland Fleet made news.

The naval architects and marine engineers who worked on the *Sykes* were clearly looking to the future when they designed it. Personnel at Inland had made an economic survey of the iron ore trade and reached the conclusion that the best ship for their needs would be the largest and fastest vessel that yards on the lakes were capable of building that would still fit through the locks at Sault Ste. Marie. The *Sykes* was designed for a maximum draft of 25 feet, 6 inches, even though the channels connecting the lakes were at that time capable of handling vessels with drafts of only up to 24 feet, 6 inches. In that respect, the *Sykes* was designed for the future and would not be able to reach its maximum designed capacity until channels on the lakes were deepened.

When the *Sykes* was launched, the best designs that were used for lakers were capable of producing ships that could operate at a maximum of about 14.5 miles an hour, while the average for the fleet on the

Spectators lined the banks of the St. Clair River at Port Huron to watch Inland Steel's 678-foot *Str. Wilfred Sykes* pass upbound on its maiden voyage, April 21, 1950. The largest ship on the lakes when it went into service, the *Sykes* embodied many unique design innovations. Converted to a self-unloader in 1975, it is now one of the smaller U.S. ships operating on the lakes. (Institute for Great Lakes Research, Bowling Green State University)

A progress photo of the construction of the *Wilfred Sykes* at American Ship Building in Lorain, Ohio, in early 1949. Ten weeks after the keel was laid, a section of the *Syke's* midbody is well along, clearly showing the cargo hold, side tanks and double bottom. The tunnels that will run from bow to stern can be seen above the side tanks, blocked off with sheets of plywood. (Institute for Great Lakes Research, Bowling Green State University)

lakes was only about 11.5 miles an hour. The 7,000 horsepower produced by the *Sykes's* two steam turbines, combined with improvements in hull design, allowed it to operate at the almost astonishing speed of 16 miles an hour when empty. That represented a 13 percent improvement over the next fastest ship on the lakes, and a 39 percent increase over the average for the Great Lakes fleet.

In terms of both speed and carrying capacity, it was obvious to observers that the *Sykes* would not soon be outclassed. At the same time, people in the industry marvelled at the extent to which designers and builders of the *Sykes* were able to perfect virtually every aspect of the design that had gradually evolved over a period of more than nine decades on the lakes. The *Sykes* had the boxy, flat-bottomed hull that had always been a unique characteristic of the lakers, dictated by the shallow channels of the lakes and the desire of owners to maximize the tonnage their vessels could haul. From the standpoint of maximizing the carrying capacity of a ship, the best possible design would be a cube, or block, similar in shape to a shoebox, with no rounded edges. A hull in the shape of a shoebox would not move through the water very well, however, so some curvature of the hull is necessary at both the bow and stern to reduce the hull's resistance to the water. The extent to which a ship achieves the carrying efficiency of a shoebox is reflected in its *block coefficient*. The block coefficient of a shoebox would be expressed as 1.00, indicating a perfect cube. On the lakes, vessels built prior to the *Sykes* had block coefficients ranging from a low of about 0.800 to a high of 0.875, meaning their hulls would fill from 80 percent to 87.5 percent of a perfect cube of their length, width, and height. While it was usually necessary to reduce the block coefficient in order to achieve higher speeds, designers of the *Sykes* were able to make significant improvements in its speed while maintaining the block coefficient at 0.875, the top of the range found on the lakes.

The midsection of the *Sykes* consists of three cargo holds separated by screen bulkheads that run transversely across the ship and aid in distributing cargo. The midsection is virtually a perfect cube, except for a slight curve where the sides and bottom of the ship meet. The lines of the bow are similar to those used on the Maritime boats built during the war. The bow cross-sections are basically U-shaped and do not flare outward at the top as they would on an ocean vessel. While a flared bow aids in rolling seas away from the ship, it is impractical on lakers primarily because of the design of the loading docks. Anything sticking out from the flat sides of the ships is likely to come into contact with the structures on the loading docks, which are often set back only four or five feet from the dock face.

Ocean vessels also normally have raked stems, or bows that jut forward, to better cut through the water. While the stem on the *Sykes* is raked more than those of most previous lakers, it is much more perpendicular than those of saltwater ships. This is because ships on the lakes often find it necessary to turn around alongside docks by stemming. Stemming involves holding the ship's bow against a dock while the stern is swung around. Any dramatic rake would cause the bow to foul on dock structures when stemming.

The *Sykes* is fitted with a cruiser stern similar to those used on some of the Maritime boats. Model tests run before the design of the *Sykes* had shown that cruiser sterns cause less resistance and improve the flow of water to the propeller, while reducing squat. The overhang of the fantail also protects the rudder and propeller when the vessel is maneuvering in congested waters.

In the Great Lakes tradition extending back to the *Hackett*, the *Sykes* has its pilothouse and accommodations for the deck crew forward. In addition, there are four staterooms for guests and a lounge and observatory on a Texas deck, located above the main or spar deck and below the captain's stateroom and pilothouse. On the main deck and poop deck aft are crew accommodations for engine and galley personnel, and galley and dining facilities, including a separate owners' dining room for use by company officials and guests.

The engine room is located at the stern and encompasses three decks below the main deck level of the vessel. Forward are two decks below the spar deck. The first of these contains accommodations for some unlicensed personnel from the deck department, a laundry room, and storage spaces for equipment used by the deck department. The second, or lower, deck provides some work area, although most of the space is devoted to ballast tanks.

While retaining the basic traditional lines of lake freighters, the designers of the *Sykes* at-

The 633-foot *Str. McKee Sons,* upbound on the Detroit River at Windsor, was launched on the East Coast in 1945 as a C-4 type ocean cargo vessel. Of the saltwater ships rebuilt for service on the lakes during the Korean War, it was the only one converted to a self-unloader. (Author's collection)

tempted to modernize the appearance as much as possible. For the most part, this involved subtle modifications to the hull and superstructure that made the appearance of the ship more aesthetically pleasing to the eye. The most significant manifestation of the owner's interest in aesthetics is the smokestack, which is much larger and more streamlined than on most lakers, where the stack is considered merely a pipe to carry away boiler gases.

Designers also sought to eliminate all superfluous details that tend to give the decks of lakers a cluttered appearance. Ventilators and storage tanks normally found atop the stern were designed in such a way that they became part of the basic structure of the stern, rather than appendages to it. Masts atop both the bow and stern were given a sleek appearance and built to be self-supporting, eliminating shrouds and stays that are normally used. The owners even agreed to a new painting scheme, which was eventually used on all Inland vessels, that further enhanced the ship's appearance. Bands of color extending the length of the *Sykes* just below deck level add to its streamlined look.

Structurally, a 5-foot to 6-foot high inner bottom for water ballast extends the full length of the *Sykes,* with additional ballast tanks located along the sides of the hull for most of the length. Above the ballast tanks that are sandwiched between the hull and cargo holds are passageways, or tunnels, for use by crewmembers and passengers during inclement weather.

The bulkheads between the sidetanks and the cargo holds are sloped inward at the bottom to aid in distributing cargo and to keep cleanup time to a minimum when unloading. Because it was intended that a bulldozer or front-end loader would be lowered into the cargo hold to assist in cleanup when unloading, large openings were left in the screen bulkheads that separate the cargo holds so the heavy equipment can move from one hold to the next.

Both longitudinal and transverse framing was used in construction of the *Sykes.* Overlapping seams of the hull's outer shell were riveted, as were the deckhouses and connections to stringers. To reduce weight and speed construction, welding was

69

used throughout most of the rest of the ship, including all of the internal structures and butt joints in the hull plating. Steel plating used on the *Sykes* ranged from ⅜ inch to about 1½ inches in thickness, with the heaviest plating used on the exterior of the hull, particularly from the waterline to the deck, the areas where the hull comes in contact with docks. Hull plates were also overlapped and riveted to increase the strength of seams in vital areas. Although generally lighter steels were used inside the hull, areas of the cargo hold that are subject to damage by unloading equipment have been reinforced with thick plates of special steel alloys to help minimize damage.

To further increase the watertight integrity of the ship, both the forepeak and the engine room were separated from the midbody by watertight bulkheads. The bulkheads are fitted with watertight doors with automatic closers designed to resist water pressure even when they are not properly dogged shut. The side tanks of the *Sykes*, which protect the cargo hold from flooding if the sides of the hull are holed, were made a minimum of 8 feet wide, rather than the 5 or 6 feet normally found on lakers. This means that the side of the hull would have to be breached to a depth of at least 8 feet before the holds would be flooded.

The *Sykes* was fitted with nineteen hatches, each of which is 44 feet wide and 11 feet long, spaced on 24-foot centers. Hatch coamings are 24 inches high, 6 inches more than is required, to reduce the chance of a crewmember falling into an open hatch while working on deck. Hatches are fitted with one-piece hatch covers that can be dogged down securely with self-locking, toggle-type clamps; they can be dogged down or released by a simple upward or downward motion of a special lever used by deckhands. About fifty clamps secure each hatch cover. Hatch covers are moved by a hatch crane that operates on tracks that run the length of the main deck on both sides of the hatches. A 25-horsepower electric motor propels the crane, while the two lifting hooks operate off a 10-horsepower motor.

The owners of the *Sykes* wanted crew accommodations that would remain adequate throughout the life of the ship. Private staterooms were provided for all licensed officers, with double rooms for unlicensed personnel. Each room has a private bathroom, and the captain and chief engineer have private offices adjoining their staterooms. Recreation rooms were included in both the forward and after cabin areas for the use of crewmembers during their off-watch hours. Stairways and passageways were also designed so that it is possible to go anywhere on the ship without having to go outside, an important convenience during foul weather.

The *Sykes*'s steam boilers were designed to burn Bunker-C fuel, a heavy oil, rather than coal, and it was fitted with wing tanks in the engine room that have a combined capacity of 165,000 gallons. The size of the bunkers provides a cruising range of 4,500 miles; the round trip from Inland's mills at Chicago to Duluth and back is only about 1,700 miles. The size of the fuel reserve provides a generous margin of safety in case the ship must ride out a storm.

Before selecting a propeller for use aboard the *Sykes*, designers conducted extensive tests of both solid and built-up propellers. Solid propellers are cast as a single unit, while the blades on built-up propellers can be removed from the hub that attaches to the vessel's drive shaft. A built-up model with blades cast from an aluminum, manganese, and bronze alloy was chosen for use on the *Sykes* because ships on the lakes frequently suffer propeller damage as a result of striking ice, docks, or the bottoms of channels. With the built-up propeller, damaged blades can be changed without drydocking the ship, saving both time and money. The imposing propeller chosen for use on the *Sykes* has four blades and a diameter of 18 feet, 6 inches.

Just aft of the propeller is the ship's large slab rudder, several feet taller than the propeller and approximately 8 feet wide. The rudder is attached to a heavy rudder post that connects to the keel skeg below the propeller, protecting the bottom of the propeller. The rudders on Great Lakes ships differ dramatically from those used on saltwater vessels, both in their size and the bulk of their supporting structures. The massiveness of the rudders makes them much sturdier and less likely to be damaged if they bang against a dock or the side or bottom of a river or harbor channel, as often happens. Because of the size of the rudders used on Great Lakes freighters, they are much more maneuverable than ocean vessels, which generally have to use tugs to assist them in maneuvering in confined waters. Rudder size on saltwater ships is limited because of the extreme sea conditions they commonly encounter on the oceans. A rudder the size of those used on the lakes would present too much surface area to a following sea, making it extremely difficult to steer the ship and increasing the risk of wave damage to the rudder.

The *Sykes* was fitted with two 12,000-pound bower anchors that fit inside special anchor pockets on each side of the forward bow. The pockets are designed to carry the anchors inboard so they cannot foul on docks. Each forward anchor is fitted with 540 feet of 2⅛-inch diameter forged alloy steel chain. The electrically driven anchor windlass is located in the ship's forepeak on the main deck level. The *Sykes* also carries a single stockless stern anchor of 10,000 pounds, fitted with 540 feet of 1⅞-inch diameter steel chain. The stern anchor windlass is on the main deck, aft of the stern deckhouse.

A total of six 50-horsepower electric mooring winches were installed aboard the *Sykes*, a configuration that has become standard for lake freighters. Two are located at the forward end of the deck, two at the aft end of the deck, and one each in the forepeak and on the fantail. Control stations for the winches are located both fore and aft on each side of the ship. The 1½-inch plow steel mooring cables are payed out through special universal mooring chocks located at the ship's side adjacent to each winch. The sheaves in the chocks rotate within the frames on ball bearings so the chocks will automatically rotate to accommodate the angle of the mooring cables from the hull to the dock, preventing excessive strain and wear on the cables.

Lifesaving equipment installed aboard the *Sykes* consisted of two thirty-one-person lifeboats and one fifteen-person raft. The boats are carried on davits located on the port and starboard sides of the after poop deck and can be raised and lowered by power winches. The raft was stowed on the roof of the pilothouse in a rack that would allow it to float free if the ship sank. That raft has since been replaced by a number of inflatable life rafts stowed in containers on deck.

The ultramodern *Sykes*, the "ship of the future," joined a U.S. fleet on the lakes that included 260 bulk freighters operated by twenty-five companies. The average carrying capacity of the ships in 1950 was just 11,300 tons, ranging from a little over 6,000 tons for the smallest vessels to 21,700 tons for the *Sykes*.[3]

The demand for iron ore was increasing significantly when the *Sykes* made its long-awaited debut, and many fleets scampered to put new vessels into service. Shipyards soon had a backlog of orders on their books, so several fleets opted to have surplus ocean vessels converted for use on the lakes. Cleveland-Cliffs led the way with the conversion of the *Victory*, the first refurbished salty to be brought onto the lakes. Three C4-S-A4 cargo ships were also converted for Nicholson-Universal Steamship Company, which was 70 percent owned by Republic Steel. Two C4-S-B2 fast troop transports were converted, one each for Hanna Mining Company and Amersand Steamship Company. The Amersand vessel was partially owned by Boland & Cornelius, the fleet that would operate the new ship.

Conversion of the ships involved lengthening them, constructing new, fuller bows, replacing their midship pilothouses with new bow pilothouses, and overhauling their steam turbine propulsion machinery. The retrofitted vessels ranged in length from 585 to 714 feet, with Hanna Mining's new *Str. Joseph H. Thompson*, the first ship on the lakes to exceed the 700-foot mark.

Because they were too long to transit the locks on the Welland and St. Lawrence, the new ships made their way to the lakes as the *Victory* had done, being towed unceremoniously up the winding Mississippi and through the Illinois Waterway and Ship Canal to Lake Michigan. With its conversion completed in just ninety days, *Cliffs Victory* entered service on the lakes on June 4, 1951. The *Tom M. Girdler* went into operation at the end of the 1951 season, while the *Charles M. White*, *Troy H. Browning*, and *Joseph H. Thompson* began their service on the Great Lakes during the 1952 season. The *McKee Sons*, which also underwent conversion to a self-unloader, was not ready to make its maiden voyage on the lakes until 1953. Because the converted vessels were half laker and half ocean vessel, they were often referred to as "hermaphrodites." The word originally referred to a plant or animal that had both male and female sex organs, but the term had previously been used in marine circles to refer to a type of sailing ship that was square-rigged forward and schooner-rigged aft.

The *Girdler*, *White*, and *Browning* had been converted to haul iron ore to Republic Steel's mill up Cleveland's shallow and winding Cuyahoga River. Thus they had relatively modest depths and drafts,

Shown here entering Cleveland harbor at the end of its first voyage on the lakes, June 8, 1951, the *Cliffs Victory* was launched in 1945 as one of the famous Victory Class cargo ships of World War II. With one cargo hold located aft of the engine room, it had a unique profile and was always popular with boatwatchers. After its second lengthening in 1957, the 716-foot *Victory* was the longest ship on the Great Lakes until the launching in 1958 of the *Str. Edmund Fitzgerald*. (Institute for Great Lakes Research, Bowling Green State University)

over 3 feet less than that of the *Thompson*, and they could carry only about 14,000 tons. Because of their shallow drafts, the three ships could not later be economically lengthened, and when the recession hit the industry in 1980, they were among the first to be sent to the shipbreakers for scrapping.

The *Cliffs Victory*, which had been lengthened to 716 feet in 1957, survived a little longer, but when Cleveland-Cliffs got out of the shipping business in late 1984, the *Victory* was sold to a Liberian shipping company, ostensibly for service in the Asian trade. By 1987, however, it too had gone to the shipbreakers in the Pacific, far distant from the familiar waters of the Great Lakes. During its more than three decades on the lakes, the *Victory* cultivated a reputation as one of the fastest of the bulk carriers, capable of speeds of up to 20 miles an hour when empty. It was also the most distinctive ship in the Great Lakes fleet. With one cargo hold aft of the stern deckhouse, it looked for all the world like it

had midship cabins, or as if a long tail had been tacked onto an otherwise normal looking ship. The *Victory*'s distinctive appearance made it a favorite with boatwatchers around the lakes.

Captain Henry "Bud" Zeber, who was master of the *Victory* for about seven seasons said: "She was one of the best sea ships on the lakes because of her sharp, flared bow, but she was a mean one for rolling. She was also a hard handling ship around docks," he added, "because of the flare of her bow." Zeber noted that even at the end of a long and distinguished career, the *Victory* had made a place for itself in the record books—as the last of the famous Victory-class to see service, a distinction it had held for many years.

The self-unloading *McKee Sons*, 633 feet long, survived the recession, but has operated little since 1980. The *Thompson*, originally the longest of the converted salties, also saw limited service after 1980, spending most of its time laid up in a slip on

The USS Great Lakes Fleet's *Str. Philip R. Clarke* down-bound on Lake St. Clair with a cargo of limestone. The 767-foot *Clarke* is one of the eight AAA-Class boats launched on the lakes during the Korean War. Originally 647 feet long, all but one have since been converted to self-unloaders and are still in service. (Author's collection)

the Detroit River. In 1983, it was sold to Upper Peninsula Towing Company of Escanaba, Michigan, for conversion to a barge. While the converted ocean vessels were never completely accepted by many people in the Great Lakes industry, they did provide their fleets with additional carrying capacity when they badly needed it. With the coming of the Korean War, fleets on the lakes had to scramble to find additional ships to meet wartime demand for iron ore, and the converted salties were an innovative and generally successful solution to the problem.

Great Lakes shipyards produced eleven new ships during the Korean War, while three other new bulk freighters were built for Great Lakes service at East Coast shipyards and brought up the Mississippi. The ships ranged in length from 626 to 690 feet. Ten of the ships had 70-foot beams, while one, the self-unloader *John G. Munson*, had a 72-foot beam. Their cargo capacities ranged from 17,800 tons to about 22,000 tons. All were built with oil-fired steam turbine engines.

As the nature of the Great Lakes industry changed, the ships built during the early 1950s were upgraded by their owners to keep pace with the demands of the industry. When tonnages on the lakes rose to record highs during the 1970s, most of the ships were lengthened, or "stretched," by the addition of new midbody sections that increased their carrying capacities. Eventually, all but three of the fourteen ships were lengthened. One of the three that did not get stretched was the *Str. Ernest T. Weir*, which at 690 feet had been the longest of the original ships. Most of those lengthened are now 767 feet long.

While only one of the original fourteen had been launched as a self-unloader, all but three of the other vessels have since had self-unloading systems installed. Most of the conversions occurred during the early 1980s when the dramatic drop in tonnages on the lakes gave a decided advantage to the versatile self-unloaders that are not limited in the ports they can serve. Most of the ships have remained in active service and are among the only traditional lakers, with forward pilothouses, still in operation by the U.S. fleet.

The *Str. George M. Humphrey*, built in 1954 for Hanna Mining Company, was the first ship on the lakes with a 75-foot beam. The *Humphrey* also had the largest hatches on the lakes, being 48 feet long and 17 feet wide. The hatches continued to be spaced on 24-foot centers, except over the three screen bulkheads that separated the cargo holds. There the spacing was 36 feet, to provide an area of open deck large enough to stack hatch covers that had been removed for loading or unloading. The *Humphrey* was 678 feet long and had a carrying capacity of 22,605 tons. Shortly after launching, it established a cargo record that would stand on the Great Lakes until 1960.

With the opening of the St. Lawrence Seaway in 1959, allowing large ships to pass from the Great Lakes to the Atlantic Ocean for the first time, several U.S. and Canadian companies launched "maximum Seaway-size" freighters. The first of the new ships built to the dimensions of the Welland and St. Lawrence locks was the *Str. Edmund Fitzgerald*, owned by Northwestern Mutual Insurance Company and operated by Columbia Transportation. The "*Fitz*," as it was known, was 729 feet long, the "Queen of the Lakes" when launched in the fall of 1958, just a few months before the opening of the Seaway (see chapter 7). In 1959, the Canadians followed with the launching of the *Str. Menihek Lake*, owned by Carryore Limited, a Canadian subsidiary of Hanna Mining. At 715 feet in length, it was the largest vessel in the Canadian fleet.

Opening of the Seaway system had a dramatic effect on Canadian shipping on the lakes. From the opening of the Seaway in 1959 until the end of 1969, eleven years, Canadian fleets launched sixty-nine new ships. By comparison, U.S. fleets added only ten ships during the same period, and five of those were converted saltwater vessels.

Iron ore tonnages on the lakes, the staple for the U.S. fleet, fell steadily in the years following the Korean War. While almost 96 million tons of ore was shipped in 1953, less than 61 million tons moved in 1961.[4] Tonnages climbed slowly throughout the rest of the 1960s, the result of both the growing war in Vietnam and the health of the U.S. auto industry. The U.S. tonnages could, for the most part, be handled by vessels that were in operation on the lakes before the sixties. Few U.S. ships were involved in trade out the Seaway. On the Canadian side, however, the opening of the Seaway created a boom for shipping companies. For the first time in history, the

A saltwater ship passes the *Str. Edward B. Greene* in the St. Marys River. The salty's bulbous bow and cargo handling cranes are clearly visible. The *Greene* was a AAA-Class vessel, built during the Korean War for Cleveland-Cliffs and later lengthened and converted to a self-unloader. It has since been purchased by Interlake Steamship Company and operates today as the *Kaye E. Barker*. (Author's Collection)

province of Ontario, the most industrialized of all Canadian provinces, was connected by water to Quebec, the Maritime Provinces, and the Atlantic Ocean by a seaway capable of handling full-size ships.

Before the opening of the Seaway, the Canadian fleet consisted largely of small canallers, but the companies began to rapidly shift to maximum Seaway-size bulk freighters after 1959. The boom in Canadian fleet expansion was fueled by exponential increases in outbound movements of Canadian grains and inbound movements of Canadian ore from mines in Quebec and Labrador.

Grain shipments out the Seaway on full-size lakers resulted in sharp reductions in transportation costs for Canadian grains moving onto world markets. As a result, Canada began to carve out a greater share of the international grain trade, resulting in still more grain that had to be moved through the Seaway. Thunder Bay, Ontario, located at the head of Lake Superior and connected by railroads with the grain-producing provinces on the Canadian plains, became the largest grain port in the world. Grain tonnages shipped on the lakes increased from 13 million tons in 1959 to 25 million tons in 1966, with most of the increase moving aboard Canadian vessels to mills or storage facilities on the Seaway.[5] The opening of the Seaway also cut the costs of shipping iron ore from Quebec and Labrador to U.S. and Canadian steel mills on the lakes. Iron ore became the primary backhaul cargo for Canadian bulk freighters carrying grain out the Seaway, making the trade route a lucrative one for the Canadian fleets.

The opening of the Seaway completely revitalized the Canadian bulk fleet. Virtually all of the Canadian ships built after 1959 were constructed to maximum Seaway-size, which was eventually set at 730 feet. Even today, no ships in the Canadian fleet exceed the maximum sizes allowed on the Seaway, a testimony to the importance of that trade route to bulk fleet operators.

While there was little expansion in the U.S. bulk fleet from 1959 through 1969, the period is significant for several reasons. First, it was primarily during the 1960s that bowthrusters were installed on most of the U.S. bulk freighters. The thrusters are mounted in a 5-foot to 6-foot diameter tunnel that runs transversely through the ship's hull in the forepeak, just below the waterline when the vessel is empty. At each end of the tunnel is a propeller mounted parallel with the ship's longitudinal centerline. The propellers are powered by a diesel engine of about 1,000–1,500 horsepower that is located in the forepeak. The thrusters are controlled from the pilothouse and can be used to move the bow of the ship to the left or right when docking or maneuvering at slow speeds. Thrusters further increase the maneuverability of the lakers, generally eliminating the need for the freighters to be assisted by tugs when operating in confined rivers or harbors, and reducing damage to hulls caused by collisions with docks. They proved so popular with vessel personnel that there are now only a couple of ships left on the lakes that do not have thrusters.

The 1960s also marked the beginning of the end for steam propulsion on the Great Lakes. The last ships in the lakes fleet built with steam engines were launched in 1960, although five saltwater steamers were converted for use on the lakes between 1961 and 1965. In 1967, the Canadians launched their last steam vessel for service on the lakes. Since 1967, all ships added to the U.S. and Canadian bulk fleets on the Great Lakes have been powered by diesel engines. Diesels are cheaper to build than steam engines, and they require significantly fewer personnel to operate them. Those savings more than offset the higher fuel and maintenance costs associated with diesels.

The year 1969 marked the one hundredth anniversary of the unique Great Lakes bulk freighter. When the *Str. Hackett* was launched in 1869, it combined steam and sailing vessel technology of the time into a new type of ship that immediately proved so well suited to hauling bulk cargo that the basic design survived for one hundred years. Even though the Great Lakes industry has always been proud of its heritage, the centennial of the launching of the *Hackett* went largely unobserved on the lakes. Naval architects and marine engineers were already at their drawing boards designing a new class of ships that would double the carrying capacity of any vessel then operating on the lakes. At the same time, they were beginning to seriously question the efficiency of the traditional laker design that had been developed a century before by Captain Eli Peck of Cleveland.

Notes

1. Jack Parker, *Shipwrecks of Lake Huron* (AuTrain, MI: Avery Color Studios, 1986), 39–44.

2. Harry Benford, "Samuel Plimsoll: His Book and His Mark," *Seaway Review* (Jan.–Mar. 1986): 79.

3. Details on the design and construction of the *Sykes* were drawn from E. B. Williams, Kent C. Thornton, W. R. Douglas, and Paul Miedlich, "Design and Construction of the Great Lakes Bulk Freighter Wilfred Sykes," reprint, *Marine Engineering and Shipping Review*, June 1950.

4. Tonnage figures were extracted from *1981 Annual Report* (Cleveland: Lake Carriers' Association, 1981), 21.

5. Ibid.

4

Today's Freighters: "Six Decks of Ugly"

The shipwatchers view [the giant carriers] as one might look at an enormous drab building, rather than to admire a beautiful lady.

—James Clary,
Ladies of the Lakes, 1981

In past generations, Longfellow and Kipling were inspired to write epic poems about merchant ships. What sort of poetry would today's bulk carriers inspire?

—Harry Benford,
Seaway Review, 1979

In June 1970, the strangest vessel to ever enter the Great Lakes transitted the St. Lawrence Seaway enroute from Pascagoula, Mississippi, to Erie, Pennsylvania. Known officially only as Hull 1173, but nicknamed "Stubby" by its crew, the 182-foot ship consisted of the bow and stern sections of what was to become the first 1,000-foot freighter on the lakes, Bethelehem Steel's *M/V Stewart J. Cort*.

The bow and stern sections of the *Cort* were built at Ingalls Shipbuilding on the Gulf Coast, then welded together for the trip north to Erie, where the giant ship's midsection, itself longer than any ship then operating on the lakes, was being built at Litton Industries' shipyard on Lake Erie. Prior to its departure from Pascagoula, shipyard workers painted a dotted line from the deck to the waterline where the bow and stern sections had been joined.

Adjacent to the dotted line they lettered tongue-in-cheek instructions for workers at the Erie yard: "Cut here."

At Erie, shipyard workers followed those instructions and the bow and stern sections were cut apart and mated to the boxy midsection, which was more than 800 feet long. Following extensive sea trials, the *Cort* departed Erie on its first working voyage on May 1, 1972, loading 49,343 tons of taconite pellets at Taconite Harbor, Minnesota, for shipment to a Bethlehem Steel mill at Burns Harbor, Indiana. On all subsequent trips, the *Cort* carried payloads in excess of 50,000 tons, twice what could be carried by the next largest ore freighter.

Not only was the *Cort* the longest ship on the lakes, but with a beam of 105 feet, it was also the widest—fully 30 feet wider than any other laker.

"Stubby," the bow and stern sections of the *M/V Stewart J. Cort,* the first thousand-footer to operate on the Great Lakes. Built at a shipyard in Pascagoula, Mississippi, on the Gulf Coast, the two sections were welded together for the trip to the lakes via the St. Lawrence Seaway. At Erie, Pennsylvania, the two sections were cut apart and joined to the huge midbody that had been built there. (Institute for Great Lakes Research, Bowling Green State University)

Built to the maximum size that could be locked through the new Poe Lock at Sault Ste. Marie, the ship is only 5 feet narrower than the massive lock. One experienced captain remarked, "The *Cort* fills the Poe Lock like a whale in a bathtub."

The *Cort* was built to fit the Poe Lock. In fact, it was built because of the Poe Lock. Before the 1968 opening of the new lock, the size of ships operating on Lake Superior was limited by the dimensions of the MacArthur Lock. Opened in 1943, the MacArthur Lock is 800 feet long, 80 feet wide, and 31 feet deep at the sills. Because of safety considerations, ships using the lock are restricted to a maximum length of 730 feet, a beam of 75 feet, and a draft of 29.5 feet. The other two U.S. locks at the Soo are both larger than the MacArthur Lock, but they are larger in the wrong direction. The Sabin and Davis Locks, built during World War I, are 1,350 feet long and 80 feet wide, but they can only accommodate ships with pre-World War II drafts of less than 23 feet. The longest locks in the world when they opened, the Sabin and Davis were designed to lock through two or three small ships at a time. The only lock on the Canadian side of the St. Marys River was built in 1896. It is 800 feet long and 80 feet wide, but also has a severely limited draft capability. The new Poe Lock is 1,200 feet long, 110 feet wide, and can handle ships with drafts of up to almost 31 feet. Construction of the lock began in 1962 on the site of two obsolete nineteenth-century locks.

Two years before the opening of the Poe Lock, a contract was let to Marine Consultants and Designers (MC&D) of Cleveland to design the ship that would eventually become the *Cort*. Development of a design for a ship the size of the new lock was initiated by Litton Industries, the diversified multinational corporation, which had opened a shipyard in Erie. Litton's 1965 analysis of the state of the Great Lakes bulk shipping industry projected that iron ore tonnages could be expected to increase from 67 million tons in 1965 to as much as 97 million tons by 1990. There had been no new U.S. vessels built on the lakes since the 1960 launching of the *Str. Edward L. Ryerson* by Inland Steel. The number of U.S. ships in the Great Lakes bulk fleet had dropped from 266 in 1950 to only 160 in 1965. Litton officials concluded that the growth in ore tonnages would result in a need for additional ships. In 1966, they authorized work to begin on a new ship design that

would be tailored to both the capabilities of their automated ship assembly facility at Erie and the increased dimensions of the new lock under construction at Sault Ste. Marie.

Army Corps of Engineers officials, who administered the locks at the Soo, had announced that the new lock would be capable of handling ships of up to 1,000 feet in length and with beams of up to 100 feet. Personnel at MC&D, however, began design work on a ship of 1,000 by 105, anticipating that the beam restriction would be relaxed before the opening of the lock, which proved to be the case.

Several other factors entered into the initial design parameters for the new "super ship." Most significant were the capabilities of the loading and unloading docks on the lakes. Designers had to insure that the new ship would be able to get under the loading rigs and that the chutes or conveyors could discharge cargo near the centerline of the vessel, so that it could be uniformly distributed in the cargo hold without the need to turn the ship around to complete loading. Officials at MC&D concluded that the conveyor belt loaders at Taconite Harbor and Silver Bay, Minnesota, were capable of loading a ship 105 feet wide, and it was decided to design the new vessel to the configurations of those loading systems. That decision meant that the ship would not be able to load at chute-type loading docks without some modifications to either the loading equipment or the ship itself.

A second early consideration in establishing the basic design for the new ship was the limitations imposed by unloading docks that the vessel would serve. The Hulett and bucket systems in use at various ports around the lakes were found to be incapable of efficiently unloading a ship with the planned dimensions of the *Cort*, so designers concluded that the new ship would have to be a self-unloader. For design purposes, a desired unloading rate of 20,000 tons per hour was established, though existing equipment at the unloading docks on the lakes was incapable of handling that rate of discharge from a vessel.

The criteria laid down for the design of the *Cort* specified that the ship should be capable of making a speed of at least 16.5 miles per hour loaded. That was eventually relaxed to an average of 16.5 miles an hour for light and loaded trips, because available propulsion equipment would not permit a loaded

The massive *Cort* during sea trials on Lake Erie early in 1972. While the ship is 105 feet wide, its hatches are only 20 feet wide, much smaller than those on most other lake freighters. Another quirk of design is that its ballast pumps are located along the outer edges of the deck, rather than in the engine room where they would normally be located. (Institute for Great Lakes Research, Bowling Green State University)

speed of 16.5 miles an hour at the carrying capacity desired for the vessel.

The ship was intended to have a carrying capacity in excess of 50,000 tons during the midsummer draft period, which dictated that the new vessel have an extremely high block coefficient. While the largest lakers in operation at that time, like the *Str. Sykes*, had block coefficients of about 0.875, the *Cort* would need a block coefficient of 0.924 to achieve the desired cargo capacity. That, along with the speed criteria, dictated that the new ship have a blunt, transom-type stern, instead of the rounded sterns found on previous bulk carriers.

While virtually all of the ships in the bulk trade at that time had single screws, or propellers, it was decided to build the *Cort* with twin screws. That decision was compelled by the hull width and configuration, which would make it difficult to get a good flow of water to a single screw, coupled with the design of the self-unloading system, which dominates the center of the engine room area where a single engine would have had to be located. Twin screws, while improving vessel maneuverability, add substantially to construction costs for engines, propellers, propeller shafts, and stern tubes.

The decision to outfit the vessel with twin screws then dictated that the ship also would have two rudders, with one rudder located just aft of each propeller and in line with the propeller shaft. The rudders selected for use are horn rudders, rather than the more conventional spade rudders, because they provide additional support in the event the rudders strike bottom, always a potential hazard in the shallow channels of the Great Lakes. For the same reason, the rudders were kept 2 feet above the baseline of the ship.

From the outset, designers knew that the ship would be equipped with a bowthruster to improve maneuverability. It was determined that a capability of 2,000 horsepower would be needed on the thruster to allow the ship to counteract wind velocities that would be encountered at loading and unloading docks around the lakes. The size of available thrusters and the desire to keep the thruster tunnel submerged when the vessel was operating at light draft forced designers to use two bowthrusters. A single thruster would have required a larger tunnel, which would not have been completely submerged when the ship was light.

It was also decided to equip the *Cort* with two stern-thrusters to make the giant ship even more maneuverable in close quarters. Model tests showed that sternthrusters would provide about twice the side thrust that could be obtained by using the vessel's twin screws, an important consideration in docking a ship the size of the *Cort*.

Each of the four thrusters on the *Cort* is powered by a 750-horsepower electric motor that can produce up to 1,000 horsepower for brief periods. They are capable of holding the vessel against a maximum wind of 28 miles per hour when the ship is light and over 33 miles an hour when loaded. An investigation of prevailing wind conditions on the lakes revealed that those wind speeds are exceeded only about 6 percent of the time, providing an adequate level of thruster effectiveness.

A study of available main propulsion engines led designers to select four 3,500-horsepower diesel engines for use aboard the *Cort*, with two engines mounted on each propeller shaft. The engines, standard models manufactured by the Electro-Motive Division (EMD) of General Motors, operate at 900 revolutions per minute and drive four EMD generators that provide power to the propeller shafts. Two of the diesels are also connected to the thruster motors located at the bow and stern and can be shifted over to power the thrusters when the ship is maneuvering, while the other two engines continue to supply main propulsion power. The selection of main propulsion equipment was influenced by the need to achieve 14,000 horsepower and by the dimensions of the available engine room space. The engine room on the huge ship is only 78 feet long and 75 feet wide—very compact even on vessels only half the size of the *Cort*.

The engines selected were capable of being mounted side-by-side in pairs, an advantage given the short length of the engine room. They were also relatively light in weight and could be installed easily because they came mounted on skids that needed only to be lowered into the engine room and bolted in place. Since the units were standard production models for EMD, they were also significantly less expensive than engines custom built for the application, and there was a ready supply of spare parts available.

The engine room was designed for operation by a single engineer on watch in the vessel's sophisti-

At 1,000 feet in length and 105 feet wide, Bethlehem Steel's massive *Stewart J. Cort* fills the Poe Lock at the Soo "like a whale in a bathtub." The *Cort* was one of the last two U.S. freighters on the lakes built with their pilothouse forward and engine room aft in the tradition that began with the launching in 1869 of the *R. J. Hackett*. (Bethlehem Steel Corporation)

cated engine control room. Most of the major control functions, including throttle control, can be shifted to deck officers in the pilothouse when they are maneuvering the ship. Thruster controls are also located in the pilothouse. The pilothouse itself is located on the bow of the ship, in the style of lakers dating back to the *Hackett*. Designers concluded that deck officers would have enough adjustments to make in handling a ship with the *Cort's* dimensions that they did not need to be burdened additionally with a totally new frame of reference.

All crew accommodations and the galley also are located in the *Cort's* forward deckhouse, a departure from past practice on the lakes. The decision to consolidate everything forward resulted from both economic considerations and space limitations imposed at the stern by the ship's unusual self-unloading system. While an attempt was made to provide private rooms for all crewmembers, space limitations made it necessary to have eight double rooms and seventeen single rooms. Ten of the single rooms are for officers, and the balance are occupied by senior unlicensed personnel. All accommodations are air-conditioned.

The massive deck of the *Cort*, larger than three football fields laid end to end, is broken only by a row of eighteen small hatches arranged along the centerline of the ship. While hatches on most lake freighters are about 48 feet long and 11 feet wide, those on the *Cort* are only 21 by 11. Their small size results from the fact that the ship was designed to load only at the docks at Taconite Harbor and Two Harbors, both of which are equipped with loading conveyors that can extend out to the centerline of the ship. While the eighteen hatches are adequate to load the ship to the 27.5 foot draft presently available in the Great Lakes system, the design of the ship allows for seventeen additional hatches to be added later if dredging of channels allows the *Cort* to load to its maximum design draft of 30.5 feet.

In order to clear the conveyor booms at the loading docks, the hatch coamings on the *Cort* extend only 8 inches above the deck, instead of the 2 feet that is common on lakers. The single-piece steel hatch covers are opened, closed, and dogged down by means of hydraulic actuators. This eliminates the need for both a hatch crane and the time-consuming process of putting on or taking off hundreds of hatch clamps. The hatches on the ship are hinged at their forward edges. They can be rotated back 180° and stowed between the hatch openings by the hydraulic units. A system of hydraulic pins on each side of the hatch are used to dog the hatch cover down when the vessel is underway.

The immense cargo hold is subdivided into four watertight compartments by a series of watertight bulkheads, providing far greater protection against flooding than is normally found on ships operating on the lakes. Most lake freighters have watertight bulkheads only at both ends of the cargo hold, while the screen bulkheads that divide the cargo hold into compartments are not watertight. (See chapter 7 for further discussion of this.)

As in conventional lakers, ballast tanks extend along the sides and bottom of the hull the full length of the cargo hold. Instead of having the ballast tanks connected to pumps in the engine room, however, the *Cort* has a ballast pump for each of its eighteen ballast tanks located on the main deck of the ship. Each pump has the capacity to remove water from the tanks at a rate in excess of 3,000 gallons per minute, allowing the vessel to be totally dewatered in about three hours, faster than is possible on most other ships.

While the unique ballast pumping system achieved the goal of allowing the vessel to be pumped out in a short period of time, the placement of the pumps created a problem when it became necessary for engineering personnel to remove a pump for replacement or repair. Unlike the engine room, there was no overhead crane or chainfall available to lift the heavy pumps out on the main deck. A small mobile crane, referred to as a "cherry picker," is now carried on the *Cort's* main deck expressly for use in lifting pumps when necessary. (Crewmembers have since installed a basketball backboard on the end of the crane's boom, and it now doubles as the centerpiece for ball games played on deck.)

The arrangement of mooring and anchor winches is also similar to that found on conventional lakers, except that one additional mooring winch is located at both the bow and stern of the *Cort*. Also, the two bow anchors each have their own anchor windlass, instead of both being raised by a single windlass with dual heads.

While lakers usually have two lifeboats hung from davits at their sterns, the *Cort* has only one lifeboat, located forward where all of the crew-

A stern view of Bethlehem Steel's *Stewart J. Cort* unloading taconite pellets into a shoreside hopper with its shuttle boom. The boom can extend out 40 feet on either side of the ship. (Bethlehem Steel Corporation)

members are housed. In addition, while most Great Lakes lifeboats have capacities of fifteen to twenty-five persons, the single boat aboard the *Cort* can carry only nine persons. If it became necessary to abandon ship, crewmembers would instead rely on four fifteen-person inflatable life rafts located at the bow and two similar rafts located at the stern. The self-launching and self-inflating rafts are felt to be superior to lifeboats, which are difficult to launch, particularly in high seas, and provide little protection from hypothermia. (See chapter 7 for further discussion of this.)

The unloading system on the *Cort*, which was designed solely to handle iron ore in the form of partially refined taconite pellets, can handle varying unloading rates from about 6,000 tons per hour to as much as 20,000 tons per hour with fewer personnel and less cleanup than most other systems. The *Cort*'s unloading equipment was designed around a unique system of 105 metered gates, which control the amount of cargo allowed to drop onto the 10-foot-wide conveyor belt that runs the length of the cargo hold. Cargo is discharged through all of the feed gates simultaneously and a series of six scales allow the operator to control the rate of flow so that the belt is not overloaded. Each gate adds a small amount of cargo to the moving belt, but no section of the belt is fully loaded until it reaches the last gate. At the stern of the ship, the hold conveyor wraps around a rotary elevator that is 60 feet in diameter and looks like a massive waterwheel. Cargo being carried on the belt is sandwiched between the belt and compartments around the outside of the rotary elevator.

When the cargo passes the topmost point of the elevator it falls into a hopper, which transfers it to the ship's discharge boom. The boom conveyor is 99 feet long and mounted transversely across the stern, running through the center of the rotary elevator. It can be extended out from either the port or starboard side of the ship for a distance of up to 40 feet to deposit cargo into a shoreside hopper.

Since the *Cort*, a number of ships have been built with similar unloading systems, featuring use of a transversely mounted boom in place of the more common deck-mounted boom. They are generally referred to as self-discharging vessels, rather than self-unloading vessels, to distinguish them from ships with the more versatile deck booms that are usually about 250 feet long.

While the *Cort* has many unique features, nothing is more unusual than the way in which it was built. The bow and stern sections were built at Ingalls Nuclear Shipbuilding's facility in Pascagoula, Mississippi, on the Gulf of Mexico. The midbody cargo hold section of the ship was built at Litton's yard in Erie, at the east end of Lake Ontario. Construction began at both yards early in 1968.

The sophisticated Litton assembly facility was really a production line for ships. Steel coming into the system at one end was converted into 40-foot-long hull modules as the materials moved along the production line, which included state-of-the-art numerically controlled burning machines and welding machines. The completed modules were then lowered into Litton's 1,200-foot drydock for assembly. As each module was finished, the portion of the hull that had already been completed would be floated 48 feet down the drydock and positioned for connection with the new section. Accurate alignment of the modules was accomplished through use of laser surveying equipment. Once positioned, each new module would be welded on to the growing midbody.

Because the bow and stern had to be brought into the lakes through the St. Lawrence Seaway, they were limited to a maximum beam of 75.5 feet, almost 30 feet narrower than the planned beam of the *Cort*. The two sections were welded together and the necessary wiring between the bow and stern was temporarily connected, creating for all intents and purposes a completely outfitted ship—except that it had no cargo hold.

When "Stubby" arrived at the Erie shipyard, the two sections were mated with the midbody. Sponsons, or empty tanks, were added on each side of the bow and stern to fair them out to the 105-foot beam of the midbody. The ship was floated out of the drydock in January 1971, and workers began putting final touches on the new vessel, including installation of the cargo hold conveyor and discharge boom.[1]

When the *Cort* made its first working voyage a few months later, it marked the dawn of a new era in Great Lakes shipping. While over the course of the industry's long history many ships had been referred to as "super ships" or "supercarriers," the *Cort* and the thousand-footers that followed it dwarfed the previous generations of ore boats. With the *Cort*, the bulk industry on the lakes took a quantitative leap forward in the never-ending quest for greater efficiency, which has always been tied primarily to greater carrying capacity. The shift to thousand-footers would have a profound effect on the industry.

While the *Cort* proved to be a transitional vessel from the standpoint of design, it completely rewrote the industry's record books as the longest, widest, and deepest ship ever built on the lakes and as the ship with the greatest carrying capacity. It pioneered the use of self-discharging equipment and was the first modern vessel designed for service on the lakes to have all crew accommodations consolidated on one end of the ship. Crewmembers aboard the *Cort* have painted a large "#1" on its aft superstructure, and while all of its records have since been surpassed by newer ships, the designation as #1 is still accurate. It serves now to remind all who see it that the *Cort* was the first of the thousand-footers.

Including the *Cort*, the U.S. shipping companies on the lakes launched twenty-eight new ships between 1971 and 1982. The flurry of shipbuilding, which kept Great Lakes shipyards busy for more than a decade, was spurred by growing tonnages, which reached record levels in 1979, and by the U.S. Maritime Administration's Title XI ship-financing program, which went into effect in 1973.

The new ships, which include twenty-seven dry bulk freighters and one liquid bulk tanker, reflect the changed nature of the industry. All of the dry bulk ships have either self-discharging or self unloading capability, marking the end of the era of the straight-deck lakers that had been in the vanguard of the industry for one hundred years. The twenty-seven ships range in length from 630 feet to 1,013 feet, averaging 869 feet. The average length of the new ships, in fact, exceeds the length of any ship that operated on the lakes before the launching of the *Cort*. The single-trip carrying capacities of the new boats ranges from 19,650 tons, just under the maximum that could be carried before the *Cort*, to a staggering 78,850 tons, three times the capacity of the biggest ships built during the pre-*Cort* period.

Not only are the ships bigger, but they are also far more powerful. All of them are propelled by diesel engines, ranging from 5,400 to 19,500 horsepower. Steam engines, which had powered the lakers for a century, had also become a thing of the past on the lakes.

Seven of the new ships are river-class vessels,

with lengths around 630 feet. They are specifically designed to operate on the narrow and winding rivers in the system, such as the notorious Cuyahoga in Cleveland and the treacherous Rouge at Detroit, without assistance from tugs. All of the river-class boats have beams of only 68 feet, instead of the relatively standard 75-foot used on most vessels of their size. Their narrow beams, combined with their short lengths and improved maneuvering capabilities, allow them to operate efficiently in confined waters. While their carrying capacities are limited by their dimensions, they carry substantially more than ships of their size built before the 1970s. Most of them are rated at just under 20,000 tons, while older self-unloaders of similar size would carry at least 1,000 tons less per trip.

Thirteen of the new bulkers are thousand-footers, ranging in size from 1,000 to 1,013 feet. All have 105-foot beams. Each of the goliaths is capable of carrying as much cargo as four or five of the 600-footers they replaced, at greatly reduced fuel and crew costs. While most of the ships were built, like the *Cort*, specifically for the taconite trade, several, including American Steamship's *Indiana Harbor* and *Belle River*, were designed to carry coal. The boats intended solely for the taconite trade could use the short self-discharging booms, but vessels also designed for service in other trades were equipped with conventional self-unloading systems, including the familiar deck-mounted booms.

The *M/V Roger Blough* was the only new ship intended solely for service in the taconite trade that was less than 1,000 feet long. Owned by the USS Great Lakes Fleet, the *Blough* was launched a year after the *Cort*. It is 858 feet long, has a beam of 105 feet, and is equipped with self-discharging equipment. The *Blough* and the *Cort* are the only two of the new vessels built in the traditional style with their pilothouses forward. Beginning in 1973 with the launch of the *William R. Roesch*, all ships built on the lakes have had their pilothouses and all accommodations located on their sterns, a configuration that had developed earlier on saltwater. The *Roesch* and its "sister ship," the *Paul Thayer*, are river-class vessels built for Kinsman Marine and designed for use on the Cuyahoga River. The two ships were built at American Ship Building's yard in Lorain, Ohio. Both the yard and the Kinsman fleet were owned at that time by George Steinbrenner,

best known as the controversial owner of the New York Yankees.

While the Canadians had operated package freighters and some bulkers with stern pilothouses for a number of years, it wasn't until the launch of the *Roesch* that U.S. companies followed suit and broke with their century-old tradition. Many people in the industry, including most deck officers, were slow to accept the new design. They argued that the forward pilothouses were necessary because they provided better visibility for the captain when making docks or entering locks. While there is some credibility to that claim, economics won out in the end. Ships with a single deckhouse at the stern are capable of carrying slightly more cargo, and they cost less to build. According to Gavin Sproul, a naval architect at American Ship Building at the time the *Roesch* and *Thayer* were built, the design change saved about $500,000 per ship. Most of the savings resulted from not having to run electrical and plumbing systems from the engine room up to the bow area. The dramatic change in vessel appearance was particularly difficult for many sailors to adjust to. Most prefer the lines of the older, traditional lakers, and it is common to hear sailors refer to the new ships as "six decks of ugly," a disparaging reference to the towering superstructures on the stern-enders.

Maneuvering the new ships, particularly the thousand-footers, differs significantly from the experience most officers had gained aboard traditionally designed vessels. On a thousand-footer, for example, a captain must try to ease the bow of the ship against a dock or lock wall that is 800 to 900 feet ahead of his or her position and which usually can't be seen because the high bow of the ship blocks the view. To assist in maneuvering, the new ships are built with a lookout station at the bow. There, a mate can serve as a second pair of eyes for the captain when docking. Many of the ships are also built with bridge wings that extend out from each side of the pilothouse until they are parallel with the sides of the ship. From the bridge wings, the captain can sight down the side of the ship and have a clear view of the docking situation. The bridge wings are usually equipped with thruster and throttle controls so that the captain can actually maneuver the ship from that vantage point, rather than from the center pilothouse window where he or she would normally stand.

Visibility is also a problem when operating in

The 630-foot *M/V William R. Roesch* was the first modern ship built with its pilothouse and all accommodations on the stern. It is shown here departing the Lorain Pellet Terminal at Lorain, Ohio, with a load of taconite pellets for a steel mill on the Cuyahoga River at Cleveland. Built in 1973, the *Roesch* is operated by Oglebay-Norton's Pringle Transit. (Author's collection)

American Steamship Company's 680-foot *M/V Roger M. Kyes* downbound on the St. Clair River, followed by the 723-foot Canadian freighter *John A. France,* operated by Misener Steamship. They show the change from the traditional *Hackett*-inspired bulk freighters that dominated the lakes from 1869 to 1973 to the current design that emerged in 1973. (Author's collection)

winding river channels because the deck officer conning the ship must start the long ships around turns while still a long way from the corner, as much as 800 to 900 feet away if the vessel is a thousand-footer. On traditionally designed lakers, the deck officer would normally signal to begin a turn when the pilothouse came abreast of the turning mark. After years of following that procedure, deck officers on stern-enders had to make a major readjustment in the procedures they used to navigate the rivers.

Other adjustments were necessary as well. Crewmembers needed to get used to the distances involved in moving around aboard the thousand-footers. Golf carts and bicycles were adopted for use both on deck and in the long tunnels beneath the cargo hold, not just for the convenience of crewmembers, but to reduce travel time involved in performing various tasks aboard ship. With four to six decks above the main deck of the ship, and three or four decks below it, the trip from the engine room to the galley or pilothouse can be arduous climb. Some companies have gone so far as to install elevators aboard their thousand-footers to reduce the need for crewmembers to use the stairs, particularly when they are moving a heavy piece of equipment or boxes of supplies.

After reaching record levels in 1979, tonnages on the lakes began to drop precipitously in 1980, falling by more than 40 percent in just three years. By 1982, U.S. shipbuilding on the lakes had ground to a halt. The last ship launched by the U.S. fleets was the 1,000-foot *Columbia Star*, which came off the ways in 1981. Since then, the only U.S. construction on the lakes has involved tugs and barges, which many industry observers feel may eventually replace freighters in much of the Great Lakes trade. While construction costs for the tug-barge systems are similar to costs for construction of a conventional ship, the tugs are required to carry far fewer crewmembers. The integrated tug-barge *Amoco Michigan/Amoco Great Lakes*, which was launched in 1982, has a greater capacity than the tankships it replaced and a total crew of eleven; the tankships carried about thirty personnel. With the average cost of a crewmember's wages and fringe benefits in the $50–$75,000-a-year range, a reduction in crew size can cut vessel operating costs and increase profitability and competitiveness considerably.

Litton Industries attempted to take advantage of the relaxed crewing standards for tug-barge units when it built the *M/V Presque Isle*. Launched in 1973, the 1,000-foot vessel is actually an integrated tug and barge. The two units are held together securely by large hydraulic pins. The *Presque Isle*, however, did not qualify for reduced manning. The Coast Guard ruled that the tug portion of the vessel was not seaworthy enough to operate independently as a tug, therefore it did not qualify for tug-manning standards. Its short length combined with the height of its superstructure made the tug unstable.

At the close of the 1973 shipping season, officials of Pickands-Mather's Interlake Steamship Company announced plans to build two thousand-footers for use in the ore and coal trades. While initial plans called for the ships to be built along the lines of the *Cort*, with forward pilothouses, economic considerations compelled the naval architects to alter their plans and locate the pilothouse and all accommodations over the engine room at the stern.

The keel was laid for the first of the two ships, the *M/V James R. Barker*, at American Ship Building's facility in Lorain on October 14, 1974. The vessel was floated out of drydock in late May 1976 and delivered to the owners on August 7, following extensive sea trials. The design became standard for the ten thousand-footers that followed, all of which were built with single superstructures located on their sterns.

Like the *Cort* and *Presque Isle*, the *Barker* has a boxy hull, with a block coefficient of 0.94, indicating that the ship's hull would fill 94 percent of a block of the same length, width, and depth as the vessel. The only curvature of the hull occurs at the bow and stern. Looking at a cross-section of the ship's long cargo hold area you would find that it is almost perfectly square. The deck has a 6-inch camber to aid in shedding water and the bilge, where the sides and bottom of the ship are joined, is curved on a tight 17-inch radius. The cross-section, 105 feet wide and 50 feet high, would fill 99 percent of a square.

Built as a conventional self-unloader with a long boom on deck instead of the short, transversely mounted boom used on the *Cort*, the *Barker*'s seven cargo holds feed three conveyor belts that run the length of the ship. At the stern, the cargo is elevated by what is referred to as a loop belt elevator. The loop belt elevator sandwiches cargo between two belts, both more than 8 feet wide, and carries it up to

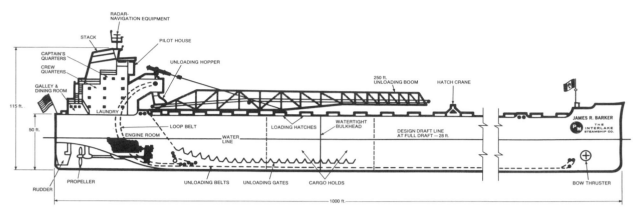

Cutaway drawing of the 1,000-foot self-unloader *James R. Barker* that was launched in 1976. Unlike the *Cort*, the *Barker* was built with a traditional self-unloading system with a boom on its deck. Ore is carried from the cargo hold to the boom by three belt conveyors that are located beneath the floor of the hold. (Interlake Steamship Company)

Interlake Steamship's 1,000-foot *James R. Barker* downbound in the Detroit River with a load of taconite pellets. The original plans called for the *Barker* to look much like the *Cort,* but before construction it was decided to build it with a single cabin on her stern. (Author's collection)

The *M/V Columbia Star* and *M/V Edgar B. Speer,* two thousand-footers, passing in the narrow St. Marys River. The deck of the *Star* is 105 feet wide and its self-unloading boom is 260 feet long. (Author's collection)

the level of the deck boom. The *Barker* is capable of unloading at rates of up to 10,000 tons per hour.

Primary propulsion for the *Barker* is provided by two 16-cylinder, 8,000-horsepower engines, each of which drives a 17-foot controllable pitch propeller. Loaded, the giant ship is capable of a maximum speed of 15 to 16 miles an hour. To enhance maneuvering at low speed, the *Barker* also has a 1,500-horsepower bowthruster, the propeller of which is almost 8 feet in diameter.

While use of the powerful thruster makes it possible for the *Barker* to virtually turn around in its own length, maneuvering is more sluggish when the vessel is underway. When operating at full speed, the ship travels 2,200 to 2,400 feet ahead before completing a 90° turn to the left or right with the rudder hard over. It takes an even greater distance to stop the massive ship.

During sea trials, when the *Barker* was operating in ballast and at full speed, it took 2,600 feet to stop the ship, even with the engines reversed at full speed. That's analogous to an automobile skidding for half a mile with its brakes locked. Loaded, the

Barker would take an even greater distance to stop or turn.[2] The stopping and turning characteristics of the *Barker* are not unusual, however. Most freighters on the Great Lakes demonstrate similar characteristics. As a result, deck officers who pilot the big ships must always anticipate any need to stop or turn well in advance. There are many instances recorded where the failure to do so has resulted in a collision or grounding.

The leviathans like the *Cort, Presque Isle,* and *Barker* are expensive to build and operate. The most recent of the thousand-footers cost approximately $60 million to build. A 1984 study by the U.S. Maritime Administration reported that they cost about $13,842 a day to operate. Operating costs included $9,275 a day in wages and fringe benefits for crewmembers and $1,118 for insurance. The big diesel engines aboard the thousand-footers reportedly burned about 410 barrels of fuel a day, another major operating expense.

One other U.S. vessel built during the last two decades deserves some special note. The *M/V American Republic* is a river-class bulk freighter launched in 1981 for the American Steamship Company. The ship was specifically built to haul taconite pellets from the LTV taconite terminal at Lorain, Ohio, to LTV's steel mill complex on the Cuyahoga River at Cleveland. The mill was at that time owned by Republic Steel, from which the ship got its name.

In an article about the *American Republic*, Professor Harry Benford of the University of Michigan School of Naval Architecture and Marine Engineering graphically described the infamous Cuyahoga:

> Paul Bunyan, so the story goes, once described a certain river that was rather useless for navigation. For half its length it was a mile wide but only a foot deep. Then it suddenly changed and was a mile deep but only a foot wide. Cleveland's contribution to navigable waters, the Cuyahoga, is not much better. It is a turbid, twisting, narrow, bridge-infested creek fit only for navigation by small canoes or large innertubes. Whoever attached "River" to its name was suffering from delusions of grandeur.[3]

Four to five miles up the meandering Cuyahoga are several steel mills that located there at a time when ships were only about 300 feet long and had no difficulty navigating the river. As ships grew longer, the river was constantly dredged to accommodate their deeper drafts, but when ships topped 700 feet it was impossible for them to negotiate the tight turns of the Cuyahoga.

The inability of mills on the river to be served by the largest bulk freighters in the industry put them at a competitive disadvantage with mills that could take advantage of the economies of scale that result from use of ships with large carrying capacities. When the thousand-footers emerged in the 1970s, the situation for the Cuyahoga mills reached unacceptable limits. In an effort to reduce lake transportation costs and increase its competitiveness within the steel industry, Republic Steel proposed establishing an iron ore terminal along the Cleveland waterfront that could be served by thousand-footers. Ore deposited at the waterfront dock would then be moved the last few miles to the Republic mill by trucks, trains, barges, or a conveyor belt.

When Cleveland politicians quashed the plan, Republic decided to develop its ore transshipment dock at Lorain, 30 miles west of Cleveland along the south shore of Lake Erie. That plan necessitated using small ships to shuttle the ore from Lorain along the coast to Cleveland and up the Cuyahoga. Republic would still save on shipping costs by being able to move ore from Lake Superior to Lorain aboard thousand-footers, but it was questionable whether an efficient shuttle service could be established for the Lake Erie-Cuyahoga River leg of the trip.

American Steamship won the Republic Steel shuttle contract, partially as the result of its plan to construct a highly specialized ship for use in the shuttle service. The ship was designed to be more maneuverable than any other ship on the lakes, capable of negotiating the Cuyahoga without the assistance of tugs. Deckhouses and bridge wings were stepped back from the sides of the hull so that they would clear the numerous bascule bridges along the river, which jut out over the river when they are in a raised position. Because it is impossible for a ship to turn around in many of the narrow stretches of the upper river, the vessel was designed with enhanced capabilities to back down the river whenever necessary. The carrying capacity of the river-class vessel was maximized, and it was designed to be versatile enough to compete on other trade routes if necessary.

Launched in 1981, the *American Republic* is 635 feet long and has a standard river-class beam of 68 feet. Operating at maximum draft the ship is capable of carrying almost 25,000 tons of ore. The shallow limits of the Cuyahoga restrict it to about 20,000 tons when the vessel is in service on the shuttle run.

The ship has twin propellers, which increase its maneuverability. To protect them from possible bottom damage in the shallow river, the propellers are encircled by stout structural shrouds that also increase their thrust at low speeds. The little vessel has an extremely high block coefficient for ships of its size, 0.932. This was achieved partially by filling out the afterbody more than usual and using very short twin rudders behind each propeller, rather than the larger single rudders that would normally have been used. This allowed designers to move the propellers further aft, maximizing the area devoted to cargo hold. The *American Republic* can carry about 1,000 tons more per trip than most ships of equivalent size. Since it is capable of making a round-trip between Lorain and Cleveland each day, the added cargo capacity on each trip amounts to hundreds of thousands of tons of additional cargo that can be moved each season.

American Steamship's highly specialized *M/V American Republic* being loaded with taconite pellets at the Lorain Pellet Terminal for the shuttle run up the Cuyahoga River. Ahead of it, Columbia Transportation's *Wolverine* prepares to unload iron ore pellets it has brought down from Lake Superior. (Author's collection)

The ship has 1,000-horsepower bow and stern thrusters, which add to its turning ability. To improve control when backing, the boat is fitted with two small flanking rudders forward of each propeller. The flanking rudders are in the slipstreams of the propellers when the vessel is moving astern, whereas the normal rudders are of little use in those situations. To further enhance the vessel's backing ability, the pilothouse was placed as far aft as possible, giving deck officers the best possible view of the river when moving astern.

The sophisticated maneuvering system aboard the *American Republic* can be operated from any of four control stations located in the pilothouse. They allow deck officers to control engine speed, propeller pitch, bow and stern thrusters, and rudder angle from whichever pilothouse location gives the officer the best view of the river at any particular time. Not having to rely on engineers to control engine speed or direction, or on the wheelsman to control the rudder angle, reduces lag times that normally occur when maneuvering a ship. It has long been standard practice on the lakes to have the captain in control of the vessel whenever it is maneuvering in confined waters like those of the Cuyahoga. Because the *American Republic* spends much of its operating time in maneuvering situations, two experienced captains are assigned to the ship and they alternate at the helm.[4]

The sophisticated ship is an excellent example of

the Great Lakes industry's ability to respond efficiently to shipping opportunities under less than optimum conditions. While the industry is not generally viewed as being highly creative, preferring instead to stick with time-tested operating procedures, the *American Republic* demonstrated the industry's ability to innovate in order to take advantage of reasonably long-term cargo carrying opportunities.

The *American Republic*'s operations on the Cuyahoga also provide a graphic example of why the Great Lakes industry doesn't convert totally to the use of thousand-footers. While many ill-informed industry observers have predicted that the industry will eventually consist solely of highly efficient thousand-footers, the vast majority of present ports on the Great Lakes cannot be served by the giant ships. Furthermore, it is questionable whether it will ever be economically feasible to conduct the extensive dredging program necessary to make it possible for most of the ports around the lakes to be served by thousand-footers. The Cuyahoga, for example, would need to be widened and deepened to make passage of thousand-footers possible. Costs of such an undertaking would be astronomical. Much of the riverbed is lined with solid rock that would have to be removed, and most of the bridges that cross the river would have to be replaced.

While the high tonnages moving up the Cuyahoga each year might justify the costs that would have to be incurred to make the river navigable by larger ships, most ports around the lakes do not handle enough cargo to justify even modest dredging programs. An excellent example of such a case is the power plant at Advance, Michigan, on Lake Charlevoix. The coal-fired plant is served by small freighters that must negotiate the narrow confines of the Pine River Channel, which connects Lake Charlevoix with Lake Michigan. River-class vessels have to inch their way along the 90-foot-wide channel and through a bascule bridge to get into Lake Charlevoix. Water depth in the channel is only about 18 feet, inadequate to float a thousand-footer even when it is in ballast. Since the tonnages shipped to Advance each year are very modest, it would be difficult to justify the improvements necessary to accommodate a thousand-footer.

The majority of the cargo moved on the lakes each year goes to and from ports that cannot be served by thousand-footers. The overall importance of those

ports to the industry insures that the fleets will always operate ships in a variety of size classes, while striving to use the largest ships possible on any particular trade route. Ships on the lakes have historically grown at an average rate of only about 2.5 percent per year, controlled by both the ability of the system to accommodate larger ships and the limits of shipbuilding technology. Our shipyards are already capable of turning out bulk freighters that would dwarf even the thousand-footers. The largest bulk freighter in the world is the Dutch-flag *M/V Berge Stahl*, launched in early 1987. The ship is over 1,100 feet long and more than 200 feet wide, about twice as big as the Great Lakes thousand-footers. With a design draft of over 75 feet, the *Berge Stahl* is capable of carrying over 200,000 tons of cargo, three times the capacity of our thousand-footers.

Given that the technology already exists to dramatically increase the size of bulk freighters, the industry on the Great Lakes is still limited by the widths and depths of harbors and operating channels and by the size of locks available in the St. Marys River. Given the high costs of lock construction and dredging, and the environmental issues raised by major dredging programs, it is probably realistic to expect that the size of Great Lakes ships will continue to inch upward, as it has in the past, rather than to make any dramatic leaps forward.

Several years ago the Corps of Engineers changed the limitations on the size of ships that can transit the Poe Lock, authorizing the passage of vessels up to 1,100 feet in length. That change suggests that the next supercarrier we see on the lakes will probably be 1,100 feet long, with the same beam and draft of the largest of the current ships. It is reasonable to assume that a freighter of that size could operate on the routes currently open to the thousand-footers without any significant problems. To go beyond that length, however, would require major improvements to the system.

In addition to the twenty-eight new ships added to the U.S. fleet on the Great Lakes since 1969, twenty-one older vessels were upgraded through lengthenings or conversions to self-unloaders. Most of the ships had been built during the early 1950s, when ships using the Soo Locks were limited to under 700 feet in length and when most unloading was still being done by shoreside equipment. The eleven ships built for the U.S. fleet during the Korean War,

Interlake Steamship's *M/V Paul R. Tregurtha,* today's "Queen of the Lakes," downbound in the Rock Cut Channel of the St. Marys River. At 1,014 feet in length, the *Tregurtha* has been the longest ship on the Great Lakes since it was launched in 1981. Because of its size, it can only call at a limited number of Great Lakes ports. (Interlake Steamship Company)

for example, ranged in length from 626 feet to 690 feet. Only one of the boats, the *Str. John G. Munson,* was built as a self-unloader.

During the 1970s and early 1980s, all but three of the Korean War–vintage ships were lengthened, in addition to one ship that had been brought into the lakes from saltwater in 1961 and three ships built on the lakes between 1958 and 1960. Four of the ships were lengthened 96 feet, while the other eight had 120 feet of new midbody added. Eight of the ships that were lengthened were also converted to self-unloaders, as were nine other lakers. A total of seventeen straight-deckers were converted to self-unloaders during the 1970s and 1980s, while twenty-seven new self-unloaders were turned out by U.S. shipyards on the lakes. Those forty-four ships now represent well over half of the total U.S. fleet.

In addition to the lengthenings and self-unloader conversions, three other aging lakers were given new leases on life during the 1980s. During the winter of 1984–85, the *Str. George A. Sloan,* built in 1943, was converted from steam to diesel propulsion. During 1986 and 1987, the Medusa Cement Corporation converted the former tanker *Amoco Indiana,* built in 1937, to a cement carrying barge. At the same time, the former *Str. Joseph H. Thompson,* built in 1944, underwent conversion to a self-unloading barge. The *Thompson,* originally built for ocean use, was the first ship on the lakes to exceed 700 feet in length when it was lengthened and converted for use on the lakes in 1952. The *Thompson* is now owned by Upper Lakes Towing Company, which also operates the barge *Buckeye.*

The Canadian bulk industry has undergone an even more dramatic transformation since the 1959 opening of the St. Lawrence Seaway. Of the 133 ships presently in the Canadian fleet on the lakes, 116 have been built since 1959, representing an overwhelming 87 percent of the total. The high number of "newbuilds" in Canada resulted from both the need to replace the little canallers that dominated the Canadian industry before the opening of the Seaway and significant increases in Canadian cargo movements through the Great Lakes and Seaway system.

Canadian fleets, however, operate under even more restrictive size limits than their U.S. counterparts. Because most of the Canadian trade routes involve transitting both the Welland Canal and the locks in the St. Lawrence Seaway, their ships have been limited by the 730-foot by 75-foot limits of those systems. The longest ship in the Canadian bulk fleet is 736 feet in length, while no ship in the fleet has a beam of more than 75 feet.

During the 1970s and '80s, while American fleets added twenty-eight new ships, the Canadian fleets built thirty-six vessels, the newest of which was launched in 1985. Twenty-one of the new Canadian ships were self-unloaders, nine were straight-deck bulk carriers, and eight were tankers. Fully twenty-five of the new ships were built to the maximum dimensions of the Welland and St. Lawrence. The new Canadian ships have carrying capacities ranging from a low of 23,900 tons to a high of 38,900 tons at maximum drafts, half the capacity of the U.S. thousand-footers. While operating in the Welland and Seaway, however, few ships are capable of carrying more than 28,500 tons, due to the restricted drafts that can be handled by the locks. Like the U.S. ships built during the same period, all of the Canadian ships were powered by diesel engines. They range from 6,665 to 12,000 horsepower.

The most significant new development during the period for the Canadian industry was the emergence of what has been termed the "salty-laker." Salty-lakers are maximum Seaway-size bulk carriers that are strengthened so they can be used in ocean service during the winter months when shipping on the lakes comes to a standstill because of ice conditions. Three Canadian fleets—ULS International, Canada Steamship Lines, and Misener Trans-portation—are currently operating salty-lakers, trading in Europe and South and Central America during the winter months. The salty-lakers have been built as both self-unloaders and straight-deck bulk carriers. The former generally haul coal or iron ore, while the latter are designed primarily for the grain trade.

In addition to their strengthened hulls, the salty-lakers also differ from most bulk carriers on the lakes in that they have bulbous bows. Their stems have more rake than normally seen on the lakes, and the bow juts forward below the waterline to form a rounded snout. Bulbous bows improve water flow around the hull of the vessel and reduce fuel consumption. Vessels on the lakes don't use them because they reduce the ship's block coefficient slightly.

Because they are designed for ocean service, most of the salty-lakers are equipped with satellite communication and navigation equipment. Radio equipment is located in a radio room, staffed by radio officers, rather than in the pilothouse, as on ships limited to service on the lakes. In addition, the ships have fully equipped hospital rooms in case a crew-member becomes ill or is injured while the vessel is at sea and cannot easily be transferred to shoreside medical facilities. On the lakes, ill or injured crew-members are normally evacuated from ships by Coast Guard vessels or helicopters.

The salty-lakers also have desalinators and sewage treatment systems that are not found on Great Lakes vessels. The ships cannot carry enough potable water to meet the needs of crewmembers during ocean passages, so desalinators are used to convert saltwater to freshwater. On lakes vessels, freshwater is generally taken on dockside or while the ships are operating on the northern lakes where the lake water is pure enough to drink. Because of state laws prohibiting the overboard discharge of sewage, even treated sewage, most Great Lakes ships have holding tanks to contain their wastes until they can be pumped out into a municipal sewage system while they are dockside. Since holding tanks are not feasible on ocean vessels, the salty-lakers are equipped with onboard sewage treatment equipment. The treated sewage is discharged overboard while the vessel is at sea.

Canadian shipping companies benefitted from a

government program to subsidize ship construction that was in effect from 1977 until 1985. From 1977 until 1980, shipping companies received subsidies amounting to 20 percent of the cost of building a new vessel. In 1980 the subsidies were reduced to 9 percent. The subsidies provided an encouragement to build their new ships in Canadian yards, rather than foreign yards, thereby creating jobs and stimulating the economy. No new bulk carriers have been ordered from Canadian yards since the subsidy program ended. At least one Canadian company has, in the meantime, placed orders with a Brazilian yard for construction of one new self-unloader and conversion of a second ship. Both ships will reportedly be used in the ocean trades.

The downturn in shipbuilding activity has dealt a severe blow to the Canadian yards. Several large shipyards have experienced severe financial difficulties, and one yard, the Collingwood, Ontario, operation of Canadian Shipbuilding, was closed permanently in early 1987. Eighteen of the twenty-eight bulk freighters launched on the lakes between 1970 and 1985 had been built at Collingwood.

U.S. yards, too, have been hurt by the lack of shipbuilding activity since 1982. American Ship Building Company yards in both Lorain and Toledo, Ohio, were closed, as was the sophisticated Litton yard at Erie, Pennsylvania. While the Toledo yard was subsequently reopened under different management, it has continuing financial problems. Only one yard, Bay Shipbuilding at Sturgeon Bay, Wisconsin, is now capable of providing drydock services for thousand-footers. The Bay yard, which built fourteen of the twenty-eight new U.S. ships launched between 1970 and 1982, including six thousand-footers, shut down most of its operations in 1988, but will still accept some repair jobs requiring use of its giant drydock. (See chapter 8 for further discussion of this.)

Not only have no new ships been launched on either side of the lakes since 1985, but the size of both U.S. and Canadian fleets has also been reduced through the sale of older, less efficient vessels that were deemed to be "excess tonnage" by their owners. Most of the ships have gone to the shipbreakers here or overseas. Shipbreakers specialize in dismantling vessels for sale largely as scrap metal.

Many of the once-proud ships that have gone to the shipbreakers would, during normal economic times, have been only middle-aged by Great Lakes' standards. While a few of the ships dated back to the early 1900s, or even the late 1800s, many of them were built in the 1930s and '40s, including most of the Maritime boats. Even some of the ships built in the 1950s and '60s were disposed of, including the *Detroit Edison*, *George M. Humphrey*, and *Arthur B. Homer*. Under normal circumstances, those ships could have remained in service on the lakes for another twenty to forty years, and perhaps even longer. While many industry observers bemoan the loss of so many ships that have played major roles in the history of the industry, the vessels that remain in operation are truly among the most efficient bulk freighters in the world. They are the most modern ships in an industry that has established a reputation for leadership in the movement of bulk cargoes.

As the industry struggles to throw off the economic shackles that have plagued it since 1980, it can look with due pride on the contributions it has made to marine bulk transportation. All of the world's bulk freighters owe at least some debt to the Great Lakes industry for its ongoing pioneering contributions to vessel design. The Great Lakes self-unloader is still the most efficient self-unloading vessel in the world, and marine transportation officials in other nations are now beginning to understand the value of that unique technology. The European, Caribbean, and South American operations of self-unloaders owned by ULS and Canada Steamship Lines have attracted substantial attention, as has the unique topping-off technology that Canada Steamship and American Steamship developed to load oceangoing coal colliers that are too large to enter the St. Lawrence system.

Maritime officials from the People's Republic of China, a nation that is just beginning to develop its marine transportation industry, have called on Great Lakes officials for advice in building self-unloaders for use on their extensive coastal and inland systems. Personnel from Canada Steamship Lines, American Steamship, and Bay Shipbuilding have all had a hand in acquainting the Chinese with the superior capabilities of the Great Lakes self-unloaders. The first of the Chinese self-unloaders are just now coming out of the shipyards; they clearly bear the stamp of the Great Lakes self-unloading technology.

In the past the Great Lakes bulk industry has survived many recessions and several depressions, and there have been prolonged periods when no new ships were built. No matter how bleak things have looked, the industry has always been there, and it is safe to assume that it will continue to be there for many years to come. At the same time, every lull in shipbuilding activity has always been followed by the launching of a new generation of ships that were larger, more sophisticated, and more efficient than those built previously. In that respect, too, it is safe to assume that the pattern will repeat itself again on the lakes.

Notes

1. Information on the design and construction of the *Cort* was extracted from C. E. Tripp and G. H. Plude, "One Thousand Foot Great Lakes Self-Unloader—Erie Marine Hull 101," paper presented to the Great Lakes and Great Rivers Section, Society of Naval Architects and Marine Engineers, January 21, 1971.
2. *M/V James R. Barker* (Cleveland: Pickands Mather & Co., 1976), 5–8.
3. Harry Benford, "Tight Corners: The Innovative American Republic," *Seaway Review* (Autumn 1981): 33–41.
4. Details on the design, construction, and operation of the *American Republic* are from ibid.

5

From Iron Men to Microcomputers

The authors and poets of the world have honored the salt
water sailors, but our freshwater sailors they have ne-
glected. Our Great Lakes sailors are largely inarticulate
and do not consider themselves heroic. Nor is there much
romance in their make-up. They are hard workers who
often place a higher value on duty than on life.
—Frank Barcus,
Freshwater Fury, 1960

During the 1978 and 1979 seasons, many Great Lakes shipping companies experienced personnel shortages, the most serious within the officer ranks, involving mates and assistant engineers. Since Coast Guard regulations prohibit a ship from beginning a voyage without a full crew, the industry faced the prospect of not being able to operate enough vessels to move all of the available cargo. A 1978 staffing study conducted by the U.S. Maritime Administration, based on confidential data supplied by the shipping companies, projected a need for 90 new deck officers and 153 new engine officers in both 1979 and 1980 to meet the industry's personnel needs. After that, the study predicted that at least 61 new deck officers and 88 engine officers would be needed annually through 1987.

The crew shortages, or predicted shortages, were

the result of a number of converging factors. Tonnages hauled on the lakes, particularly by the U.S. fleets, reached post-World War II record levels in 1978 and 1979. Iron ore tonnages alone rose from 67 million tons in 1977 to 88 million tons in 1978 and more than 92 million tons in 1979. Since most ships on the Great Lakes are capable of carrying between 1 and 1.5 million tons in a season, the increase in ore tonnages between 1977 and 1979 meant that twenty to twenty-five additional ships had to be put into service.

At the same time that the shipping companies were being forced to put more vessels into operation, a generous vacation plan negotiated by the major labor union on the lakes was being implemented. The plan called for officers to receive twenty days of paid vacation for every sixty days they spent aboard ship. Within two years, the officers would be entitled to thirty days of paid vacation for every sixty days aboard ship. Implementation of that labor-management agreement meant that it would actually take 1.5 officers to fill each shipboard billet. For every two officers actually serving aboard ship, one additional officer would essentially be employed, but on vacation. Shipping company data also showed that the industry could expect a higher than normal number of retirements during the 1978 to 1987 period. Many officers who began their careers on the lakes during, or just after, World War II would reach retirement age during the ten years covered by the Maritime Administration study.

The Great Lakes Maritime Academy (GLMA), located in Traverse City, Michigan, became the focus of industry efforts to avert a crippling shortage of officers. The academy, which opened in 1971, is one of six state maritime academies recognized by the Maritime Administration and the Coast Guard for the training of merchant marine officers. The six state academies and the U.S. Merchant Marine Academy at King's Point, New York, together have become the primary sources of new officers for U.S. fleets.

The program offered at Traverse City is thirty-six months long. Students enrolled as cadets in the deck or engine programs at the academy combine twenty-seven months of classroom study with two "seatime" experiences, during which they spend a total of nine months aboard operating freighters on the Great Lakes. Upon graduation and successful completion of the necessary Coast Guard examinations, deck graduates are licensed as first class pilots (Great Lakes), while engineering grads receive unlimited licenses as third assistant engineers, good for service on steam or diesel ships of any horsepower. Only forty-five students were enrolled in GLMA's programs in 1978, and the small number of graduates being produced each year was not adequate to meet the industry's growing needs.

While the industry could recruit engineering graduates from the larger coastal academies, deck graduates of those schools, licensed as ocean third mates, could not serve aboard Great Lakes vessels without obtaining pilotage endorsements on their licenses. Because Great Lakes ships operate so extensively in congested waters, deck officers have always been licensed as first class pilots. In order to obtain the necessary pilotage endorsements, a deck graduate from a coastal academy would have to actually be aboard a lake freighter in an observer capacity while it made three trips across each of the Great Lakes and ten trips on the Detroit, St. Clair, and St. Marys Rivers, and then take a very detailed Coast Guard pilotage exam.

The powerful Lake Carriers' Association (LCA), the trade organization representing U.S. fleets on the lakes, decided that sharp increases in enrollments at GLMA would afford the industry the best long-term prospect of obtaining the needed officers. Working in conjunction with Governor William Milliken of Michigan and the Upper Great Lakes Regional Commission, an economic development agency, the LCA generated substantial additional funding for the academy. The money was earmarked for expansion of GLMA's classroom facilities, the acquisition of needed training equipment, and implementation of an aggressive recruiting program designed to increase the number of applicants for the school's programs. The expansion plans called for GLMA to admit 100 to 200 new students each year, with 60 percent of each new class to be made up of engineering students and 40 percent of deck students.

The shortage of officers on the lakes received extensive media coverage throughout the Great Lakes area, often focusing on the claim that GLMA graduates were assured of starting pay of $37–$46,000 a year and extensive paid vacations after only three years at the academy. The academy itself hired a public relations firm to produce a slick, twenty-minute film and videotape and slide programs for use in recruiting new students.

The recruiting program proved so successful that 600 to 700 applications were received in both 1979 and 1980. Most applicants were attracted by the prospect of high pay, the generous fringe benefits offered by the industry, and the certainty of employment upon graduation. Many of the applicants were already college graduates, a few had master's degrees, and one even had a Ph.D. In 1980, 100 new students were admitted to GLMA, and the school appeared to be on its way to resolving the shipping industry's crew shortages.

During the 1980 shipping season, however, tonnages fell by more than 32 million tons from the prior year. By 1982, annual tonnages had dropped 86 million tons from the 1979 high. Only 45 to 50 U.S.

ships operated during the 1982 season, compared to 144 in 1978.[1] None of the students who had entered GLMA in 1979 were able to get jobs on the lakes when they graduated in 1982. In fact, thousands of *experienced* sailors were unable to find work on the lakes after 1979; many would never sail again. Throughout the early 1980s, few graduates of the academy were able to find work on the lakes.

A 1982 update of the Maritime Administration's work force projections for the Great Lakes industry continued to forecast shortages of both deck and engine officers, based on data supplied by the fleets. The academy continued its aggressive recruiting campaign and admitted more than one hundred new students in 1982, claiming that the industry would rebound and that the projected shortages would materialize in the immediate future. They didn't.

In retrospect, it is possible to identify several factors that contributed to the erroneous forecasts of impending shortages of officers on the lakes: First, nobody in the industry in 1978 or 1979 anticipated the dramatic downturn in tonnages that began in 1980. Second, once the downturn occurred, nobody anticipated that it would last as long as it did. Third, there were several major flaws in the Maritime Administration study. For example, it projected that the 1,000-foot freighters being added to the fleet would generate a need for officers with more sophisticated training, providing an employment advantage to academy graduates. In reality, the addition of the thousand-footers to the fleet on the lakes reduced the number of ships needed to carry the available cargo; each thousand-footer replaced about four older ships, resulting in a net decrease in jobs. Further, available jobs generally were filled first by experienced sailors who had worked their way up to the officer ranks aboard ship, rather than by academy graduates who possibly were better trained, but far less experienced.

In addition, the Maritime Administration study was based on erroneous data supplied by personnel officers at the shipping companies. Some of the personnel officers, who are responsible for insuring that adequate crews are available to staff their ships, undoubtedly inflated the demand they anticipated for new officers. From the standpoint of a personnel officer for a shipping company, it is far better to have an excess of officers than a shortage. There is no cost to your company if there is an excess, but high costs if shortages actually occur and your ships have to sit idle because you don't have enough crews.

After 1980, the number of applications for admission to the academy dropped dramatically. In addition, many of those already in training dropped out to pursue non-maritime careers. The greatest number of drop outs occurred after students spent their first tours aboard ship, undoubtedly as a result of the "doom and gloom" picture painted for them by the experienced crewmembers, many of whom were themselves worried about the security of their jobs. Other cadets dropped out of the academy because they found that they didn't like life aboard ship. The academy and the maritime industry have always been plagued by a high rate of attrition. Many people are attracted to the industry by romantic notions about life aboard ship, a result of having watched too many segments of "Love Boat," or too many Old Spice commercials. They soon find, however, that there isn't anything very romantic about life aboard a freighter on the Great Lakes.

Historically, many sailors have been social misfits. A lot of thieves, alcoholics, and other sociopaths escaped jail, bad marriages, or financial destitution by going to sea. In fact, Samuel Johnson reportedly once compared life aboard ship to "being in jail . . . with the chance of being drowned."[2] Shipping companies would obviously have preferred a higher caliber of sailor, but few people would voluntarily submit to the rigors of life aboard ship. Crews aboard Great Lakes vessels have probably always been a cut above those found aboard ocean ships, but they too have tended to be a hard lot.

Even today, most sailors on the Great Lakes come from middle or lower-middle income groups in port cities around the lakes. Most sign on as sailors to avoid a life of working in the mines, factories, or steel mills, or to escape the family farm. Few have more than a high school education, including most of today's captains and chief engineers. That's changing, however, as companies look increasingly to the maritime academies for new officers. With the possible exception of the captain, the jobs of all the crewmembers aboard a lake freighter fall into the blue-collar category. In addition, their jobs tend to be highly repetitive most of the time. If you ask them to describe life aboard ship in a single word, most sailors will respond with "boring." For most, it's just a job.

The biggest negative to the job and the aspect of life aboard ship that is the single largest cause of attrition in the industry is the isolation that must be tolerated by crewmembers. While the liberal vacation plans have helped to make the time spent aboard ship more tolerable, sailors must still struggle through two-month stints aboard ship without being able to see their families or friends or to go down to the corner tavern for a cold glass of beer at the end of the work day.

What draws many people to the industry and keeps them coming back year after year is the high pay. Today, a deckhand, one of the lowest ratings aboard ship, can expect to make $30–$40,000 a year, while a captain is likely to make $70–$90,000. Much of that pay is the result of overtime work. When they are aboard ship, sailors work seven days a week without any time off. They also commonly get called out for overtime work when their ship is making a dock, or while loading or unloading. For most crewmembers, the hourly rate of pay is not necessarily that high, only $7–$12 an hour for unlicensed personnel; their high annual incomes are rather a function of the amount of overtime they work, combined with their generous vacation pay and end of the season bonuses.

On the other hand, there are others who just love sailing, and who get great satisfaction from their jobs and the camaraderie aboard ship. Sailing is in their blood, and they would probably sail regardless of the pay or fringe benefits. They're a unique breed and represent a minority of the sailors who crew the lake freighters.

It takes about thirty people to crew a modern laker, considerably fewer than were needed two or three decades ago. The gradual and continuing downsizing of crews results from the drive for more economical operations and the installation of equipment and automated systems that are less labor intensive. The crews are organized into three shipboard departments, all under the control of the captain, whose formal title is *master*. The captain personally directs the operations of the ship's deck department, which is primarily responsible for navigation of the vessel, loading and unloading, and maintenance of deck areas. The engine department is headed by the chief engineer. Personnel in that department are responsible for the operation and maintenance of the ship's propulsion system, auxil-

iary equipment, and hotel systems, including lights, water, and sewage. The steward, or chief cook, is in charge of the galley department, usually the smallest aboard the ship, which feeds the crew and handles the vessel's linen service.

The size of the crew aboard a particular ship is a function of minimum Coast Guard requirements, labor-management contracts, and the number of personnel actually needed to operate the vessel. Coast Guard staffing requirements are specified on the ship's certificate of inspection, which is posted in the pilothouse. On Great Lakes vessels, Coast Guard requirements usually account for no more than about two-thirds of the total crew carried. Most of the balance are required by labor-management contracts between the ship's owners and unions representing officers or unlicensed crewmembers.

With the exception of officers serving aboard ships owned or operated by the M. A. Hanna Company, Inland Steel, and Inland Lakes Transportation, all officers and unlicensed crewmembers in the U.S. fleet are members of labor unions. Most of the officers belong to the Marine Engineers Beneficial Association (MEBA) or the American Maritime Officers (AMO). MEBA-AMO is a federated union that bargains jointly for both deck and engine officers. Deck personnel belong to AMO, while engineers belong to MEBA. The union is affiliated with the AFL-CIO. All unlicensed personnel aboard U.S. vessels on the Great Lakes are members of labor unions. Depending upon which shipping company they are employed by, they belong to either the National Maritime Union (NMU), Seafarers International Union (SIU), or the Steelworkers. Unionization of the crews began with unlicensed personnel around the time of World War II. The big push by the officers' unions occurred from the mid-1950s to the early 1960s, starting with the crews of U.S. Steel's Pittsburgh fleet, then the largest on the lakes.

The situation was a little different on the Canadian side of the lakes, according to George Miller, president of the Canadian Lake Carriers' Association, the organization that bargains with the Canadian labor unions on behalf of the ship owners. Miller said that the Canadian sailors began to be represented by labor unions before World War II, but the major unionization occurred after the war when ship owners invited the SIU to come in to purge the communist-affiliated unions that were

The captain of the *Str. Edward B. Greene* "in the window" as his ship approaches the ore dock at Marquette, Michigan. The wheelsman who actually steers the ship is located behind the captain on a raised platform. (Author's collection)

making inroads in the industry. Today, most unlicensed crewmembers on Canadian freighters belong to either the SIU or the Canadian Brotherhood of Railway and Transport Workers (CBRT). Most mates belong to the Canadian Merchant Service Guild, while engineers are represented by the Canadian Merchant Officers Union, an offshoot of the SIU.

Canadian crews are slightly smaller than those on the U.S. freighters. According to Miller, crew size will range from twenty-one to thirty-one personnel, depending on the type of ship and the trade it is in. Most straight-deckers carry about twenty-one crewmembers, five to seven fewer than on similar U.S. vessels; Canadian self-unloaders have an average of twenty-seven personnel, three to five fewer than on comparable U.S.–flag ships. Miller says that pay is slightly higher aboard U.S. ships, but that fringe benefit packages are very similar. The Canadian sailors are covered by their country's social medicine program, however, so insurance costs run about 15 percent less for the Canadian fleets.

In addition to representing their members in collective bargaining with the shipping companies, most of the unions also provide a variety of other services. In most cases, the unions manage the pension funds of their members, provide job placement services, operate training programs, and lobby elected officials and government agencies on behalf of both their membership and the maritime industry in general.

Great Lakes sailors build up both union and company seniority. Many tend to stick with a single company during their entire careers on the lakes to the extent that is possible. If their seniority with that company is not sufficient for them to get a job aboard one of their ships during a specific season, they can go through their union's hiring hall to try to find work with another company covered by their union. Shipping companies on the lakes only hire from the union halls when they do not have enough sailors on their own seniority list to fully crew their vessels. During boom periods, such as occurred in 1978 and 1979, the union hiring halls weren't able to supply enough sailors to meet the needs of the shipping companies. In that instance, the companies instituted their own recruitment program, but the personnel hired had to join the union after a short period of time in order to keep their jobs.

Prior to unions, shipping companies were free to do their own hiring. When unexpected vacancies occurred aboard a ship, and they were very common, the captain was often given the authority to fill the vacancy from the labor supply available at whatever port the ship was in. If a replacement could not be found at the port or if a crewmember missed the boat when it departed the port, the captain would often attempt to hire someone when the ship got to the Soo Locks. It was not uncommon for dozens of job seekers to hang around the locks day and night, all hoping to obtain jobs aboard passing freighters.

Those practices resulted in a disproportionately large number of sailors in the industry coming from ports on the northern lakes, communities far distant from the offices of the shipping companies in Cleveland, Buffalo, Detroit, and Chicago. Many companies actually preferred to hire sailors from ports on the northern lakes, feeling that they were more likely than their counterparts from the cities on the lower lakes to be sober, hard-working employees.

Perhaps the most homogeneous crews on the lakes, from the standpoint of where crewmembers come from, were those aboard ships operated by the Bradley Transportation Line. The grey-hulled self-unloaders in the Bradley fleet carried limestone from the Port of Calcite at Rogers City, Michigan, to ports around the lakes. Virtually all of the Bradley sailors were from either Rogers City or the other small communities in Presque Isle County on northern Lake Huron. Although the Bradley fleet was later absorbed by U.S. Steel's Great Lakes Fleet, the ships today continue to be crewed primarily by sailors from Rogers City, which continues to be home port for the vessels.

On a per capita basis, Rogers City has produced more sailors than any community on the lakes. Residents of the small town, which is promoted as "Nautical City, U.S.A.," have twice been devastated when ships from the small fleet were lost. In 1958, twenty-three of the thirty-three crewmembers who lost their lives when the *Str. Carl D. Bradley* sank in a November storm on Lake Michigan were from Rogers City. Five others were from the nearby communities of Onaway and Posen. In 1966, nine of the ten sailors who died in the sinking in the Straits of Mackinac of the *Str. Cedarville* made their homes in Rogers City. (See chapter 7 for further discussion of this.)

In addition to supplying crewmembers for the shipping companies, most of the unions operate training programs that are primarily geared to helping members either qualify for higher shipboard ratings or perform their duties more effectively. Schools have traditionally been held during the winter months to prepare crewmembers to write the Coast Guard exams they must pass to qualify for higher ratings. For unlicensed deck crewmembers, the schools have aided ordinary seamen—deckhands and maintenance personnel—to prepare to take the test for the able-bodied seaman's rating or to prepare experienced able-bodied seamen to obtain licenses as deck officers. Unlicensed engineering personnel have attended schools to upgrade from the entry-level wiper's rating to oiler or qualified member of the engine department (QMED) and to move from oiler or QMED to third assistant engineer.

Most officers on Great Lakes ships have "come up the hawsepipe" or moved up from unlicensed ratings, rather than graduating from maritime academies. Requirements for advancement are set by the Coast Guard and involve a specified amount of experience in a rating and passage of an exam or series of exams. Officers who have come up the hawsepipe have substantially more practical experience aboard ship than those graduating from maritime academies and a proven employment record with their companies. Academy graduates, on the other hand, may have a better technical education, a factor of growing importance. Today's ships are equipped with much sophisticated equipment, including Loran and satellite navigation systems, satellite communications systems, loading computers, and complex engine control systems. In addition, some ships are even equipped with microcomputers that are used in ship-to-shore communications or to maintain records and prepare reports. Hawsepipers often find it difficult to adjust to the operation of high-tech equipment of that sort, and it is often hard to pick up the necessary expertise in an on-the-job training environment.

Union training programs, however, are rapidly expanding into high-tech areas. Instead of the wall charts and schematics supplied by equipment manufacturers, which used to be the only training aids available at the schools, MEBA-AMO now operates elaborate simulators for use in training its members. The MEBA-AMO's Maritime Training and Research Center in Toledo, Ohio, opened in 1984 and is equipped with state-of-the-art simulators for use in training deck personnel. The simulators are similar to those used for the training of commercial airline pilots. The MEBA-AMO deck officer simulator, built at a cost of $6 million, is designed to improve the shiphandling abilities of sailors who participate in the training program. Through the use of computer graphics, the simulator can familiarize officers with what it is like to navigate ships of various sizes in the rivers and harbors of the Great Lakes. Instructors can analyze the decisions made by the students to insure that they are making sound judgments and not putting their "vessel" in jeopardy.

Such training is particularly valuable if a deck officer is going to be assigned to an unfamiliar trade route or to a ship that differs from those that he or she has experience on. For example, an officer who has always served aboard traditional lakers with their forward pilothouses could gain simulator experience in handling a ship with an aft pilothouse. Computer-generated images projected on wide-angle screens simulate waters the officers are familiar with, adding to both the realism and value of the simulator training. While time spent on simulators can help sailors hone their skills, the only simulator training actually required is part of the continuing education needed when deck officers renew the radar observer endorsement on their licenses every five years. Both MEBA-AMO and GLMA operate radar training facilities certified by the Coast Guard.

While training has become an important priority for most maritime unions, other successes have come in the area of collective bargaining agreements on wages, fringe benefits, and working conditions for their members. The contracts they have negotiated are among the most generous maritime agreements within the U.S.-flag shipping industry, and U.S. sailors are the best paid in the world.

It is not just in the area of pay and fringe benefits that Great Lakes maritime unions have chalked up victories, however. Their greatest accomplishments may, in fact, have been in maintaining crew size aboard lake freighters at a time when U.S.— and foreign-flag fleets are making major cuts in the number of personnel carried aboard their ships. For example, while most lakers carry twenty-nine to thirty-four crewmembers, the world's largest bulk carrier, the Dutch-owned *M/V Berge Stahl*, operates with a crew of only fourteen, even though it has a carrying capacity about three times greater than the largest bulk freighters on the lakes. Similarly, the latest generation of U.S. ships built for ocean service generally carry nineteen to twenty crewmembers. There are some logical reasons why ships operating on the lakes tend to carry more crewmembers than those in ocean service. The maintenance and operation of self-unloading equipment, for example, requires more personnel than needed aboard saltwater bulk freighters, few of which have self-unloading systems. Similarly, because lakers are making docks virtually every day, additional personnel are needed to handle mooring lines and open and close hatches.

On the other hand, many of the ships added to the Great Lakes fleet since 1970 were built with automated engine rooms that would normally qualify as unstaffed or unattended. Unattended engine rooms are commonplace on saltwater vessels. Engine controls are handled from the pilothouse by the deck officers under most circumstances. One or two engineers are carried, but they are primarily involved in the maintenance and repair of equipment. A sophisticated system of engine monitors and alarms alerts the engineering personnel to any malfunctions. On the lakes, however, most ships built with unattended engine rooms carry seven to nine engineering personnel, even though their engine rooms have been certified by the Coast Guard for unstaffed operation. Of all the Great Lakes boats built with unattended engine rooms, in fact, only the tug *Michigan*, operated by a subsidiary of Amoco, is actually operating without a full complement of engineering personnel.

In the mid-1970s Cleveland Tankers attempted to operate three of their tankships with unattended engine rooms. Coast Guard certificates awarded to the three ships required a complement of only three engine officers, none of whom had to be watchstanders. MEBA, which represented Cleveland Tankers's engineering officers, sued the Coast Guard, charging that it was unsafe to operate the vessels with unattended engine rooms because they regularly operated in congested waters. The union argued that safety considerations dictate that an engineer be available at all times and actually at the throttles when the vessel is in restricted waters, in case an equipment malfunction should occur. A federal judge hearing the case decided in favor of the union, and even though the tankers are still certificated for unattended engine

rooms, they now carry a chief engineer, three assistant engineers who stand watches, and an unlicensed wiper.

Other shipping companies that built ships with automated engine rooms never seriously challenged the union regarding the level of engine room staffing, even though the extra personnel cost them a great deal of money each year. With all of the Great Lakes companies in the same proverbial boat, none is at a competitive disadvantage, and the inflated costs of operating the ships are merely reflected in the rates they charge their customers.

Historically, the reductions that have occurred in crew size have been largely the result of improvements in shipboard technology. Coal passers were the first to go, displaced by automatic stokers that feed coal to the boilers on steamboats. When oil replaced coal as the main fuel used on the steamboats, the firemen who had tended the boiler fires went the way of the coal passers. The position of deck watch disappeared when call bells and intercom systems were installed aboard ships. They eliminated the tradition of having a seaman on each watch who could wake personnel for the next watch or summon a crewmember who had received a radio-telephone call

The next shipboard position that may be eliminated as a result of improvements in technology is that of the watchman. Great Lakes ships carry a watchman on each of the three watches. Historically, the watchman has served as a lookout, posted on the bow when the ship is operating in congested waters, or when inclement weather reduces visibility. The job entails watching for ships or other navigational hazards, or listening for foghorns when visibility is limited, and alerting the mate of the watch to anything seen or heard. It is questionable whether the watchman now serves any meaningful purpose aboard ship. Today's sophisticated radars and greatly improved ship-to-ship and ship-to-shore communication systems, including traffic control systems in the Detroit, St. Clair, and St. Marys Rivers, have dramatically reduced the value of posting a lookout.

The position of watchman has been maintained, however, partly out of tradition and partly as a result of a vague Coast Guard regulation that requires vessels to "post a proper lookout" in congested waters or when visibility is limited. In reality, the primary responsibility of the watchman today is to relieve the

A fireman aboard the *Str. S. T. Crapo,* one of the last coal-fired ships operating on the Great Lakes, hoses down hot ash and clinkers he has just removed from the boiler. The automatic stoker that carries coal to the boiler can be seen just in front of the fireman. (Author's collection)

Deckhands begin removing wooden hatch covers, a backbreaking chore that had to be repeated at every loading and unloading dock. Wooden hatch covers were made obsolete in 1904 by development of the leaf-type hatch closures that were opened and closed by winches, but some ships continued to use them as late as the 1930s. (Institute for Great Lakes Research, Bowling Green State University)

wheelsman for an hourly coffee break. Most of their time on watch is spent "standing by" in the vessel's recreation room or assisting deckhands with their chores, time that is largely nonproductive. Watchmen are relics left over from the pre-World War II period when radar didn't exist and deck officers had to rely on the eyes and the ears of their watchmen to alert them to any possible hazards.

Most of the crewmembers aboard today's lake freighters stand watches, working two four-hour shifts each day with eight hours of off-duty time between each watch. For many watchstanders, "standing watch" is a painfully accurate description of what they do. During much of the time they spend on watch there is little, if anything, for them to do. When a ship is on the open lakes, for example, it is usually on automatic pilot, so the wheelsman has nothing to do. An entire four-hour watch often passes without the wheelsman ever touching the wheel or doing any other work. The time passes by reading or chatting with the mate who is also on watch in the pilothouse.

In the engine room, oilers stand watch with assistant engineers. Their primary job is to take hourly readings on equipment scattered throughout the engine room, although the equipment on the newest lakers has remote sensors that eliminate the need for the oiler to make his traditional rounds. On many ships, the main job of the oiler is to keep the engineer company and insure that there is an endless supply of fresh coffee available. They are largely there out of tradition and due to provisions in their union contracts. Even the watchstanding engineers have little to do, particularly on vessels with automated engine rooms. On those ships, the watch engineer's primary traditional function, handling the throttles, has been taken over by deck officers who can control the engines from the pilothouse.

The days of wooden ships and iron men are gone forever. There is little strenuous physical labor aboard modern ships. Coal is no longer shovelled by hand into roaring boilers, and deckhands no longer have to handle heavy wooden hatch covers, shovel cargo into buckets when unloading, or wrestle with the heavy, awkward canvas tarps that were used to cover hatches during inclement weather. The iron men who used to crew the lake freighters have been made obsolete by the modern equipment on today's ships. Today it is probably more important for sail-

STEAMBOATS AND SAILORS OF THE GREAT LAKES

ors to be capable of learning how to operate electronic equipment and microcomputers that have become standard fixtures in both pilothouses and engine rooms. The careers of many senior crewmembers serving on the lakes today have spanned the entire period from iron men to microcomputers. They began their maritime careers when the work aboard ship was so strenuous they could barely stand it at times, and today most of the work aboard ship involves mainly just standing.

Most of the physical labor aboard modern ships falls to non-watchstanders, the day workers in the deck and engine departments. In the deck department, the bosun, or maintenance man, and deckhands stay busy doing maintenance work, primarily painting, removing and replacing hatch covers when loading or unloading, and washing and scrubbing down the ship to remove the dust that settles on the deck and deckhouses during loading and unloading. In the engine room, the chief engineer and one or two assistant engineers are day workers. They primarily spend their time maintaining or repairing equipment.

The captain has the most irregular schedule aboard ship. By tradition, Great Lakes masters are in the pilothouse whenever their ship is operating in the narrow and often congested rivers that connect the lakes, even though the ship is then being navigated by the mate of the watch. The captains are there to insure that no problems occur, but really spend most of the time drinking coffee and chatting with pilothouse personnel. The captain also maneuvers the ship when entering or departing a harbor, or when transitting the Soo Locks or locks in the Welland or St. Lawrence systems. Unlike saltwater captains who build their reputations as managers, Great Lakes captains are renowned as shiphandlers. They may, in fact, be the best shiphandlers in the world.

On the five-day, 850-mile roundtrip from the lower lakes to the ore docks at the head of Lake Superior, the freighter captains guide their ships through about 160 miles of river channels that are often no more than 300 feet wide. Aboard ships operating on the Welland Canal and St. Lawrence, primarily Canadian vessels, the captains must maneuver their ships in and out of fifteen locks that are often barely larger than the freighters. Between the locks are more than 100 miles of narrow, congested

channels. Depending upon traffic conditions, the 26-mile trip through the Welland can take from twelve to twenty-four hours, with the captain at the helm or observing on the bridge during the entire stressful passage.

Unlike their saltwater counterparts, Great Lakes Captains seldom use tugs to assist in maneuvering in rivers or harbors, or when entering the narrow locks in the St. Marys, Welland, or St. Lawrence. On rivers like the Cuyahoga in Cleveland and the Rouge in Detroit, the captains guide their huge ships through a series of railroad and highway bridges barely wide enough to let the boats slip through. Because the narrow confines of the rivers often make it impossible for the ships to turn around after unloading, the captains commonly have to back their huge ships down the treacherous channels until they reach a turning basin or open water. The captains and mates who crew the ships on the Great Lakes are *pilots*, known for their talents in guiding ships through rivers and channels by relying on their remarkably detailed knowledge of the waterways. Author Joseph Conrad, himself an experienced mariner, wrote in one of his short stories that "to a seaman, [a pilot] is trustworthiness personified."[3] They are the masters' master, and few are better than those who serve on the Great Lakes.

Using landmarks along the shore, such as buildings, water towers, points of land, and even tall trees, along with buoys, lights, ranges, and other navigational aids maintained by the Coast Guard, the pilots steer their ships through the narrow and winding channels where even a minor error in judgment can result in a grounding or collision. While much of the piloting is actually done by the three mates who rotate on watch, it is almost always under the watchful eye of the captain. The captains are ultimately, even legally, responsible for everything that goes on aboard their ships, but much of that responsibility is delegated to other crewmembers. In many respects, the Great Lakes captains have fewer specific responsibilities than any of the other crewmembers. Other than maneuvering their ships, the extent to which the captains become personally involved in other shipboard activities seems to be a function of the personality of the individual captain and the extent to which he or she has confidence in the crewmembers.

There are countless stories, true stories, about

A captain atop the open-air flying bridge of the sidewheel passenger steamer *City of Chicago* shortly after its launching in 1890. The captain is in the process of docking his vessel at St. Joseph, Michigan, and he is looking off the port side of the boat. The wheelsman who is actually steering the *Chicago* is in the pilothouse below the captain. (Dossin Great Lakes Museum, Detroit, Michigan)

Great Lakes captains who have remained on the bridges of their ships continuously for several days during bad storms. During a November 1926 storm on Lake Superior, for example, Captain Henry T. Kelley stayed at the helm of the *Str. Peter A. B. Widener* for seventy-two continuous hours after his ship lost its rudder. When asked about the feat afterwards, the tired and worn Captain Kelley said only, "It's all in a day's work."[4] At the same time, there are also stories about Captains who have gone for days without ever making an appearance on the bridge. In general, however, the captain probably puts in more hours than anyone else aboard the ship.

If the captains are responsible for their ships, it is usually the first mates who run them or at least are in charge of those areas of responsibility that are assigned to the deck department. The first mate, sometimes also referred to as the chief mate, is one of three mates who stand watches. The first mate is usually in charge of the watch from 4–8 A.M. and from 4–8 P.M. The first mate's responsibilities on watch are the same as those of the other mates. They spend much of their on-watch time "in the window," standing in the center window of the pilothouse, the "driver's seat" on a laker. Behind the mate, on a slightly raised pedestal, is the wheelsman, who steers the ship based on commands from the mate.

The mate's position is surrounded by the navigation and communication equipment used to do the job. The mate is usually flanked on both sides by radar sets, which become substitute eyes at night or when fog, rain, or snow reduce visibility. A gyrocompass repeater, and often a magnetic compass, are generally located just in front of the mate, often mounted on the outside of the pilothouse just below the center window. On the bulkhead above the mate is a rudder angle indicator, which tells how much rudder the wheelsman is using to make a turn. The greater the rudder angle, the more rapid the vessel's rate of turn. The mate's work station at the center window also includes a radio transceiver, which the Mate uses to communicate with other ships or shore stations, such as those operated by the U.S. and Canadian Coast Guards. There is also an intercom station, which allows the mate to talk to crewmembers in various locations on deck or to engineers staffing the engine controls.

Controls for the ship's whistle are also located within the mate's reach. The whistle is used to ex-change passing signals with other ships, although that practice is now largely a formality as a result of improved radio communications between ships. One short blast of the whistle is also used to alert dockhands to cast off lines when departing locks. The whistle can also be set to operate continuously as a foghorn, sounding one long blast every two minutes while the ship is underway.

Controls for the ship's general alarm system are also generally located near the mate's station in the center front window. Activated in emergency situations, such as a collision or fire aboard ship, alarm bells sound throughout the vessel to alert crewmembers that danger exists. Combinations of alarm bells and blasts of the ship's whistle are used to inform crewmembers of the specific type of danger so that they know whether to report to lifeboat stations or to form firefighting squads at the bow or stern.

Within view of the mate is the boat's Loran-C receiver. The sophisticated Loran navigation system has been in operation on the lakes since 1980. It consists of a chain of radio transmitters located around the lakes, which broadcast short pulse signals. The signals are processed by the Loran receiver aboard the ship, which is really a microcomputer that can be programmed to home in on signals from two Loran transmitters and calculate the ship's precise position based on the amount of time it takes the signal from each station to reach the ship. A digital monitor on the Loran shows the location of the ship in latitude and longitude, the distance to the ship's next waypoint where a course change has to be made, and how far the ship has deviated from its planned course.

The mate also maintains the ship's trip log, a book in which the vessel's course, general location, and speed are regularly entered, along with windspeed and direction. The log is an official document, which is signed by the mate coming on and going off watch. Coast Guard regulations also require that records of fire and lifeboat drills be entered in the log, along with information on the cargo being carried, the draft of the vessel when it departed the loading dock, and any casualties in which the ship is involved during a voyage. In addition to watchstanding duties, the first mate is in charge of deck maintenance performed by the bosun and deckhands who work days, although the actual work is usually supervised by the bosun.

The first mate is also usually responsible for overseeing the loading of the ship, even though loading may occur when he or she would normally be off watch. Some ships are equipped with loading computers that can assist the first mate in determining how much cargo to stow in each hold, but most mates on the lakes merely rely upon their extensive experience. Details of each load are carefully recorded by the mate in a pocket notebook for future reference to assist in designing the optimal loading plan for a particular cargo.

Cargoes differ dramatically in how they are loaded. Some cargoes, like grain and coal, are relatively light in weight, so the holds can be completely filled without exceeding the ship's loadline. They are often referred to as "cubic cargo," meaning that the amount of the cargo that can be carried will be determined by the cubic capacity of the ship, rather than the tonnage capacity. Other cargoes, like iron ore, are heavier and the ship's holds cannot be completely filled without exceeding the loadline or draft limitations on the lakes. From the standpoint of volume, a surprisingly small amount of iron ore can actually be loaded aboard a ship. A full load often takes up no more than two-thirds of the available space in the cargo hold.

When loading a heavy cargo like iron ore, the ship's holds are not evenly loaded. Because the hull of a laker is somewhat flexible, extra cargo must be placed at the extreme ends of the cargo hold to counteract the buoyancy of the forepeak and engine room. If an insufficient amount of cargo is placed in the ends of the holds, the ship will sag in the midship area because the center of the ship will have less buoyancy than the bow and stern. If too much cargo is placed at the ends, the ship will hog—the bow and stern will be deeper in the water than its midships.

It is the responsibility of the first mate to see that the vessel is properly trimmed, without any hog or sag, and that it does not list to either port or starboard as a result of cargo being unevenly distributed within the cargo holds. The first mate tells operators of the loading docks how much cargo to load in each hatch and constantly watches the ship's draft marks at the bow, stern, and amidships to insure that the vessel is properly trimmed and does not exceed either its assigned loadline or the maximum draft available on the route to the unloading dock.

The first mate also is often responsible for maintaining payroll records for the crewmembers. In most fleets that only involves recording the number of regular, overtime, and premium pay hours each crewmember has worked during a pay period. On some ships, however, the mate also calculates the pay and deductions and actually prepares payroll checks for the crew. In some fleets, each of the three mates are responsible for payroll records for part of the crew.

The first, second, and third mates also divide responsibility for a variety of other paperwork that has to be done. This includes the preparation of trip reports, cargo manifests and bills of lading, customs documents, purchase orders for deck supplies, accident reports, paperwork that has to be submitted when going through the Soo Locks or the Welland or St. Lawrence systems, and discharges for crewmembers who are signing off the vessel. Some captains also share in the paperwork responsibilities aboard their ships.

When the captain is at the helm during a maneuvering situation at the locks or approaching or departing a dock, the mate on watch and one of the other mates staff the winch control stations at opposite ends of the spar deck. If deckhands have to be put on the dock to handle lines, a mate is also in charge of the landing boom that is used to swing the deckhands over the side and drop them onto the dock. On self-unloading ships, the mate on watch is also responsible for supervising unloading, including control of the unloading boom. On some ships, primarily thousand-footers, an extra mate is sometimes carried, and the first mate becomes a day worker with primary responsibility for loading and unloading the vessel.

When standing watches, each of the mates is assisted by a wheelsman and a watchman, both of whom are able-bodied seamen or A.B.s, as they are called. The wheelsman actually steers the ship, based on commands from the mate or captain. The commands are usually given in the form of a new heading the mate wants the wheelsman to steer or, when rounding a bend in a river, how much rudder the mate wants put on. Rudder commands may be given in specific degrees of left or right rudder angle, but mates often use a sort of shorthand, such as "some right" or "hard left." Those shorthand commands often have specific meanings within each fleet.

Deckhands painting the *Str. Benson Ford* before the start of the 1984 shipping season, the last year the vessel operated. Even the ship's massive anchor got a fresh coat of paint. (Author's collection)

A deckhand being lowered to the dock at Escanaba, Michigan, on a bosun's chair. Once on the dock, he will assist in handling the heavy steel cables used to moor the vessel. (Author's collection)

Deckhands in foul-weather gear washing down the deck of the *Str. Edward B. Greene* after loading taconite pellets at Marquette, Michigan. (Author's collection)

The directions *left* and *right* are always used in giving rudder commands, rather than *port* and *starboard*. That practice, which is used throughout the world maritime community, is intended to minimize the possibility of error by either the mate or the wheelsman. When operating in rivers or harbors, the failure of the wheelsman to respond rapidly and correctly to a rudder command could place the ship in danger.

As noted previously, the watchman serves as lookout whenever conditions require one and relieves the wheelsman for hourly rest breaks. During the day, the watchman usually assists the bosun and deckhands in their ship maintenance activities. When at loading or unloading docks, the watchman generally assists in operating winches or staffing the ship's ladder or gangway, as does the wheelsman.

Day workers in the deck department who do not stand watches include the bosun and three deckhands. The bosun is usually an experienced ablebodied seaman, while the deckhands need only be ordinary seamen. The day workers are responsible for maintenance of all deck areas, including the deck itself, the exteriors of the deckhouses, passageways, stairways, recreation rooms, and the ship's windlass and dunnage, or storage, rooms. They also maintain the ship's lifeboats and are responsible for insuring that the hatch clamps that secure the hatch covers are working properly.

Before loading, the bosun and deckhands remove all of the ship's hatch covers, which involves first removing all of the hatch clamps. Using the iron deckhand, the hatch covers are lifted off the hatch coamings and stacked on the deck. On straight-deck freighters, hatch covers must also be removed before unloading. On self-unloaders it is common to remove only a few hatch covers from each of the ship's cargo holds before discharging the cargo. Those give the mate on watch a view of the flow of cargo in the hold.

During loading and unloading, the bosun or one of the deckhands must also regularly "sound the tanks," measuring the amount of water in the ship's ballast tanks. Loading cannot be completed until all of the ballast water has been pumped out of the tanks. Any water left in the tanks will reduce the amount of cargo that can be loaded before the ship reaches its loadline. When unloading, it is common to start putting in ballast water so that the ship is adequately ballasted when it is empty and ready to leave the unloading dock. Soundings are taken with a metal measuring rod that is lowered into the ballast tanks in the bottom and sides of the ship through sounding tubes, or pipes, located around the deck. After loading or unloading, the deck crew replaces the hatch covers and secures them with hatch clamps. Any cargo spilled on the deck is shovelled over the side, and deck areas and deckhouses are scrubbed and washed down to remove dust and dirt.

Much of the deck crew's time is devoted to the time-honored seafaring tradition of chipping and painting, the modern equivalent of holystoning the decks on old wooden ships. Old layers of paint are removed, generally through use of an electric or pneumatic chipping hammer, and new paint is applied over the bare metal to protect it from rusting. Most ships on the lakes are completely repainted every few years, with areas of heavy wear, such as the sides of the deck, done every season. Ship owners on the lakes take pride in the appearance of their vessels, but they also know that regular painting will help extend the longevity of the hull and delay the need for costly shipyard repairs.

When docking, three deckhands usually are landed on the dock to handle the ship's heavy steel mooring cables. Before 1913, they had to leap from the ship to the dock, a practice that was always dangerous and occasionally fatal. In 1913, Captain Benjamin Bowen of Canada Import Company's *Str. Compton* devised the first landing boom in an effort to make the practice of landing crewmen on docks safer.[5] The booms have been refined over the intervening years, and they are now standard equipment on all U.S. and Canadian ships operating on the lakes. Today's booms consist of a 15- to 20-foot length of heavy pipe that can be swung out over the side of the ship. A flat seat is attached to a rope that runs through a pulley at the end of the boom. A deckhand sits on the seat and is swung over the side as the ship slowly approaches the dock. The crewmembers tending the boom rapidly pay out the line so that the deckhand is lowered swiftly to the dock below. Once the linehandlers are on the dock, the end of a light heaving line is thrown to them, which they use to pull out one of the ship's heavy mooring cables. The mooring cable is slipped over a chock or bollard on the dock so that the powerful mooring winches can be used to help bring the ship to a stop and position it along the dock.

On self-unloading vessels, the normal complement of deck personnel is usually augmented by two additional unlicensed crewmembers who operate the self-unloading equipment. These include the conveyorman and a wiper-gateman. The conveyorman is responsible for maintenance of the complicated unloading system that carries cargo up and out of the ship's holds. The wiper-gateman assists the conveyorman and works in the tunnel below the cargo hold when unloading, opening and closing the gates that allow cargo to flow onto the belts. After the vessel has been unloaded, the conveyorman and the wiper-gateman are responsible for cleaning the tunnel area, which involves removing any cargo that has spilled off the belt during unloading operations. The wiper-gateman's responsibilities extend beyond the unloading system, however, to cleaning chores in the engine room and assisting the engineers when fueling the vessel.

The engine department is headed by the chief engineer, who is normally a day worker. Like the captain, however, the chief is usually on duty in the engine room when the boat is maneuvering or in a river, where an equipment malfunction or throttle error could imperil the ship. The chief supervises the engine staff and often gets personally involved in the repair and maintenance of machinery and equipment that are the responsibility of the engine department, which includes all of the machinery aboard the ship except the equipment located in the pilothouse. In addition to machinery located in the engine room, the engine department is responsible for the maintenance and repair of deck winches and anchor windlasses, the bowthruster, engines and motors driving the self-unloading equipment, galley equipment, the ship's electrical, water, and sanitary systems, and even the washing machines located in the laundry room.

The first assistant engineer is also generally a day worker, who assists the chief and has primary responsibility for performing maintenance and repair work on equipment located outside of the engine room. The three second and third assistant engineers who stand watches are restricted to the ship's throttle board or control room, so they are not available to do much maintenance or repair work unless the vessel is dockside. Some self-unloading vessels also carry an assistant engineer who is responsible for the unloading system. In those cases, the conveyorman and wiper-gateman work directly under the engineer's supervision.

On older boats, particularly steam vessels, the throttles that control the direction and speed of the ship are located in the engine room. When deck officers want to change speed or go from ahead to astern, or vice versa, they signal the watch engineer on the engine order telegraph, sometimes referred to as the Chadburn. The watch engineer then moves the indicator on the engine order telegraph in the engine room to signal back to the bridge that the order has been received and understood. With the improvements in shipboard communications, it is common for the deck officers to communicate their intentions to the watch engineer on the ship's intercom system before signalling on the engine order telegraph.

In addition to manning the throttles, engineers on steam vessels tend to the boilers, making sure that they are receiving the correct proportions of fuel and air to insure efficient combustion. If the boilers are not receiving the proper mix of fuel and air, billows of black smoke can be emitted from the smokestack as the incompletely burned fuel escapes through the stack. Watch engineers on steam vessels are also responsible for periodic operation of the ship's soot-blowing system to rid the stack of any accumulations of soot that represent a potential fire threat. Soot is blown out of the stack through the use of jets of compressed air.

On oil-fired steam vessels, it is also standard practice to have one of the watch engineers clean the fuel strainers each day. The strainers filter impurities out of the heavy Bunker-C fuel so that the burners inside the boilers do not get clogged up.

Like their counterparts in the pilothouse, the engineers also maintain a trip log. In it they record the time of speed changes, except for the changes that take place when the vessel is maneuvering. When maneuvering, speed and direction of the engines often change so frequently that it is impossible for the engineer to take the time to record them. The log also includes a record of when freshwater was taken on and when ballast tanks were filled or emptied. When ships are travelling light, or without any cargo, they often take on ballast in the side and bottom tanks to sink them deeper in the water and reduce the amount of surface area exposed to the wind. The more severe the weather, the more ballast will be taken on.

While ballasting decisions are made by the deck officers, the ballast pumps are located in the engine room and operated by engine department personnel, usually an oiler or QMED. To fill a ballast tank, a valve is opened that allows water to flood into the tank from a seacock below the ship's waterline. Large electrically driven pumps are used to remove the water from the tanks and pump it back out through discharge ports in the side of the hull above the waterline.

The oilers or QMEDs also make rounds of the engine room, usually every hour, and take temperature or pressure readings from the various machinery that is in operation to insure that it is functioning properly. Engineers will tell you that an experienced oiler can often hear or smell when a piece of equipment is beginning to malfunction. Since many of the vessel casualties that occur on the lakes are the result of equipment malfunctions, such as the loss of power or failure of the steering gear, an oiler with good hearing and a keenly developed sense of smell can be a real asset.

Engine rooms used to be referred to disparagingly as "black holds" and engine personnel were called the "black gang," both throwbacks to the days of coal-fired steamships when black dust and ash coated everything in the engine room, crewmembers included. Conditions are much improved today. Engine rooms aboard steamships can still be the hottest places this side of Hades during the summer months and they are constantly noisy, but since the shift to oil for fuel they are much cleaner. On the newer, diesel-powered ships, engine rooms are not only clean, but they often have control rooms that are air-conditioned. And in the finest tradition of the lakes, the coffee pot is always on.

Few sailors miss a scheduled meal aboard ship. Mealtime is in many respects a social occasion, providing an opportunity for crewmembers to talk with people who are on different watches or who work in different departments. In addition, the food prepared by the crew in the galley is always hot and plentiful. The galley department is headed by the steward or chief cook, assisted by the second cook, who traditionally has also been the ship's baker, and a porter. The porter helps with food preparation and galley cleanup, including washing dishes and pots and pans. Traditionally, crewmembers have been waited on by the second cook and the porter, but in recent

115

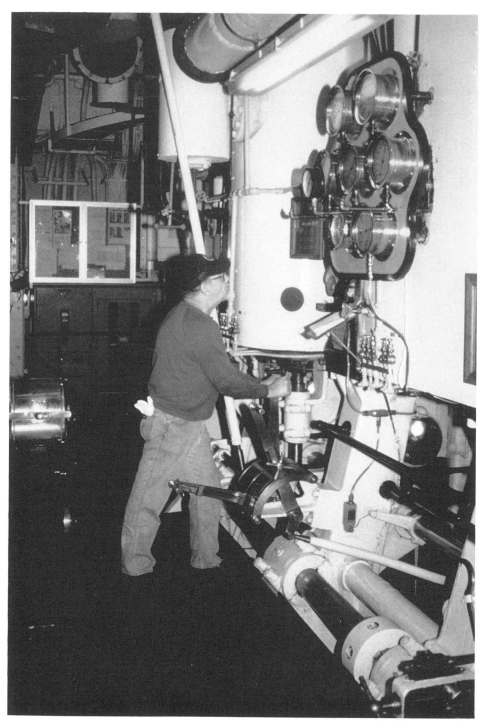

An engineer eyes a bank of gauges as he adjusts the throttles aboard the *Str. S. T. Crapo*. Built in 1927, the *Crapo* is powered by a 1,800 horsepower, coal-fired, triple-expansion steam engine, one of the last in operation on the Great Lakes. (Author's Collection)

The chief cook preparing dinner aboard Interlake Steamship's *Elton Hoyt II*. Food is always plentiful aboard ships on the Great Lakes. (Author's collection)

years many fleets have converted to cafeteria-style service to reduce costs.

On most ships there are two or three entrees available at every meal, along with assorted vegetables and salads, soup, freshly baked bread and rolls, pastries, fresh fruit, ice cream, and assorted beverages. For crewmembers, it is like eating every meal of every day in a restaurant or, perhaps more accurately, a cafeteria. The food on lake freighters is usually well-prepared. It is not gourmet fare, but home cooking, the type you would find on the dinner table of a farmer or factory worker, except that more expensive cuts of meat are generally used. Steak, prime ribs, and seafood are usually on the dinner menu each week, a long-standing Great Lakes tradition. It is a laborer's diet, high in fats and carbohydrates, even though there are few physically demanding tasks aboard the modern ships.

The combination of a rich diet and limited exertion has led to serious problems of obesity among the crews. To counter the growing problem, a number of fleets have installed salad bars aboard their vessels and enlisted the aid of nutritionists to design menus better suited to activities aboard ship.

For some crewmembers, eating is a favorite pastime, and they can tell you which ships on the lakes have reputations as "good feeders." In addition to the three hearty meals served each day, crewmembers also have access to what is referred to as the "night locker," a refrigerator packed with cold cuts, cheeses, leftovers, and frozen entrees that can be heated in the galley's microwave. In the past, many fleets also had a night cook to prepare full meals for personnel coming on and going off watch at midnight.

The most elaborate meal of the year aboard the lake freighters is generally Thanksgiving dinner. The following is a menu from the Cleveland-Cliffs fleet's 1983 Thanksgiving feast:

Appetizers

Chicken Consomme	Waldorf Salad	Shrimp Cocktail
Stuffed Celery	Relish Tray	Hot buttered rolls

Entrees

Roast Young Tom Turkey with Cranberry Sauce	Baked Virginia Ham with Raisin Sauce
Roast Long Island Duckling with Orange Sauce	Lobster Tails with Drawn Butter

Wild Rice Dressing

Savory Dressing

Broccoli in Cheddar Cheese Sauce

Whipped Potatoes

Giblet Gravy

Candied Sweet Potatoes

Desserts

Pumpkin Pie with Whipped Topping

Hot Mince Pie

Fruit Cakes

Apple Pie a la Mode

Plum Pudding with Brandy Sauce

Condiments

Assorted Chocolates

After-Dinner Mints

Hard Candies

Assorted Nut Meats

Fresh Fruits

Beverages

Assorted Soda Pop

Apple Cider

Coffee

Tea

Milk

Until Christmas 1973, wine was also always served aboard the Cliffs's vessels on special occasions, like Thanksgiving and Christmas. That year, however, a crewman fell overboard from the *Str. Frontenac* and drowned, possibly after having consumed too much wine at Christmas dinner. In addition, six crewmembers who launched a lifeboat in an effort to save their shipmate were almost lost when the high seas and fierce winds made it impossible for them to row back to their ship. Had another freighter not been in the area and able to get to the lifeboat, its six hands might also have been died.[6] As a result of the incident, Cliffs discontinued the prac-

tice of serving alcoholic beverages aboard its ships on holidays. Some fleets still continue the tradition, however.

Alcohol abuse has always been a serious problem in the merchant marine, even though Coast Guard regulations prohibit crewmembers from consuming alcohol aboard ship, and persons applying for Coast Guard licenses must supply letters attesting to their sobriety. With little to do during off-duty hours, however, crewmembers often resort to drinking to occupy their time. The problem is not as serious now as it once was, as many fleets have cracked down on the use of alcohol aboard their ships. Over the years, though, many sailors have been injured, some seriously, when they have fallen while trying to carry several six-packs of beer up a boarding ladder.

Falls are one of the most common causes of injury to crewmembers. There are a lot of steep ladders and stairways aboard the ships, and the steel decks can be very slick when wet. Occasionally a crewmember falls into the cargo hold through an open hatch when the ship is at a loading or unloading dock, a constant hazard for deck workers. In addition to injuries stemming from falls, burns are a common hazard for engine room personnel, particularly on steamboats where crewmembers work amid hot boilers and piping.

First aid is used to treat minor injuries aboard ship, but crewmembers who are seriously injured or ill are either put off the ship at the nearest dock or evacuated by the Coast Guard. Most medical evacuations are done by Coast Guard search and rescue vessels stationed at ports around the lakes, but in the case of life-threatening situations a Coast Guard helicopter may be called in to airlift the crewmember from the ship. In those instances, the helicopter hovers over the deck of the ship, and the crewmember is hoisted up in a special basket.

The most popular off-duty activities aboard ship are sleeping, watching television, talking, and reading, probably in that order. It is also common for crewmembers to pursue hobbies when they are off watch, including building model ships and making stained glass lampshades. One chief engineer went so far as to have a complete woodworking shop set up in the no-longer-used coal bunker aboard his ship. One avid golfer spent much of his spare time practicing his swing, driving old golf balls off the deck into the lake. To get exercise, some crewmembers use

Thanksgiving dinner aboard the Cleveland-Cliffs flagship *Edward B. Greene* in 1983. The captain sits at the head of the table, with the mates on his right and an assistant engineer on his left. The holiday meal is traditionally the most elaborate of the year aboard ships on the Great Lakes. (Author's collection)

weights, rowing machines, or stationary bicycles aboard ship. Others walk or jog around the deck. On a thousand-footer, one trip around the sprawling deck is about one-third of a mile.

To fight the boredom so common aboard ship, most crewmembers who are not on watch when the vessel is loading or unloading will try to get away from the ship for a few hours, going "up the street," as they say. In some ports, like Taconite Harbor, Minnesota, and Stoneport, Michigan, however, there really isn't any place close for sailors to go. In most ports, though, sailors can usually walk or catch a cab to go uptown. Time ashore is often spent shopping or sightseeing, particularly if the ship is at a port that it does not regularly call at. Other crewmembers will go out to eat or spend a few hours drinking at some tavern.

At the twin ports of Duluth, Minnesota, and Superior, Wisconsin, "bum boats" still tie up alongside the freighters while they are loading or unloading. The bum boats are really floating general stores where crewmembers can buy clothing, candy, beer, pop, magazines, books, stationery supplies, toilet articles, and even jewelry. Bum boats used to operate at all the major ports around the lakes, but with the downsizing of the fleet, most have gone out of business in recent years. They are, however, a colorful part of the industry's history. (See chapter 8 for further discussion of this.) Crewmembers can purchase newspapers at the Soo Locks or at the mailboat in Detroit. They also receive and send mail from both locations, and a merchant marine library at the Soo regularly puts boxes of books and magazines aboard the freighters.

The ship's laundry is sent off to commercial laundries that serve the ports around the lakes. Crewmembers launder their own clothes in laundry rooms provided aboard the ship or save up their dirty clothes until they get home. Generally speaking, crewmembers aboard Great Lakes ships do not wear uniforms. Blue jeans and T-shirts or flannel shirts are standard attire, although many officers opt for tan, grey, or blue work uniforms. Some fleets supply their officers with dress uniforms, similar to Navy dress blues, but they are worn only when important guests are aboard the ship. Baseball caps and hardhats are the normal headgear. Galley personnel generally wear white shirts and pants, similar to those worn by cooks in most restaurants.

If there are women in the crew, they are most likely to be employed in the galley. In recent years, a few women have also been employed in the deck or engine departments, although few of them had enough seniority to survive the personnel cuts that occurred in 1980. Since the late 1970s, each class at the Great Lakes Maritime Academy has included from three to six female cadets, a few of whom obtained shipboard jobs after graduation, at least on a fill-in basis.

The first female captain on the lakes was Lillian Kluka, who sails for N. M. Paterson & Sons, a Canadian fleet. Joining the Paterson fleet in 1976 as a cadet, Kluka made her way up through the officer ranks and was promoted to captain of the *M/V Ontodoc* on July 7, 1986, at the age of thirty-one.

A graduate of the navigation program at Owen Sound College in Ontario, Captain Kluka says that she has always been treated fairly aboard ship. "I've never been passed over in favor of a man," she remarks, "although there are those who are just waiting for me to make a mistake." Captain Kluka bears excellent testimony to the ability of women to serve effectively aboard ship in virtually any capacity, rather than being limited to jobs in the galley. A few decades ago, women might have shied away from entry-level positions that required the lifting of heavy hatch covers or shovelling tons of coal into a fiery boiler. Today, however, there is little strenuous physical labor left aboard the lake freighters.

It is not hard work that drives people away from careers aboard ships. Rather, it is the long hours of monotony, the highly restricted lifestyle, and the need to be separated from families and friends for extended periods of time. The situation has improved significantly in recent years with the adoption of liberal vacation plans. It wasn't too many years ago, however, that sailors often stayed aboard ship for the entire season, from early April until Christmas. They missed many important family events, including birthdays, graduations, and marriages.

During 1981 and 1982, Professor Harriet E. Gross and two of her graduate students at Governors State University in Illinois studied the ways in which the separations imposed by a sailor's life affected his family relationships. Dr. Gross and her research assistants interviewed thirty Great Lakes male officers and fifty wives of officers. They found that only

Captain Lillian Kluka of N. M. Paterson & Sons, a Canadian shipping company, was the first woman to command a freighter on the Great Lakes. Captain Kluka became master of the *M/V Ontodoc* on July 7, 1986, at the age of thirty-one. (Thunder Bay Harbour Commission)

21 percent of the women indicated a high level of satisfaction with their lifestyles, while 62 percent expressed moderate satisfaction, and 17 percent ranked their satisfaction as low. The sailors' wives said they often felt like single parents, solely responsible for managing their households during much of the year. They were often lonely, frequently excluded from couples' activities in their communities, and most found it impossible to hold jobs because their husbands expected them to be waiting for them at the dock whenever their boat came in, regardless of the time of day.

The relationships between the sailors and their families were also strained when the sailors were home during the winter. Wives reported that their husbands seemed like strangers to them when they were reunited at the end of the sailing season. After being primarily responsible for their family during the sailing season, the wives found it difficult to relinquish control to their husbands during the winter months.

Many of the sailors tended to be autocratic in dealing with both their wives and children, undoubtedly a carryover from the quasi-military authority they were used to aboard ship. One freighter captain commented: "I'm God on the boat. All I have to do is mention something and it's done, and that's the way it's supposed to be on the boat, that's the way it has to be. I come home and I'm only a deckhand." Other sailors were too lenient with their children, reluctant to discipline because they were only going to be home for a brief period and wanted to have good relations with the children during that time. The sailors acknowledged that their children missed out on a lot because they were gone so much of the time, but many felt that the children also had some advantages. One sailor noted: "Although they missed a lot in not having their father, I guarantee you, they had a very good living. I guarantee you that. Monetarily they had anything that was reasonable."

The sailors' wives, too, saw their husband's relatively high incomes as the best aspect of working on the boats. In addition, many felt that their marriages were actually strengthened by not having their husbands around all of the time. The frequent separations maintained a freshness in their personal relationships that prevented them from becoming boring or dull. Many used the term *honeymoon* to describe what it was like when their husbands came home from the boats.[7]

The inability of sailors to adjust to the frequent lengthy separations from their families is a prime cause of the high attrition within the maritime industry. At the same time, it is difficult for many sailors, and particularly officers, to give up their jobs aboard ship for jobs ashore. While engine officers can often find jobs at power plants or operating boiler systems that provide heat for hospitals, schools, or other commercial facilities, the pay falls far short of what they are used to in the maritime industry, and they would probably have to work harder than they do aboard ship. One captain seemed to sum up the situation when he commented, "A guy could probably find a job on shore if he hustled, but you couldn't sit around like you do out here." A chief engineer nearing retirement said, "I've missed a lot of stuff over the years by being out here, but you've got to give up something to get something. Where else could a guy like me with an eighth-grade education accomplish as much as I have." He added that he has made up to $60,000 in a single season. Deck officers generally find that their experience aboard ship doesn't qualify them for many positions outside of the maritime industry. If they are able to find a job ashore, they are generally forced to take a significant cut in pay and give up the status associated with their positions aboard ship.

Many of the deck and engine officers who have graduated from maritime academies have found it easy to find good jobs ashore, however. Many of those who attend academies, in fact, have no interest in a career aboard ship. They intend to sail for a few years, in order to build a financial nest egg, then find jobs ashore in management positions, often with shipping companies, shipyards, or other businesses within the marine transportation industry. The maritime academy graduates have the advantage of having college degrees, an essential credential for most jobs ashore. A growing number of hawsepipers have also recognized the value of obtaining a college degree in terms of career opportunities and are attending college during the winter months when their ships are not operating. With more sailors obtaining educations that increase their marketability for shoreside jobs, many observers feel that attrition within the maritime industry is likely to increase.

Some fleets would clearly prefer to hire personnel, particularly officers, who do not have college educations, feeling they are less likely to lose those employees to jobs ashore. Some industry executives, for example, have objected to developing baccalaureate degree programs for cadets at the Great Lakes Maritime Academy for that very reason. GLMA graduates receive only a two-year associate's degree, while graduates of the other maritime academies earn bachelor's degrees. During the 1980–87 period when the shipping industry on the lakes was in the grip of a severe recession, few GLMA graduates were able to find jobs aboard ships. At the same time, their lack of four-year degrees made it difficult for them to find jobs outside of the marine industry or to compete with graduates of the other academies for shoreside jobs within the industry.

Many sailors, however, are wedded to their jobs aboard ship, not just because of the high pay, but because they genuinely love their work and their lifestyle. Regardless of what other career opportunities existed for them, they would prefer to continue sailing. At a very basic level, they are sailors . . . and they love life aboard ship. Life is not always easy for sailors. In addition to the stress of being separated from their families, they spend a great deal of time basically out of touch with society. Most of the time, their "society" consists only of their shipmates.

Deck department personnel also are exposed to extreme weather conditions. In the fall and spring, they battle subzero temperatures, bitter winds, snow, and bone-chilling rain. In the summer, they bake under the inescapable glare of the sun. Engineering personnel don't have to work out on deck very often, but they spend their hours in a windowless engine room. Noise constantly assaults their eardrums, and in the summer they swelter in the hot, stifling humidity. The smell of hot oil permeates the engine room and, in the heat of summer, can be almost overpowering.

These sailors are heirs to a seafaring tradition that is thousands of years old. Their profession is memorialized by King David in the familiar words of Psalm 107, written almost three thousand years ago:

They that go down to the sea in ships,
and occupy their business in great waters;
These men see the works of the LORD,
and his wonders in the deep.[8]

The remaining verses of the Psalm are less familiar to us. They speak of the stormy winds and fierce waves that carry the sailors "up to heaven, and down again to the deep." Like the seamen of David's era, today's sailors carry on their proud tradition with the full knowledge that thousands who have gone before them lost their lives in shipwrecks. No sailors have been lost on the lakes since the 1975 sinking of the *Edmund Fitzgerald*, but the men and women who sail the lakes know that it is only a matter of time before the old bell at the Mariners' Church of Detroit will again toll mournfully for sailors lost at sea.

Notes

1. *1982 Annual Report* (Cleveland: Lake Carriers' Association, 1983), 18.
2. The line was supposedly delivered by Samuel Johnson's Boswell in *Life*, 1759.
3. Joseph Conrad, "Heart of Darkness," in *Tales of Land and Sea* (Garden City, NY: Hanover House, 1953), 34.
4. "An Historic Thirty-Six Hours of Superior Seamanship," *Inland Seas*, Summer 1984, 82–88.
5. R. D. Graham, "Benny and the Boom," *Telescope*, Nov.–Dec. 1980, 154–56.
6. "Stmr. McKee Sons Cited for Outstanding Seamanship," *The Bulletin* (Cleveland: Lake Carriers' Association, 1974), 3–6.
7. Harriet Engel Gross, Marie Van Gemert, and Christine Thomas, "A Distance Between Worlds," *Seaway Review* (Winter 1983): 83–87; "The Ongoing Dilemma," *Seaway Review* (Spring 1984): 53–58; "The Limitations They Cannot Ignore," *Seaway Review* (Summer 1984): 49–53.
8. Revised Standard Version.

6

Ports and Cargoes: Moving Mountains

Oh, we're bound down from Marquette my two hands are sore; I've been pushing a wheelbarrow and I'll do it no more.

—Nineteenth Century Great Lakes Chantey

There is currently some controversy as to whether Mount Everest or K2 is the tallest mountain on earth. Measurements made by satellites seem to indicate that the summit of K2 may actually be higher than Everest, which has been recognized throughout this century as the tallest peak on our planet. Regardless of the outcome of the debate, the name *Mount Everest* will always hold some special magic for both the generations of mountain climbers who have been challenged by the lure of its towering summit and the Nepalese and Tibetans who live in the shadow of the great mountain and refer to it as Chomolungma—"Mother Goddess of the World." K2 may inch out Everest in the record books, but Everest will always retain its reputation as the most imposing and awe-inspiring peak on the planet, the mother of all mountains.

Mount Everest rises out of the tropical forests and rolling foothills of the Indian subcontinent to a height of 29,028 feet, its rocky summit standing more than 5 miles above sea level. In geologic terms, it is a new mountain, formed during the past sixty-five million years by the collision of the African and Eurasian crustal plates. Composed of 906 million tons of rock, Everest is the largest structure on earth, dwarfing anything humans have built.

During the five shipping seasons from 1975–79, the Great Lakes shipping industry moved 986 million tons of cargo. If put into a single pile, perhaps somewhere along the south shore of Lake Erie, the resulting peak would have surpassed both Everest and K2. It took millions of years for Everest and the Himalayan chain to be formed, but in just over 150 years, the bulk industry on the lakes has moved enough iron ore, grain, coal, limestone, and liquid bulk products to form a mountain chain that would rival the great mountain ranges of the world.

The amount of cargo the industry moves in even a single season defies our comprehension. Since World War II, total tonnages moved each year have ranged from a low of 125 million tons in 1982 to a high of 214 million tons in 1979. To carry 214 million tons at one time, you would need 8,560 ships, each with a carrying capacity of 25,000 tons. Placed end to end, the ships would form a convoy that would stretch for over 1,180 miles, the distance from Duluth, Minnesota, to the east end of Lake Ontario. If that is hard to comprehend, it might help you to know that it would take 2,675,000 80-ton rail cars or more than eight million 25-ton trucks to carry the same amount of cargo. End to end, the rail cars, without engines, would stretch for more than 60,000 miles. The trucks would make a bumper-to-bumper convoy more than 90,000 miles in length. That's a convoy! The trucks could circle the earth at the equator almost four times.

In a single trip, a 1,000-foot ore freighter can carry more than 60,000 tons of iron ore, enough to make all of the steel needed to build sixteen thousand automobiles. A single Seaway-size, 730-foot bulker can load over 500,000 bushels of grain. It takes almost 20,000 acres to grow that much grain. Ground into flour, the cargo from that one ship would be sufficient for your local bakery to turn out fifty million loaves of bread. The modern tankers that operate on the Great Lakes can carry more than 70,000 barrels of fuel oil or gasoline, enough to supply the needs of more than three thousand motorists for a full year, even if they weren't driving economy cars.

Of the total cargo moved each year, a little over 40 percent, 51 to 94 million tons, is iron ore—the "river of red" that has been the industry's key commodity for a hundred years. Mines in the Lake Superior region produce about 78 percent of all the iron ore mined in the U.S. In Canada, the provinces of Quebec and Ontario that border the Great Lakes and St. Lawrence River account for close to 60 percent of all the country's iron ore.

Humans have been using iron since about 3,000 B.C., when people in the Middle East began making tools and ornaments by working iron-laden meteors. Iron obtained from meteors and meteorites was rare, so the metal was expensive; only kings and ranking warriors could afford it. True iron working, involving the smelting of ore to remove impurities and increase the quality of the iron began in Asia Minor about 1100 B.C., ushering in the *Iron Age*. Iron ore was found there in great abundance, so iron was cheap. It had the added advantage of being stronger than other metals that were then in wide use, such as copper and bronze.

Iron is one of the key elements in the core of the earth and makes up about 5 percent of the crust of the planet. Scientists believe that deposits of iron began to form over a billion years ago when violent volcanoes spewed iron laden dust into the air in massive quantities, covering much of the earth. The iron was gradually dissolved from the dust by water, and it settled to the bottom of the expansive oceans that then covered much of the surface of the planet, forming vast subterranean deposits of ore. Later, many of the ore deposits were forced to the surface as a result of earthquakes and the shrinking of the earth's crust. Then, during the Ice Age, the retreating glaciers deposited a layer of sand and gravel over the beds of iron ore, what the mining industry refers to as "overburden."

The ores differ significantly in the amount of iron they contain. The most common commercial ores are classified as either magnetite, hematite, or taconite, based on their physical characteristics and iron content. All three are found in the Great Lakes region.

Magnetite is a black mineral that accounts for about 60 percent of the ore mined in the U.S. As suggested by its name, magnetite, or lodestone as it is often called, has magnetic properties. About 1200 A.D., Europeans discovered that elongated pieces of the stone would point to the north if suspended by a string, leading to the first compasses and totally altering navigation.

About 40 percent of the ore mined in the U.S. is hematite, which can be as much as 70 percent iron and normally occurs as a red-colored mineral, the color of rust. The mineral's name is derived from the Greek word *haimatites*, meaning bloodlike.

The third commercial ore, taconite, contains iron in specks and streaks and has an overall iron content that is often as low as 25 percent. While taconite is not commercially viable until some of its impurities have been removed and its iron content has been concentrated, it is growing in importance

Modern iron-mining operations at LTV Steel's pit at Hoyt Lakes in Minnesota's Mesabi Range. The electric-powered shovel is shown loading the "King of the Lode," a 240-ton payload truck that is the largest in use on the Mesabi or Marquette Ranges. (Cleveland-Cliffs Iron Company)

as supplies of higher quality ore are being depleted. Much of the ore produced today in the Great Lakes region is taconite.

Iron is presently the most widely used of all commercial metals because it is cheap, it is found in large quantities throughout the world, and it is the basic mineral used for the production of steel. As Rudyard Kipling wrote in his poem *Cold Iron*:

"Gold is for the mistress—silver for the maid—
Copper for the craftsman cunning at his trade."
"Good!" said the Baron, sitting in his hall,
"But Iron—Cold Iron—is master of them all."

To make one ton of pig iron, the basic ingredient in steel or cast iron, it takes about 1⅞ tons of ore, ⅞ ton of coke, and ¼ ton of limestone. Coke—coal which has been burned in special ovens to remove gasses—is ignited in the bottom of a blast furnace. The charge of ore and limestone is then dumped into the furnace and heated to around 3,000° Farenheit, which causes the iron in the ore to melt. To achieve those temperatures, large quantities of air are injected into the furnaces, up to 100,000 cubic feet per minute. This is the blast of air from which the blast furnace takes its name.

When the iron in the blast furnace has melted, it settles to the bottom, because it is heavier than the other materials in the furnace. Impurities that were in the iron, along with the limestone that has served as a flux to aid in the melting and separation of impurities, float to the top of the furnace. At regular intervals, the iron is tapped off by burning out a plug near the bottom of the furnace. The white hot stream of iron flows through a trough to ladle cars, also known as bottle cars or hot metal cars, which hold 40 to 160 tons of molten iron. As much as 400 tons of iron can be removed from the furnace at a time. The limestone and impurities that form a slag floating on top of the molten iron are tapped off through a hole located above the level of the iron in the furnace. The slag, too, is carried away in ladle cars.

In the past, the iron removed from the blast furnaces would have been taken to a pig-casting machine where it was cast into pigs, or bars of iron. Today, however, most of the molten iron goes directly into the production of steel. Steel is an alloy of iron and small amounts of carbon and other minerals. It is stronger than iron and can be shaped into many useful products. The steelmaking process is basically one of removing excess carbon and other impurities from the iron and adding other desired materials, such as manganese, dolomite, chromium, or vanadium, in small quantities. The materials added

Molten iron from the blast furnace is charged into one of
two basic oxygen furnaces as Bethlehem Steel's plant in
Bethlehem, Pennsylvania. After the charge has been completed, the vessel will return to its upright position for the
oxygen "blow" during which the blast furnace iron, combined with scrap steel and additives, will be refined into
steel. (Bethlehem Steel Corporation)

to the iron in the steel-making process determine the type of steel alloy that is produced. Stainless steel, for example, is a corrosion-resistant steel that has had chromium added to it.

Most steel made in the U.S. today is produced by the basic oxygen process developed in Europe shortly after World War II. A basic oxygen furnace, called a BOF, can produce up to 300 tons of steel in less than an hour, compared to the five to eight hours needed in the older, open hearth process. The BOF furnaces are cauldrons that look much like gigantic thermos bottles. The furnaces are open at the top, like a thermos, so that raw materials can be added, and they are mounted on pivots so they can be tipped to pour out their contents.

About 30 percent of a BOF's charge consists of scrap metal. Molten iron from blast furnaces is poured in on top of the scrap to melt it, and pure oxygen is injected into the BOF at supersonic speeds to burn away carbon and other impurities and convert the metal into steel. Limestone is then added to act as a flux and gather impurities into a layer of slag that floats on top of the molten steel in the furnace.

The slag can be drawn off the top of the BOF and discarded. Then alloying materials can be added to the steel in the furnace before the BOF is tipped to pour its contents into molds or feed a continuous casting process that forms the steel into billets or slabs. The resulting ingots, billots, or slabs can then be shaped into finished steel products, such as sheets, bars, wires, pipes, or beams.

In the older open hearth process, still in wide use in the industry, the furnaces are about as large as a two-story building. The furnace is filled through a door on the top level, while the molten steel is tapped through a door on the other side, where the floor is one story lower. In one melt, an open hearth furnace can produce 100 to 300 tons of steel in five to eight hours.

To charge the furnaces, a special machine with a long arm dumps boxes of limestone and scrap steel into the furnace. The materials are heated until they are melted, then molten pig iron is added to mix with the molten scrap iron. Mill workers constantly test samples of the molten metal to determine when it has reached the desired purity, then small quantities of other minerals can be added to produce the desired alloy.

The open hearth furnaces are tapped by shooting out the tap-hole plug in the lower level of the furnace with a device much like a bazooka rocket. The molten steel and slag run off into a ladle, with the slag rising to the top. The slag overflows into an adjacent smaller ladle, known as a slag thimble. The ladle with the molten steel can then be lifted by a crane and poured into ingot molds mounted on railroad cars. Each resulting ingot weighs about 115 tons.

The third steel-making process, involving the electric furnace, accounts for about 10 percent of all steel produced, primarily the more exacting grades of alloys and carbon steel. The electric furnaces are saucer-shaped and, like the BOFs, they can be tipped to pour off slag and molten steel. The charge used in electric furnaces is primarily scrap steel, with little or no pig iron being used. Massive electrodes in the top of the furnace are lowered until they are almost in contact with the charge, then the electricity is turned on. The electricity arcs from the electrodes to the charge in the furnace, causing temperatures to rise to about 3,500° Farenheit. The furnace can then be tipped to rake off the layer of slag and pour the steel into a ladle.

About 75 percent of all the iron ore that moves through the Great Lakes and St. Lawrence system each year is shipped from iron ranges south and west of Lake Superior through ports in Minnesota, Wisconsin, and Michigan. Currently, the largest ore ports on Lake Superior are Two Harbors and Duluth in Minnesota and Superior, Wisconsin.

Duluth and Superior are often referred to as the twin ports, because they share a common harbor that straddles the Minnesota-Wisconsin border at the west end of Lake Superior. Until 1871, the only entrance to the sprawling, 24-mile long harbor was through a break in the sandbar on the Superior side. Wanting to create a direct access to its side of the harbor, Duluth began excavating a channel through the sandbar in 1871. Officials from Superior attempted to block the excavation by obtaining a federal court injunction. Before the injunction could be issued, however, thousands of angry Duluth residents armed with shovels worked day and night for two days to finish the channel and link their side of the harbor with Lake Superior.[1]

French explorers first visited the Duluth-Superior area in about 1634, led by Chippewa Indians who lived there. The first permanent settler may have been George Stuntz, the surveyor and amateur geologist who discovered iron ore on the Vermilion range north of Duluth around 1852. The importance of the two ports increased significantly during the 1890s when ore first began moving off the Mesabi Range. Shipyards were eventually established in both cities, including Captain Alexander McDougall's famous American Steel Barge Company in Superior. Most of McDougall's unique whaleback barges and steamers were built there between 1888 and 1896. The only surviving whaleback, the *Str. Meteor*, is now a maritime museum at Superior, just a few miles down the shore from the shipyard where it was launched. Today, between 12 and 30 million tons of taconite pellets move across the ore docks in Duluth and Superior each year, accounting for about 40 percent of the total shipments from U.S. ports on the Great Lakes.

East of Duluth and Superior along the north shore of Lake Superior are the Minnesota ports of Two Harbors, Silver Bay, and Taconite Harbor. While Two Harbors dates to about 1884, when George Stuntz's Duluth and Iron Range Railroad connected the twin bays of the port with the Vermilion Range, Silver Bay and Taconite Harbor are among the newest ports on the lakes. The three ports are among the largest and most modern in the system. All capable of accommodating thousand-footers, together they handle 10 to 30 million tons of taconite each year. Silver Bay was opened in 1955 as the outlet port for Reserve Mining's Davis Works at Babbitt, Minnesota, the first facility developed by Republic Steel and Armco Steel to concentrate low-grade iron ore into taconite pellets. A second taconite processing plant was subsequently built at Hoyt Lakes, Minnesota, by a consortium of steel companies, including U.S. Steel and Youngstown Steel.

The process for concentrating low-grade taconite ores into pellets with an iron content in excess of 60 percent was developed by faculty at the University of Minnesota. Referred to as "benefication," the low grade ores are pulverized until they are the consistency of dust, then the iron is drawn off by magnets. The concentrated iron powder is then moistened and rolled into balls the size of marbles that are fused solid in mammoth ovens. A second process, developed for use with non-magnetic ores, involves a flotation process that separates the heavier ore-bearing

particles from impurities that would make the shipment of the low grade ore uneconomical. The concentrated iron ore is then rolled into balls and hardened in ovens. Today, virtually all of the ore moving off Lake Superior is shipped in the form of taconite pellets. They provide the steel mills with a uniform, high-quality product that is generally considered to be superior to raw ore.

Taconite Harbor, the newest of all ore ports on the Great Lakes, was opened in 1957 to handle pellets from a beneficating plant at Aurora, about 100 miles west of Taconite Harbor. Operated by LTV Steel, the country's second largest steel producer, the facility uses a conveyor belt loading system, similar to those in use at Silver Bay and Two Harbors. The Taconite Harbor loading system is among the most efficient in the world, capable of loading the giant freighters at rates up to 10,000 tons per hour. By comparison, most of the older style chute docks cannot exceed more than 3,000 tons per hour.

Along the south shore of Lake Superior, at Marquette, Michigan, is the oldest of the Great Lakes iron ore ports. The first ore ever shipped on the lakes was loaded by hand at Marquette in 1855, largely by crewmembers aboard the ships that carried it. The sailors loathed the indignity of being pressed into service for the arduous work of loading iron ore, a task they viewed as demeaning to their status as mariners. While the first cargoes of ore were small, the wheelbarrows loaded with ore were heavy and it was backbreaking work. Most sailors would rather have been called on to weather a gale on Lake Superior than to load the dirty red ore.

In 1859, the first chute-type ore dock was built at Marquette by the Cleveland Iron Company, forerunner to the present Cleveland Cliffs Iron Company. The prototype for all subsequent ore docks, it was 22 feet wide and 25 feet tall and could load up to four ships simultaneously. A newer dock was constructed at Presque Isle Point on the the outskirts of Marquette in 1896. While the pockets of the original dock could hold only 50 tons apiece, those in the new dock each held 160 tons. To keep pace with the growth in the size of the ore boats, the dock stood 54 feet high, twice the height of its predecessor.

The chute-type docks were built so that rail cars loaded with ore could be pushed to the top of the dock trestle. Gates in the bottom of the hopper-shaped cars were opened and the ore would spill into the

A worker replaces grinding plates inside one of the twelve crude ore grinders at the Tilden Mine on Michigan's Marquette Range. The cavernous 32-foot grinding mill breaks down chunks of raw ore so that the iron can be removed for use in the benefication process that produces taconite pellets. (Cleveland-Cliffs Iron Company)

The *Str. Benson Ford* loading taconite pellets at the belt-type ore dock at Escanaba, Michigan. The articulated boom of the loader can be moved about to distribute cargo evenly in the cargo hold. The operator rides in a cab near the end of the boom. (Author's collection)

A freighter being loaded at the chute-type ore docks at Marquette, Michigan. The dock workers standing on each side of the ore chute open and close the trap doors that allow ore to flow from the storage bins above them into the hold of the ship. (Author's collection)

pockets under the tracks. At the bottom of each pocket was a gate that could be opened to let the ore slide down the loading chute and into the hold of the ship moored alongside the dock. It was an ingenious system that allowed a large quantity of ore to be loaded very rapidly, with little manual labor. Needless to say, the system was an instant hit with the sailors who crewed the ore boats.

By 1899 there were twenty-two ore docks serving the Lake Superior District. In addition to the docks at Marquette, there were five docks at Two Harbors; two docks at Duluth; one dock at Superior; three docks at Ashland, Wisconsin; four docks at Escanaba, Michigan; one dock at Gladstone, Michigan; one dock at L'Anse, Michigan; and one dock at St. Ignace, Michigan. The twenty-two docks contained a total of 4,624 pockets, with an aggregate capacity of 633,804 tons. The docks ranged in length from 559 feet to 2,304 feet. Laid end-to-end, they would have stretched for more than 5 miles.

The present chute dock at Marquette was completed in 1912 at Presque Isle. Handling ore mined in Michigan's Upper Peninsula, the dock now loads 2 to 8 million tons a year. The only other ore dock now operating in Michigan is at Escanaba, on Little Bay de Noc at the northern end of Lake Michigan. The first ore dock was built at Escanaba in 1863. Today, the conveyor belt loading system there handles 5 to 10 million tons of taconite each year. The loading system is rated at about 3,700 tons per hour.

Because ships loading at Escanaba do not have to transit the Soo Locks, the port has traditionally held the record for the largest cargoes of ore loaded on the lakes. The current record of 72,351 gross tons of taconite was loaded aboard Bethlehem Steel's *M/V Lewis Wilson Foy* during the 1986 shipping season at Escanaba. The record cargo aboard the *Foy* was made possible partially as a result of record high water levels that existed on the Great Lakes.

On the Canadian side, shipments of iron ore originate from Thunder Bay on Lake Superior and Little Current on Lake Huron. Thunder Bay, known as the "Canadian lakehead," is primarily a grain port, but it ships 1 to 2 million tons of ore each year. Little Current is the home of International Nickel, which ships only 15 to 16,000 tons of ore annually. The other Canadian ore moved through the Great Lakes and St. Lawrence system is ore shipped from mines in Eastern Canada to mills on Lake Ontario and at Sault Ste. Marie. More than 6 million tons of ore moves into the system each year from port facilities at Contrecoeur, Pointe Noire, Port-Cartier, and Sept Iles, all in Quebec.

Since the earliest days of the iron ore industry on the Great Lakes, most of the ore carried aboard the lake freighters has been destined for Ohio ports along the south shore of Lake Erie. Both Cleveland and Lorain developed early as steel-making centers as a result of their accessibility to ships bringing ore and limestone down from the northern lakes. Coal, the other vital raw material needed to make steel, was shipped in from the coalfields of Kentucky, West Virginia, Pennsylvania, and southern Ohio by rail. Andrew Carnegie reportedly felt that northern Ohio was the natural center for the world's iron and steel industries because all of the necessary raw materials could be shipped there so economically.

The LTV Steel mills on Cleveland's infamous Cuyahoga River and the U.S. Steel plant on Lorain's Black River are still major consumers of ore mined on the northern lakes. Lorain is also the site of LTV's pellet transshipment terminal. The terminal was opened in 1972 to serve thousand-footers carrying ore destined for the LTV mills in Cleveland, which cannot navigate the narrow and winding Cuyahoga. Pellets discharged at the terminal at the mouth of the Black River are loaded aboard smaller ore carriers, like the *M/V American Republic*, for movement to Cleveland and up the Cuyahoga. Other ore discharged at Lake Erie ports is destined for steel mills inland, primarily in southern Ohio and western Pennsylvania. Ore unloaded at ports like Toledo, Ashtabula, Huron, and Conneaut often moves by rail to steelmaking centers like Pittsburgh and Youngstown.

Accessibility to raw materials also led to the construction of steel mills along the southern shore of Lake Michigan at South Chicago, Illinois, and Burns Harbor and Gary, Indiana. Gary, in fact, was developed in 1905 by U.S. Steel, turning sand dunes and marshland into what was for years the largest steel manufacturing facility in the world. The city was named for Judge Elbert H. Gary, a lawyer and industrialist who helped form U.S. Steel in 1901. The port of Burns Harbor in Portage, Indiana, is home to Bethlehem Steel's Burns Harbor mill. The port of South Chicago, on the Calumet River, serves an LTV Steel mill and facilities of Acme Steel.

Three steel mills are also located in "downriver" suburbs of Detroit. Trenton is home to McLough Steel, while Ecorse is the site of National Steel's Great Lakes Steel Division. In Dearborn is Ford Motor Company's Rouge Steel subsidiary, which supplies much of the steel used by the auto manufacturer. The Ford complex is connected to the Detroit River by the Rouge River, a narrow, twisting industrial channel that is crisscrossed by rail and highway bridges. Like Cleveland's Cuyahoga and Chicago's Calumet, it challenges the skill of the sailors who must regularly guide their giant ships up and down the treacherous channels.

Three major steel mills are located on the Canadian side of the lakes in the province of Ontario. On Lake Ontario are the Hamilton and Nanticoke mills of the Steel Company of Canada (Stelco) and Dofasco Steel. At Sault Ste. Marie, within view of the Soo Locks and just a few miles from the entrance to Lake Superior, is Algoma Steel, the only steel mill on the northern lakes.

Most of the iron ore moved on the Great Lakes and St. Lawrence is now carried aboard self-unloaders, eliminating the need for shoreside unloading equipment. Historically, most of the ports receiving shipments of ore had shoreside unloading systems. While small ports around the lakes could not justify the installation and maintenance of unloading equipment, the iron ore ports handled sufficient quantities of material to develop their own unloading systems. They could then be served by traditional Great Lakes straight-deckers, which have a slightly greater carrying capacity per load than comparably sized self-unloaders.

During the 1986 shipping season, however, no straight-deckers were assigned to the ore trade. A few that were primarily engaged in grain movements also carried some iron ore during the season, but for the first time in the industry's long history, the regular iron ore trade was limited to self-unloaders. Self-unloading equipment can unload a ship faster than shoreside equipment and eliminates the need to maintain and operate expensive and aging dockside equipment at a time when the tonnages being handled by the industry are at a low level. It had also become difficult and expensive to maintain crews of dock workers to operate equipment that was not in regular use.

For a hundred years, however, the efficiency of the shoreside unloading systems used around the lakes contributed significantly to the overall efficiency of the Great Lakes bulk industry. It didn't take long for the industry's early pioneers to conclude that the efficiency of their vessels would be forever limited by the speed at which they could be loaded and unloaded. High volume chute docks were developed within a few years of the opening of the iron ore trade on the lakes, but efficient unloading proved to be a more difficult challenge.

The greatest breakthrough in unloading technology didn't come until 1899, forty years after the first chute-type loading dock was opened at Marquette, when an eccentric genius named George H. Hulett built an unloader that looked something like a giant prehistoric grasshopper. The Hulett unloader consisted of a huge clamshell bucket mounted at the end of a heavy articulated arm. The unloading rig was operated by a worker who rode in a cab just above the bucket itself.

Powered first by steam and later by electricity, a Hulett could be guided into the hold of a ship, where it would take a 15-to-18 ton bite of cargo. Because the operator rode into the hold atop the bucket, he was able to do a much better job of cleaning out the cargo hold than systems where the operator was stationed on the dock and could not see into the hold. Those systems, like conventional cable cranes, relied on laborers in the cargo hold to move material to the bucket, making cleanup of the hold a slow process.

During their heyday, the Hulett unloaders were the most efficient in the world. In 1937, for example, port officials in Liverpool, England, bragged that they had set a European record when they unloaded 4,960 tons of iron ore from the Str. Tregarthen in twenty hours. By comparison, at about the same time Hulett unloading rigs at Conneaut, Ohio, scooped 13,586 tons of ore from the hold of the Str. William A. Irvin in just two hours and fifty-five minutes![2] Even today, cargo loading and unloading "efficiency" has a totally different meaning on the Great Lakes than it does elsewhere in the world. While a lot of international ports ballyhoo loading and unloading systems that can handle 3,000 tons or less an hour, ships on the lakes are commonly loaded and unloaded at rates of up to 10,000 tons per hour without any fanfare.

Over the years, the efficiency of the Great Lakes bulk industry has had a tremendous impact on the steel industry within the region and the overall economic vitality of the U.S. A 1980 study by Michigan Technological University showed that lake shipping saved the steel mills around the lakes about $15 per ton over what it would cost to ship the ore by rail. Those savings amounted to $240-$475 million a year for the steel industry, representing 29 percent of the industry's net income during the 1970–78 period.[3] A large share of the savings documented were the result of the highly efficient loading and unloading systems that had been developed on the lakes, like the Huletts.

Today, Huletts remain in operation at only two Great Lakes ports, Cleveland and Chicago, and they see only limited use. There are still Huletts at Toledo, Huron, and Conneaut, but they are all idle and may never be used again. Many other lower lake ore ports are equipped with some sort of crane-type unloading equipment, primarily bridge cranes. Like the Huletts, bridge cranes have been largely made obsolete by the industry's reliance on self-unloaders. If the demand for ore forced the industry to put the few remaining straight-deckers back into operation, the shoreside unloading equipment could again see some use.

In terms of tonnages, the second most important commodity moved on the lakes today is coal, much of which is destined for use as fuel by steel mills along the lower lakes. Power plants and other industrial facilities in both the U.S. and Canada are also prime customers for coal moved through Great Lakes ports.

Before the late 1960s, when coal was still the primary fuel used in home heating, freighters moved 50 to 60 million tons each year. With the shift to natural gas for residential heating and low fuel oil prices, tonnages dropped to a low of just under 35 million tons in 1974. Then, when oil prices skyrocketed in the early 1970s during the Arab oil embargo, coal tonnages began to creep upward again, reaching almost 46 million tons during the 1979 shipping season. In 1980, primarily as a result of the downturn in steel production, tonnages again dropped to around 34 to 35 million tons per year.[4]

The majority of the coal shipped on the Great Lakes and St. Lawrence is Appalachian bituminous coal or soft coal, which is shipped by rail from the mines to ports on Lake Erie and Lake Michigan. More than 60 percent of the total coal moving in the system is shipped from the Ohio ports of Conneaut, Ashtabula, Sandusky, and Toledo. Conneaut and Toledo are the largest of the Great Lakes coal ports, both moving approximately 10 million tons a year. In addition, substantial amoounts of coal are moved out of South Chicago on Lake Michigan and from Superior, Wisconsin, and Thunder Bay, Ontario, on Lake Superior. Between 1.5 and 2 million tons of Appalachian coal move through South Chicago annually, while Superior has handled up to 7 million tons a year and Thunder Bay has reached 1.9 million tons. Coal moved through the Lake Superior ports is made up largely of low sulphur Western coal mined in Wyoming.

Most of the coal shipping docks on the Great Lakes, including most of the major facilities on Lake Erie, are owned and operated by railroads, including CSX, Norfolk Southern, Bessemer & Lake Erie, and Pittsburgh & Lake Erie. The railroads are extensively involved in marketing coal to consumers in the U.S., Canada, and overseas, often in conjunction with the shipping companies.

While iron ore shipments are received at only a limited number of ports around the lakes, coal goes to more than fifty facilities. Major coal consumers include utility companies that operate power plants that burn coal, steel plants not located on Lake Erie or Lake Michigan, paper manufacturing plants, auto plants, cement manufacturers, and coal retailers.

Much of the coal that is loaded aboard ships at Lake Erie ports, totalling 8 to 12 million tons a year, is destined for Canadian ports. One to 2 million tons a year go to the Algoma Steel plant in Sault Ste. Marie, Ontario, and 6 to 8 million tons are shipped to ports east of the Welland Canal, primarily to the major steel plants on Lake Ontario. Virtually all of the coal exported to Canada is carried aboard Canadian ships, a fact that has attracted the attention of many government and shipping officials in the United States.

In 1953, before construction of the St. Lawrence Seaway, U.S. vessels carried 30 percent of the cross-lakes cargoes. By 1986, the U.S. share had dropped to only 5 percent. A 1985 study by the U.S. Government Accounting Office (GAO), done at the request of the House of Representatives Merchant Marine Committee, blamed much of the disparity on government policies that put U.S. fleets at a competitive disadvantage. The government investigators cited

The *Str. Wyandotte* loading coal at Toledo. A conveyor system feeds coal to the ship loader, whereas the older loader visible in the right foreground lifts railroad cars full of coal and dumps them into the hold of a ship. (Institute for Great Lakes Research, Bowling Green State University)

Canadian tax incentives and financial assistance to their fleets, and their ability to build ships overseas cheaply, as contributing to the economic competitiveness of the Canadian fleets.[5]

Coal shipments out of the Lake Erie ports, as well as incoming iron ore shipments are coordinated by an organization known as the Ore and Coal Exchange. Based in Cleveland, the Ore and Coal Exchange was established by the government during World War I to insure that delays were not experienced in the movement of raw materials critical to the U.S. war effort. At the end of the war, the operation was taken over by the railroads, and it operates today as the agent for thirteen railroads involved in ore and coal movements in and out of Lake Erie ports. Through the efforts of the personnel at the Ore and Coal Exchange, delays are dramatically reduced for vessel operators, the railroads, and the customers waiting to receive the coal or ore. Partially as a result of their coordination of cargo movements, Great Lakes shipping companies seldom experience the demurrage, time spent waiting to load or unload, that is an everyday part of doing business at many saltwater ports in the U.S.

Demurrage problems at U.S. East Coast coal ports in the early 1980s, due partially to a growing demand for coal on world markets, led to development of a unique coal transshipment technology, which has resulted in international shipments of coal from Lake Erie ports. The system was pioneered in 1980 by the Bessemer & Lake Erie Railroad (B&LE), which operates modern dock facilities at Conneaut, Ohio. When ocean vessels were delayed for thirty days or more waiting to load at East Coast ports, B&LE arranged to move coal by self-unloaders to the deep water at the mouth of the St. Lawrence River. There, the self-unloaders discharged their cargoes directly into the holds of the giant coal colliers, which are too large to enter the St. Lawrence and Great Lakes system. Almost a million tons of Lake Erie coal was shipped overseas during 1981 as a result of the midstream transfer technology. Included was the single largest cargo of coal ever shipped from North America. The record was set when six self-unloaders from Canada Steamship Lines (CSL) loaded 165,000 tons of metallurgical coal aboard a massive Japanese collier at anchor in the bay off Sept Iles in the St. Lawrence. The coal was loaded aboard the CSL vessels at Conneaut and Sandusky for the 900-mile trip to the mouth of the St. Lawrence. The ultimate destination for the coal was Nippon Steel in Japan.

CSL subsequently established a regular monthly top-off service at Sept Iles, servicing large foreign ships that could not be completely loaded at East Coast or St. Lawrence River ports because of draft restrictions. The vessels, which were often capable of carrying 150,000 tons, would load to the maximum draft available at the East Coast or St. Lawrence River port, then sail to the deep waters off the St. Lawrence to be topped-off to their full capacity by Great Lakes self-unloaders.

While the cost of shipping coal overseas from Great Lakes ports would normally be more expensive than costs from East Coast ports, such as Norfolk, Baltimore, Philadelphia, or Hampton Roads, demurrage at the coastal ports tipped the scales in favor of the Great Lakes system when demurrage costs added as much as $10 per ton. Ship operators whose vessels had to wait a month or more to load at the coastal ports billed their customers up to $20,000 for each day they were delayed. By taking advantage of the opportunities for the midstream loading of coal that came from Lake Erie ports, at which there were no delays, coal customers were able to reduce their costs and speed up receipt of the coal they needed.

As delays were minimized at East Coast ports, as the result of both improvements in their facilities and some reduction in world demand for coal, tonnages transshipped declined. In the long term, however, Great Lakes operators are optimistic that midstream transfers can allow them to share in the international coal market, though their share of the market will vary from year to year depending on the capacity of the coastal ports to meet demands without costly delays.

The record coal shipment on the Great Lakes occurred in 1986 when Columbia Steamship's 1,000-foot *Columbia Star* carried 70,706 net tons of western coal from Superior, Wisconsin, to St. Clair, Michigan. The largest shipment of coal from a lower lakes port took place on September 3, 1988, when American Steamship Company's *Indiana Harbor* broke its own record by loading 59,058 net tons at Sandusky, Ohio, for delivery to Marquette, Michigan. Over 600 rail cars of coal were emptied into the hold of the *Indiana Harbor*.

Coal is the second most important bulk cargo shipped on the Great Lakes. Most of it moves from ports on Lake Erie to steel mills and power plants around the lakes. Here Algoma Central's *Algosteel* is shown loading coal at Toledo, Ohio for shipment to Algoma Steel's mill at Sault Ste. Marie, Ontario. Canadian shipping companies control most of the coal traffic between the U.S. and Canada. (Author's Collection)

The *Indiana Harbor*, one of two 1,000-foot coal colliers owned by ASC, also holds the record for the largest load of stone ever shipped on the lakes. During the 1984 season, it loaded 44,841 tons of limestone at Presque Isle Corporation's dock at the Port of Stoneport, located on the north shore of Lake Huron between Alpena and Rogers City. The record set by the *Indiana Harbor* surpassed the previous record by more than 9,500 tons and represented the first time that a thousand-footer had been used in the stone trade on the lakes. Because the dock at Stoneport is designed to handle ships only up to 826 feet in length, the *Indiana Harbor* first backed in to load its after holds, then turned around and went into the dock bow first so that it could finish loading.

The shiploader at Stoneport is typical of the modern conveyor belt systems used at most ports around the lakes for loading stone, iron ore, or coal. The loader at the sprawling limestone quarry is capable of loading ships at rates of up to 1,800 tons per hour, while similar equipment at other ports can achieve rates as high as 5,000 tons per hour for stone or 10,000 tons per hour for the heavier iron ore.

At Stoneport, limestone from the open pit mining operation is crushed and sorted according to size in a mill. Conveyor belts carry the sized stone to various storage piles adjacent to the loading dock. Each of the storage piles sits atop a concrete "tunnel" that houses a conveyor belt. Gates in the ceiling of the tunnel can be opened to allow stone of a particular size to drop onto the moving conveyor belt and be carried out to the shiploader.

The shiploader itself is a steel structure taller than the ships that call at the dock. It is mobile, operating on railroad tracks so that it can move back and forth along the dock to load each hatch of a ship. The conveyor belts carrying cargo from the storage piles connect with a belt on the loader's boom. The boom can be extended out so that it reaches to the centerline of the ship being loaded, just above the hatch openings, insuring that the limestone will be evenly distributed in the hold.

In terms of tonnages, stone has traditionally been the third most important bulk product moved on the lakes, although the slowdown in the steel industry caused shipments to drop below those of grain after the 1979 season. Only 15 million tons of stone was moved in 1982, compared to about 43 million tons in the record years of 1973 and 1974.[6] Stone is the most diverse of all the commodities carried by the Great Lakes bulk industry. The overwhelming majority of the stone is limestone, with the balance made up of dolomite, a closely related mineral. The stone is used by the steel, construction, agricultural, cement, and chemical industries.

Limestone, chemically calcium carbonate, formed in the Great Lakes region when the area was covered by shallow seas. All water, fresh and salt, contains quantities of dissolved calcium carbonate, which eventually either settles out of the water or is extracted from the water by aquatic organisms that use it to make their shells and bones. When the organisms die, the shells and bones break down and form beds of calcium carbonate that harden into limestone or dolomite over a long period of time.

Major commercial limestone and dolomite quarries on the lakes include the Michigan Limestone Calcite Plant at Rogers City, Michigan; the USX Port Dolomite plant at Cedarville, Michigan; the Presque Isle Corporation quarry between Rogers City and Alpena, owned by a consortium of steel companies, including LTV; the Drummond Island quarry of Drummond Dolomite; and the Port Inland facility at Gulliver, along the Lake Michigan shoreline on Michigan's Upper Peninsula. The Port Inland facility was developed by Inland Steel, but it was sold in 1989 to St. Mary's Cement Company of Toronto.

The grey stone is crushed and sorted, with the larger rocks, pieces 4 to 5 inches in diameter, primarily used as flux in the making of steel. Smaller stone is commonly used as construction aggregate, with much of it going into the production of concrete for paving. The versatile mineral also has many applications in the chemical and agricultural industries, including use as lime by farmers to reduce the acidity of soils.

Limestone is shipped to hundreds of ports around the lakes and even to places where no port exists. When the massive concrete caissons that support the Mackinac Bridge were being constructed, they were filled with limestone from self-unloaders that tied up alongside them. When the Michigan Department of Transportation contracted for the repaving of the road that circles Mackinac Island in northern Lake Huron, a self-unloader was used to discharge the needed limestone directly onto the shore of the island. The first self-unloaders on the lakes, in fact, were primarily used in the limestone trade, a prac-

The foreign-flag *Federal St. Laurent* loading grain at a terminal in Superior, Wisconsin. Its cargo booms, used to handle breakbulk cargo, can be seen along the deck. (Author's collection)

tice that caught on because of the demand for stone at ports around the lakes that did not have shoreside unloading equipment. Today, most of the ports to which limestone is delivered are totally dependent on self-unloaders for service.

While iron ore, coal, and stone have been the staples for the U.S. shipping companies on the Great Lakes, grain is the most important cargo for the Canadian fleets. Grain tonnages moved on the lakes have been showing a generally upward trend since the opening of the St. Lawrence Seaway in 1959. Before 1959, only about 9 to 15 million tons of grain were shipped annually on the lakes. Since the Seaway opened, however, volumes have ranged from 13 to 32 million tons, averaging more than 25 million tons a year for the past decade. In 1978, more than 32 million tons were shipped from Great Lakes ports, setting a record that still stands. Wheat accounts for more than 50 percent of the total grain shipped on the Great Lakes, followed by corn, which

represents about 10 percent of the total. Other grains include oats, rye, barley, flax, soybeans, sunflower seed, and rapeseed.

About 60 percent of the grain is shipped from Canadian ports, primarily aboard Canadian ships. By contrast, of the grain moving out of U.S. ports, only 10 to 15 percent is carried by U.S. ships. Around 35 percent of the U.S. grain is shipped on Canadian vessels, while 50 percent or more goes out of the lakes in foreign ships.

Virtually all of the grain carried by U.S. ships goes to elevators in Buffalo, New York, still the most important grain receiving port on the American lakes after more than a hundred years. U.S. and Canadian grain carried by Canadian bulk freighters is generally bound for mills or transshipment facilities in Eastern Canada. Grain shipped to storage facilities in Montreal, Quebec City, Port-Cartier, Baie-Comeau, and Sorel is often subsequently loaded onto foreign-flag vessels for overseas shipment. Much of that grain moves overseas during the winter months when the system is icebound west of Montreal. About 60 percent of all the Canadian grain is sold on the international markets.

Most of the grain is grown on the great prairies that straddle the U.S. and Canadian border between the Great Lakes and the Rocky Mountains. It is shipped by rail from storage elevators on the prairies to terminal elevators at the ports, where it is cleaned and stored for eventual shipment by water. The largest grain port on the Great Lakes, and one of the largest in the world, is Thunder Bay, Ontario. There are fourteen grain terminals at Thunder Bay that can store more than 2 million tons of grain at a time and process and ship over 20 million tons a year. Over the last decade, grain shipments from Thunder Bay have averaged about 15 million tons a year, with a high of more than 17 million tons in 1983.

On the U.S. side, the twin ports of Duluth and Superior account for more than half of all grain shipments, moving 4 to 10 million tons a year. The other major U.S. grain ports include Toledo, Chicago, and Milwaukee, basically in that order.

With most of the grain that is shipped on the lakes destined for foreign markets, tonnages can vary significantly from season to season. Foreign sales of U.S. and Canadian grain are affected by the size of foreign harvests, prices on the international markets, and the strength or weakness of U.S. and Canadian currency. During the five-year period from 1979–1984, the best international customer for U.S. grain moved through the Great Lakes and St. Lawrence was Spain. It accounted for 17 percent of all shipments, or about 1.9 million tons a year. Holland was the second best customer during the period, the destination for almost 11 percent of the shipments from U.S. Great Lakes ports, about 1.2 million tons a year. Other major foreign customers for U.S. grain were Algeria, Belgium, England, Italy, Canada, Portugal, the Soviet Union, Japan, Mexico, and West Germany.

The Soviet Union is Canada's top grain customer, buying 4 to 5 million tons a year. Most of the grain purchased from Canada by the Soviet Union has moved out the Seaway. In addition to the Soviets, the People's Republic of China, Brazil, Japan, and the United Kingdom are major customers for Canadian grain.

Unlike the other dry bulk commodities carried by U.S. and Canadian fleets on the lakes, most grain is shipped on straight-deckers, rather than on self-unloaders. Because grain is a light product, with about 36 bushels to a ton, it is most efficiently transported by ships with high cubic capacity cargo holds. Even then, a ship's cargo hold generally can be completely filled with grain and the ship will still not have reached its maximum loadline draft. More weight could be carried, but not more volume.

On a self-unloader, some cargo hold volume has to be sacrificed because there must be room beneath the cargo hold to accommodate the conveyor belt system. In addition, the interior walls of the cargo hold angle from the sides of the ship toward the bottom center of the vessel where the conveyor belt is located, so that cargo will slide down onto the belt. As a result, the cargo hold of a self-unloader is shaped like an inverted triangle, while the cargo hold on a straight-decker is cube-shaped, like a giant shoebox. For the carriage of grain, the boxy cargo holds of the straight-deckers are more efficient. Unloading is not a problem, because all of the grain terminals are equipped with special unloading systems for grain.

To observers, the bulk freighters on the lakes may look very much alike. However, some are better suited to certain cargoes than others. Maximum Seaway-size straight-deckers do the best job of carrying grain. Thousand-footers outshine the smaller ships in the iron ore trade, except in those instances when the ore has to be moved up a river like the Cuyahoga or Rouge. The smaller self-unloaders have carved out a niche in the river trades and in delivering coal and stone to small ports around the lakes. The most highly specialized ships on the Great Lakes are those designed to carry a single type of commodity, such as cement or petroleum products.

In an industry that has always been dominated by iron ore, grain, coal, and stone, the cement and tanker fleets have often been viewed as stepchildren by industry insiders. Until recently, the annual report of the Lake Carriers' Association totally ignored cement shipments and devoted only one line to liquid bulk cargoes. Together, cement and petroleum shipments account for less than 5 percent of the total cargo moved on the lakes each year. During the boom years, such as 1978 and 1979, they represented less than 2 percent of the total carried by the U.S. and Canadian fleets.

Shipments of petroleum products, primarily gasoline and fuel oil, range from 6 to 15 million tons a year. On the U.S. side of the lakes there are two tanker fleets, Amoco's Coastwise Trading operates one vessel; Cleveland Tankers has three. Some liquid bulk is also moved by tug companies using barges. On the Canadian side, there are five fleets operating tankers. They include Sofati-Soconav, Enerchem, Shell, Gulf, and Texaco. Together, they operate about twenty tankers. Liquid bulk cargoes move mainly from refineries or shipping terminals on the lower lakes and Seaway to terminals on the upper lakes or in the Maritime Provinces of Canada, where the products are stored in large tanks for local distribution by truck.

Cement shipments on the lakes total 3 to 8 million tons a year. There are two U.S. cement fleets, serving manufacturing plants in Alpena and Charlevoix, Michigan. On the Canadian side, two cement companies operate their own tug-barge delivery equipment, while a third charters a cement ship operated by Canada Steamship Lines. Cement is delivered to terminals in the major cities around the lakes, where it is stored in silos similar to those used for grain. From the storage silos, the cement is delivered to retail or commercial markets. Cement for retail sale is generally bagged, while deliveries to commercial users, such as redi-mix concrete plants, is primarily in bulk quantities shipped in special trucks or rail cars.

Regardless of how it is shipped, the key consideration is to protect the cement from exposure to water. Instead of large rectangular hatches like those used on ships in the ore or stone trades, cement boats load through small, circular hatches, generally no more than a foot or two in diameter. Use of the small hatches reduces the likelihood that water will get into the cargo hold, even if waves roll across the vessel's deck during a storm on the lakes.

The cement boats and barges are all self-unloaders, but do not have deck booms like ships designed to handle stone or ore. The cement is carried up and out of the cargo hold by either mechanical or pneumatic conveyors and elevators, but when it reaches deck level it is usually pumped into the shoreside storage silos. When aerated, cement will flow like a liquid, so it can be moved effectively by pumps like those that would be used for water or other liquid bulk commodities. The link from the ship to the silo is usually a large-diameter rubber hose, similar to those used to unload bulk products from tankers. In loading cement, a similar sealed connection is made between the loading spouts on the storage silos and the hatches on the deck of the cement boat or barge, protecting the cargo from exposure to moisture. The largest cement carrier on the lakes can carry 65,000 barrels of cement per trip, about 12,000 tons. That amount of cement will produce enough concrete to pave 10 miles of two-lane highway or manufacture close to seven million concrete blocks.

Other bulk cargoes moved on the lakes in small quantities include road salt, sand, coke, fertilizer, and gypsum. Canadian ships occasionally carry deck loads of automobiles from ports in southern Ontario to Thunder Bay.

Autos were once a major cargo for a number of U.S. and Canadian shipping companies on the lakes. There were more than half a dozen ships engaged primarily in hauling new cars from Detroit to Cleveland, Buffalo, Chicago, and other major ports, while many bulk freighters would take deck loads of automobiles every once in a while. The special auto haulers had decks installed in their cargo holds and racks on their main decks so they could carry hundreds of autos at a time. The last ship on the lakes solely engaged in carrying automobiles was the *M/V Highway 16*. The 328-foot vessel was operated by the Wisconsin and Michigan Steamship Company, carrying automobiles between Muskegon, Michigan, and Milwaukee. Placed in service in 1948, the ship was capable of hauling 190 cars in a single trip. By the early 1960s, most of the auto trade had been taken over by the railroads, although lakers continued to carry an occasional deck load of cars as backhaul cargo on their trips up the lakes. It is a sight that is seldom seen anymore, however.[7]

Most American bulk freighters "deadhead" on their trips up the lakes, lacking return cargo. If any cargo is hauled on their upbound trips it is generally coal. On the other hand, the trade routes operated by the Canadian fleets commonly involve cargo movements in both directions. For the most part, the ships carry grain out the Seaway and iron ore on the return voyages into the lakes. Most of the ore is destined for mills in southern Ontario or the Algoma Steel plant at Sault Ste. Marie, so they generally run empty for at least a part of their return trip to the grain terminals at Thunder Bay or the ore docks at Duluth and Superior.

The *Str. Medusa Challenger,* operated by Medusa Cement, loads cement at the firm's Charlevoix, Michigan, manufacturing plant. Launched in 1906 as a straight-decker, the 552-foot ship was converted to a cement boat in 1967 and is the largest vessel on the lakes in that trade. Cement stored in the silos spills into the ship through the loading spouts that connect to small, round hatches on the deck of the ship. (Author's collection)

The *Str. S. T. Crapo* loading cement at LaFarge Corporation's Huron Cement plant at Alpena, Michigan. The loading spouts insure that the cement flowing from storage silos into the hold of the *Crapo* is protected from moisture. (Author's collection)

With the general decline in cargo movements on the lakes, a number of Canadian fleets have recently put some of their ships into international service, primarily during the winter period when the Great Lakes and St. Lawrence system are shut down because of ice. The ships that have been engaged overseas are called salty-lakers, vessels built to ocean standards. Self-unloaders owned by both Canada Steamship Lines and ULS International have been extensively involved in ore and coal movements in Europe. With their relatively shallow drafts and self-unloading capabilities, the ships have carried cargo to steel mills and power plants that cannot be served by deep draft ocean vessels.

ULS vessels have also been operating in the Gulf of Mexico, hauling grain from ports in Texas and Louisiana to Mexico, with backhaul cargoes of stone and fertilizer. The trade has proven so successful that ULS has reregistered several of its ships under the Mexican flag.

Misener Shipping has operated three straight-deckers in the European grain trade in recent years. Specially reinforced to operate in ice, the Misener ships even carried grain from terminals in Hamburg, Antwerp, and Rouen to Leningrad under charter to the Soviet government. With the stagnation of trade opportunities on the lakes, the Canadian fleets, particularly CSL and ULS are attempting to expand their international operations. The unique Great Lakes self-unloaders have attracted a great deal of attention from foreign shipping officials, and both companies feel they can benefit by marketing their many years of experience in operation of the versatile ships.

Few industry officials on the lakes expect any dramatic increases in cargo tonnages in the near future. With the downsizing of the domestic steel industry, iron ore and limestone tonnages are expected to remain far below their historical levels. As the economy strengthens, some increases are anticipated, but nobody expects to see the Great Lakes fleets move tonnages approaching the records set in the late 1970s.

In the long term, coal shipments appear to hold the greatest promise for U.S. fleets. If, or when, international oil prices increase, demand for coal will rise, and that should stimulate both interlake movements and opportunities for the transshipment of coal from Great Lakes ports to foreign markets. With combined capacity of almost 80 million tons a year, the ports on the Great Lakes can handle almost twice as much coal as they presently do.

The Canadian fleets, too, could benefit from increased demand for coal, but grain is expected to remain the staple of that segment of the industry. The outlook for future grain movements on the lakes is uncertain, however. Yearly grain shipments can vary dramatically, depending on world demand and how competitive Canadian pricing is. In addition, Canadian West Coast ports, particularly Vancouver, have been wresting grain shipments away from the Great Lakes ports for the past few years. Because of government subsidies to railroads hauling grain from the Prairie Provinces to Vancouver and Prince Rupert Island, the West Coast ports have enjoyed a competitive advantage over the Great Lakes and Seaway system.

What the future holds for the U.S. and Canadian fleets and ports on the lakes is unclear. The glory days of the industry appear to be past, both in terms of the size of the fleets and tonnages hauled, yet the bulk freighters continue to play an important role in moving vital industrial and agricultural products. The industry may be down, but it's far from out.

Notes

1. Harlan Hatcher and Erich A. Walter, *A Pictorial History of the Great Lakes* (New York: Bonanza Books, 1963), 157–60.
2. Walter Havighurst, *The Long Ships Passing* (New York: Macmillan Co., 1942), 147.
3. Terry D. Monson, *The Role of Lakes Shipping in the Great Lakes Economy* (Houghton, MI: Michigan Technological University, 1980), 43–49.
4. *1986 Annual Report* (Cleveland: Lake Carriers' Association, 1987), 70–75.
5. "U.S.–Canadian Cargo Disparities," *Seaway Review* (Jan.–Mar. 1986): 59–61.
6. *1982 Annual Report* (Cleveland: Lake Carriers' Association, 1983), 33.
7. For a complete discussion of the auto trade on the lakes, see Lawrence A. Brough, *Autos on the Water* (Columbus, OH: Chatham Communicators, 1987).

7

Shipwrecks: The Past Is Prologue

In this connection we have also in view the fate of the crews of the lake steamers *Western Reserve* and *Gilcher*, both having metal lifeboats, but no lives saved.

—Editorial, *Marine Review*, May 8, 1901

With the prevailing weather conditions and the quick settling of the after section, it is extremely doubtful that a launching of a lifeboat in the vicinity of the vessel's counter by use of falls fitted with common hooks could have been successfully accomplished.

—Report on the Foundering of the *Str. Carl D. Bradley*, U.S. Coast Guard, July 7, 1959

Testimony of witnesses indicated that a successful launching of a lifeboat would have been extremely difficult in the weather and sea conditions which prevailed at the time *Fitzgerald* was lost.

—Report on the Sinking of the *Str. Edmund Fitzgerald*, U.S. Coast Guard, July 26, 1977

The first ship to sail the upper lakes—La Salle's *Griffon*—disappeared with all hands on the return leg of its maiden voyage, the victim of a fierce mid-September storm in 1679. In the intervening years, the bones of thousands of ships have joined those of the *Griffon* on the bottomlands of America's Inland Seas. While there are no accurate records of shipwrecks during much of the more than three hundred-year history of shipping on the lakes, we do know that during one twenty-year period, from 1878 through 1897, 5,993 wrecks were recorded by the U.S. Commissioner of Navigation. Of that number, 1,093 were listed as total losses.[1]

For Great Lakes sailors, the threat of being shipwrecked was a clear and present danger on every voyage during that period. With a total fleet on the lakes at that time of between 3,087 and 3,761 vessels, there was about one chance in twelve that a ship would be wrecked during the sailing season, better than one chance in a hundred that the ship would be a total loss. If the Commissioner of Navigation's records are accurate, 66 to 1,607 passengers and 1,754 to 4,051 crewmembers were involved in shipwrecks on the lakes in each of the twenty years. Altogether, 1,166 of them, mainly sailors, died.[2]

In terms of lives lost, the worst wrecks on the lakes have involved passenger vessels. The single greatest loss of life occurred in Chicago in 1940 when the steamer *Eastland*, loaded with about 2,500 Western Electric employees for a Saturday afternoon

Rescue workers struggle to remove bodies from the sunken hull of the *Str. Eastland*. The *Eastland* capsized and sank at its dock in Chicago in 1915, killing 835 passengers and crewmembers in the worst marine tragedy on the Great Lakes. (Institute for Great Lakes Research, Bowling Green State University)

excursion on Lake Michigan, rolled over and sank while still tied to its dock. The horrible tragedy claimed 835 lives. The worst collision on the lakes occurred during a fierce Lake Michigan storm in 1860 when the passenger steamer *Lady Elgin* was rammed and sunk by the schooner *Augusta*. There were 400 to 500 passengers and crewmembers aboard the *Lady Elgin* at the time and 300 to 350 of them perished in the stormy waters off Winnetka, Illinois. Although the shipwrecks with the greatest numbers of casualties have involved passenger vessels like the *Eastland* and *Lady Elgin*, the vast majority of the ships wrecked on the lakes over the years have been bulk freighters. Similarly, most of those who have died as a result of marine disasters have been sailors who crewed the freighters.

When we think of shipwrecks on the lakes we immediately conjure up images of the ferocious storms that sweep across the region each year, particularly in the month of November. And rightly so.

Storms have accounted for thousands of wrecks on the Great Lakes, the furious winds and towering waves driving ships aground or battering them to pieces. The lakes are struck by dozens of gales and storms each year. During 1982, for example, records of the National Weather Service show that forty-seven gales and thirteen storms were recorded on Lake Superior, forty-two gales and ten storms on Lake Michigan, and twenty-five gales and six storms on Lake Huron.[3] The weather service defines gales as having winds of 34 to 47 miles an hour, while storms are accompanied by winds of 48 miles an hour or more. During a particularly severe storm in November 1940, winds of 125 miles an hour were recorded at Lansing Shoal in northern Lake Michigan, and instances of winds exceeding 60 to 70 miles an hour are not uncommon. Winds over 64 miles an hour qualify as hurricanes under the definitions used by the National Weather Service.

The storms, which often move rapidly over the

The 432-foot ore freighter *William H. Truesdale* taking water over its deck in a violent storm on Lake Erie in the 1930s. The cable stretching the length of the deck would normally have been used as a safety line by crewmembers during bad weather, but in a storm of this magnitude it would have been impossible for crewmembers to cross the deck. (Institute for Great Lakes Research, Bowling Green State University)

region on a generally west to east track, can pile the waters of the lakes into huge waves in a relatively short period of time. Compared to the oceans, waves on the lakes are smaller, but they build in height faster and their crests are much closer together. While it is extremely difficult to accurately gauge the height of waves from a ship, reports of 20 to 25-foot waves are common, and estimates have ranged as high as 35 feet during some particularly severe storms.

While many storms batter the lakes each year, the annals of Great Lakes shipping record a number of particularly severe storms that have occurred over the years, storms that took an especially heavy toll on shipping. The single worst of the killer storms struck the lakes in mid-November 1913. Over a three-day period, thirty-five ships were wrecked and over 248 persons died. Eight of the ships disappeared with all hands. In the aftermath of the storm, beaches around the lakes were littered with ships that had been driven ashore by the cyclonic winds, as well as flotsam and jetsam from those that sank in the waters offshore. One ship, the *Str. Charles S. Price*, was found floating upside down in lower Lake Huron, her twenty-eight crew-members gone to watery graves. A similar storm occurred on November 18, 1942. Estimates are that fifty ships were wrecked during the blow, with at least fifty sailors lost.

Many of the killer storms occurred before the introduction of ship-to-shore radio communications and before weather forecasts were available to mariners on the lakes. In those days, ships were often taken totally by surprise by heavy weather. Such was the case in late November 1918 when three minesweepers, which had been built for the French Navy, departed the shipyard at what is now Thunder Bay, Ontario, en route to the Soo on the first leg of a voyage that would eventually take them to Europe for use in the war effort. Storm clouds lurked just over the western horizon when the three 136-foot ships departed the Canadian lakehead, but the French sailors weren't concerned in the slightest. After all, the ships had been designed and built for use on the oceans and should be able to shrug off any paltry storm that the lakes could throw at them. Three days later one of the minesweepers, the *Se-bastopol*, reached the Soo. When the other two ships failed to show up a search was launched, but no

evidence was ever found of the two vessels. Seventy-six French sailors and two Canadian pilots vanished along with the ships.

Saltwater sailors who bring their ships onto the lakes often underestimate the violent nature of the storms that sweep across the freshwater seas. On November 10, 1975, for example, the captain of a German freighter scoffed at the suggestion by the Great Lakes pilot who boarded his vessel at the Soo that he not venture out onto Lake Superior in the face of seriously worsening weather conditions. "It's just a lake," the German captain is reported to have remarked. With that, the vessel departed the Soo and steamed out onto Lake Superior and into the teeth of the storm that would claim the *Str. Edmund Fitzgerald* and its crew before the day was over. Several days later, when the battered German ship finally limped into Duluth harbor at the west end of the lake, the pilot paused before departing the ship to ask the German captain what he thought of Lake Superior after having experienced it in a storm. "Damned big lake," replied the captain meekly, all of his saltwater superiority long since knocked out of him by the storm, "*damned* big lake."

As communications and weather forecasting have improved, the number of wrecks attributed to storms has declined. The advent of radar, which became standard equipment on the Great Lakes shortly after World War II, also has helped to reduce the number of wrecks stemming from both groundings and collisions. Before radar, collisions accounted for a large share of the shipwrecks on the lakes and in the river systems that connect them. Islands and shoals that dot the lakes, and points of land that intrude on the shipping lanes, had literally become graveyards for scores of unlucky ships over the years.

Traffic congestion has always been a serious problem for Great Lakes mariners. Before the turn of the century, there were three thousand to six thousand ships operating on the lakes. Without radar, radio communications, or modern navigational systems, they generally operated within sight of land, skirting the shoreline so they could seek refuge in a bay or harbor if the weather turned sour. Unfortunately, with so many ships following the same coast-hugging strategy, collisions were common, particularly if fog, snow, or rain reduced visibility.

One of the worst collisions in the history of shipping on the lakes occurred on a clear, calm August evening in 1865, however. The tragedy involved the *Pewabic* and the *Meteor*, combination passenger and freight steamers that were common at that time. The two "sister ships" were operated by the Lake Superior Transportation Company. The *Pewabic* was downbound from Lake Superior carrying a full complement of passengers, including a number of Confederate Civil War soldiers who were being repatriated to the South after having been held prisoner in Wisconsin. Below decks, the *Pewabic* carried a load of copper ore from mines in the Keweenaw Peninsula, some high-grade iron ore from the Marquette Range, and rolls of tanned animal hides.

The upbound *Meteor* met the *Pewabic* at sunset off Thunder Bay Island in northern Lake Huron. Evidence suggests that the two ships attempted to pass alongside each other so that the master of the *Meteor* could pass dispatches to the captain of the *Pewabic*. Through some error, the *Meteor* struck and holed the *Pewabic*, which sank in a matter of minutes. As blackness settled over the tranquil lake, the *Meteor*, damaged and seriously leaking, picked up what survivors it could before making a dash to Alpena for repairs. The final tally showed that 125 passengers and crewmembers aboard the *Pewabic* went down with the ship.

As the number of vessel collisions mounted over the years, there was increasing pressure to develop separate upbound and downbound courses on the lakes. By putting upbound and downbound ships on separate tracks, with a reasonable distance between the two lanes of traffic, supporters felt that the number of collisions could be significantly reduced. We know that there was strong support for the concept before 1899, but it wasn't until 1911 that separate courses were finally established. The number of vessel collisions on the open lakes immediately showed a marked reduction.

Most collisions occurred, however, at the numerous bottlenecks around the lakes, places where traffic on the open lakes is funneled down into narrow channels at the entrances to rivers or at the Straits of Mackinac, which connects Lake Huron and Lake Michigan. Ships on various courses on the lakes must merge into basically a single line of traffic to enter the narrow channels, creating serious congestion problems. Without radar, and with visibility often restricted by darkness or inclement weather,

collisions were commonplace in the numerous areas of vessel congestion around the lakes. With the coming of radar and ship-to-ship communications, combined with a significant decline over time in the number of ships in operation on the lakes, casualties resulting from collisions have declined dramatically.

With the development of radio direction-finding (RDF) after World War I and radar after World War II, a sharp reduction also took place in the number of groundings, since navigational personnel were better able to plot accurate locations regardless of weather conditions. Even before the advent of RDF and radar, major strides had been made in reducing groundings through the development of a system of aids to navigation and dredging of harbors and river channels.

The British government in Canada ordered the first lighthouse to be built on the lakes in 1804 at Fort George, on the west bank of the Niagara River, near where it enters into Lake Ontario. The first U.S. lighthouse was put into operation on Lake Erie in 1818, followed by lighthouses on Galloo Island in Lake Ontario, built in 1820, and the Fort Gratiot light at Port Huron, constructed in 1825.[4] By 1960, there were 150 staffed lighthouses around the Great Lakes, marking shoals, reefs, points of land, and islands. In addition, the U.S. and Canadian governments had developed an extensive system of aids to navigation in the rivers connecting the lakes, including buoys that defined the limits of the channels and ranges that helped navigators keep their ships in mid-channel. Together with the ongoing dredging of channels to make them deeper and wider, the installation of aids to navigation helped reduce the number of groundings that occurred within the system.

Another major cause of shipwrecks that has declined in significance over the years is fire. The early wooden ships were particularly susceptible to destruction by fires caused by sparks from the ship's boilers, wood-fired ranges used in the galleys, or careless smoking by crewmembers. Even after iron and steel became the primary building materials for ships, fires continued to be a problem because wood was used extensively in construction of cabin areas aboard the vessels. Today, however, regulations governing vessel construction prohibit the use of flammable materials. Engine rooms, the only remaining location aboard ships that presents a fire hazard, have been equipped with carbon dioxide or halon extinguishing systems, which are capable of snuffing out a blaze in a matter of minutes by depriving the fire of the oxygen needed to support combustion. Although the likelihood of fire aboard ship has been greatly reduced, Coast Guard regulations require vessel personnel to conduct fire drills on a weekly basis. A number of Canadian fleets that belong to the Canadian Lake Carriers' Association have instituted highly realistic fire drills that even include the use of smoke bombs to simulate fires in various vessel compartments.

Most of the serious casualties that occur on the lakes today involve either collisions or heavy weather damage. What is most significant, however, is the astonishing reduction that has occurred in the number of vessel casualties: During the past thirty years, U.S. ships have been involved in only six major casualties on the Great Lakes. A leading expert on risk analysis has shown that marine transportation involves far less danger than hunting, smoking cigarettes, or many of the other risks that society has accepted. Based on statistics from 1981, the marine industry on the lakes was twice as safe as the railroad industry and eight times safer than truck transportation.[5] The industry's present safety record is enviable, at least in a comparative sense. But when casualties do occur they tend to be dramatic.

Of the six major casualties the U.S. segment of the industry has experienced during the past three decades, three involved the loss of ships in heavy weather. A total of ninety-three sailors served aboard the three ships, ninety of them died. The three other major casualties involved collisions. Two of the ships were total losses, while the third was salvaged and subsequently placed back in service. Only ten of ninety-six crewmembers serving aboard those three vessels died as a result of the sinkings.

Of all the books written about the Great Lakes shipping industry over the years, none have been more popular than those about shipwrecks. Unfortunately, most of the books present highly romanticized accounts of the casualties, which are intended to play upon our morbid fascination with disasters. The shipwreck books don't capture the horror of people dying. Important facts have often been overlooked, and few, if any, of the authors have called their readers' attention to the recurring patterns that emerge from the litany of broken ships and lost sailors—patterns of sweeping complacency and in-

eptitude that complete our understanding of the wrecks that have occurred and sensitize us to the certainty that the lakes have not seen their last shipwreck.

A shipwreck is not an isolated, exclusive event that occurs to one unlucky ship and its equally hapless crew. All of the hulls that have ever gone to the bottom of the lakes and all of the sailors who have ever struggled to cling to life in their watery purgatory have arrived at death's door as a result of patterns of behavior that have evolved within their industry over a very long period of time. The recurring patterns create an environment in which the loss of ships and sailors is virtually assured. The patterns are so consistent, in fact, that we can see them clearly by looking at just four of the most recent shipwrecks, starting with the loss in 1958 of the *Str. Carl D. Bradley* in a furious Lake Michigan storm.

Death of a Queen

At about 5:30 P.M. on November 18, 1958, First Mate Elmer Fleming was on watch in the pilothouse of the *Str. Carl D. Bradley* when he heard a loud thud. Looking aft, Fleming saw the stern of the long freighter sag in the storm-tossed seas. He realized immediately that his ship was in jeopardy, as did Captain Roland Bryan, who was on the bridge with Fleming at the time. While the captain activated the general alarm bells and blew the ship's steam whistle to alert the crew to the imminent peril, Fleming broadcast a "mayday" call over the vessel's radio, giving the *Bradley*'s position as southwest of Gull Island in northern Lake Michigan. Fleming had just enough time to broadcast the distress call twice before the power failed on the forward end of the ship and the radio went dead.

As crewmembers donned their life jackets and raced for the *Bradley*'s two lifeboats, the ship heaved upward at midships and broke in two. The bow section settled in the water until the deck was completely submerged, listed to port, rolled over, and sank. The stern section, with lights still blazing,

The 640-foot self-unloader *Carl D. Bradley* upbound in the Detroit River before its sinking in November 1958. The *Bradley* was "Queen of the Lakes" from its launching in 1927 until the 678-foot *Wilfred Sykes* entered service in 1950. Thirty-three of the *Bradley*'s thirty-five crewmembers died when the ship sank in a severe storm on northern Lake Michigan. (Institute for Great Lakes Research, Bowling Green State University)

swung away from the bow, settled a little in the water, then plunged downward. Crewmembers aboard the *M/V Christian Sartori*, a German freighter that was about four miles from the *Bradley* at the time, saw a brilliant flash of light and heavy smoke coming from the location of the stricken vessel. At the same time, the radar operator aboard the *Sartori* reported that the radar image of the *Bradley* had disappeared from his scope.

Although the *Sartori*'s captain had not heard the *Bradley*'s "mayday," he immediately ordered his wheelsman to bring the ship about and head for the location of the explosion. The German captain knew that coming about in the heavy seas would put his ship in jeopardy, but he gave the order without hesitation. He was doing what any merchant mariner would do in a similar situation, going to the aid of shipwrecked sailors. He also knew that if there were survivors out there in the 40° waters, they could not survive for long.

The final voyage of the *Bradley* had begun during the evening hours of the previous day when the ship had departed Gary, Indiana, after discharging a cargo of limestone at the U.S. Steel mill there. Gale

warnings had been broadcast, but the *Bradley* was a stout ship that had weathered hundreds of similar storms in its thirty-one years on the lakes and the captain didn't hesitate to point it north.

When the *Bradley* was launched at Lorain, Ohio, in 1927, it was quickly tabbed as "the Queen of the Lakes." At 640 feet in overall length, it was the largest ship on the Great Lakes for more than twenty years. In it, the art of building self-unloading freighters had also reached perfection and during its early years, it set many cargo records. The *Bradley* was one of nine grey-hulled self-unloaders operated by the Bradley Transportation Company of Rogers City, Michigan. The Bradley boats were primarily involved in hauling limestone from the giant U.S. Steel quarry at Rogers City to ports around the lakes. Twenty-six of the *Bradley*'s thirty-five crewmembers were from that small town on the north shore of Lake Huron, and four others were from nearby communities in Presque Isle County.

As the broken hull of the once-proud ship disappeared below the raging surface of Lake Michigan, Elmer Fleming found himself in the frigid water along with many of his shipmates. He and three other *Bradley* crewmen, including Deck Watchman Frank Mayes, were able to struggle aboard a life raft that had floated free of the ship as it sank. The raft rapidly drifted away from the scene of the disaster, pushed by winds in excess of twenty-five miles an hour. The massive waves, estimated to have been twenty-five feet high, tore at the tiny life raft, flipping it over several times during the night and throwing the four shipwrecked sailors into the water. Each time, the four struggled to crawl back on, but by dawn only Fleming and Mayes still clung to the raft and to life. At 8:25 A.M. on November 19, they were plucked out of the water by the Coast Guard Cutter *Sundew*.

Fleming and Mayes were the only survivors from the *Bradley*'s crew. While the *Sartori* and numerous lake freighters and Coast Guard ships and aircraft continued searching the northern Lake Michigan area, they found only dead bodies among the flotsam from the wreck. Altogether, eighteen bodies were recovered, all wearing life jackets. Fifteen crewmembers were never found, apparently having gone down with their ship.

While the residents of Rogers City mourned the loss of fathers, sons, brothers, friends, and neighbors, the Coast Guard launched its investigation into the sinking. Their report, released in July 1959, concluded that the ship had broken in two and that the explosion observed by crew aboard the *Christian Sartori* had been caused when cold lake water hit the *Bradley*'s hot boilers. The report dispelled speculation that the ship had struck Boulder Reef near Gull Island.

The breakup of the ship was attributed to extreme hogging and possible structural weakness. While in drydock in May 1957 for the repair of damage sustained in a minor collision with another vessel, hairline cracks had been discovered in a number of the ship's bottom plates. The cracks were repaired at that time. The Coast Guard investigation also revealed that the *Bradley* had been involved in two minor groundings earlier in the 1958 season, neither of which was reported to the Coast Guard, as is required by the regulations governing commercial vessel operations. It was found that the second grounding had caused a fourteen-inch fracture in the bottom of the ship and that fleet personnel had repaired the crack by welding a piece of channel iron over it. While the Coast Guard could not determine whether damage from the two unreported groundings contributed to the sinking, there was strong evidence to suggest that the ship had suffered a lot of wear and tear since its last detailed Coast Guard inspection in 1953. The ship was scheduled to go into drydock at the end of the 1958 season to have much of the steel plate in its cargo hold replaced.

The Coast Guard report also noted that it was common practice for crewmembers aboard the *Bradley* not to completely dog shut the watertight door separating the engine room from the tunnel that ran the full length of the ship. The investigators concluded that failure to completely dog the door allowed water to flood into the ship's engine room after it broke in half. Had the watertight door been secured, additional buoyancy would have been provided for the stern section and it might not have sunk as fast as it did. None of the personnel on watch in the engine room were able to escape from the ship, probably because of the speed at which the stern sank.

Investigators also found that sea conditions probably made it impossible for crewmembers who assembled at the two lifeboat stations on the *Bradley*'s stern to launch the boats. Further, neither the lifeboats nor the life raft carried aboard the vessel were equipped with distress flares. Had the life raft had flares, Fleming, Mayes, and the two other crewmembers on the raft might have been found during the night.

The commandant of the Coast Guard, in reviewing the report, also added the recommendation that the Ninth District, encompassing the Great Lakes, implement "a program of technical evaluation to determine if there is any evidence of structural defects in other vessels of the Great Lakes fleet." Such a program was reportedly initiated soon after the report was issued.

Even though many ships that had been out on Lake Michigan the day the *Bradley* sank had sought refuge from the storm in sheltered bays or in the lee of islands, the Coast Guard commandant dismissed the board's findings that the master erred in taking his ship out in such weather. "Such reasoning," the report concluded, "would necessarily require an assumption that the waves were unique in the vessel's 31-year history of navigation in the Great Lakes." That premise, the commandant continued, must be rejected.[6]

The *Str. Cedarville* loading coal at Toledo before its loss in 1965 as the result of a collision with a Norwegian freighter in the Straits of Mackinac. The *Cedarville*'s self-unloading boom is swung out so that the loader has access to its forward hatches. (Institute for Great Lakes Research, Bowling Green State University)

Collision in the Straits

Almost seven years passed before another major casualty on the lakes. When the next sinking occurred, however, it too involved a ship from the Bradley fleet, crewed by men from Rogers City. The *Str. Cedarville* sank in heavy fog in the Straits of Mackinac on May 7, 1965, after colliding with the Norwegian freighter *M/V Topdalsfjord*. Ten of the thirty-five crewmembers aboard the *Cedarville*—nine from Rogers City—died as a result of the sinking.

On the morning of May 7, the *Cedarville* was westbound in the Straits, en route to Gary, Indiana, with a load of 14,411 tons of limestone. The northern reaches of Lake Huron were familiar territory for Captain Martin Joppich and his crew, and even though the Straits were socked in with dense fog, the

Cedarville steamed westward at full speed. Captain Joppich was in command on the bridge, along with Third Mate Charlie Cook, who watched the radar for other vessel traffic. Three or four miles from the Mackinac Bridge, which spans the Straits that separates Michigan's Upper and Lower Peninsulas, Captain Joppich established radio contact with the *Str. Weissenburg*. The German freighter was approaching the Straits from the west and its captain told Joppich that there was a Norwegian freighter ahead of him. Joppich attempted to contact the Norwegian ship by radio to arrange a passing agreement, but his radio calls went unanswered. Charlie Cook was observing the Norwegian ship on the *Cedarville*'s radar, and he kept the captain informed of its movements.

Joppich cut the speed of his vessel to half-speed and sounded one long blast on the *Cedarville*'s whistle, a signal to the approaching Norwegian ship that

153

he wanted to make a port-to-port passage. Not getting a response from the rapidly closing vessel, Joppich repeated the passing signal. As the captain of the *Cedarville* sounded one last long blast on his ship's whistle, the Norwegian freighter, the *M/V Topdalsfjord*, was observed coming out of the fog at a distance of only about one hundred feet. Joppich ordered the *Cedarville*'s engines to slow ahead. Then, as the two ships converged on an obvious collision course, he rang up full ahead on the engine order telegraph and told his wheelsman to make a hard left turn in an effort to swing the ship clear of the Norwegian freighter.

Despite Joppich's evasive action, the *Topdalsfjord* struck the port side of the *Cedarville* at an almost perpendicular angle. Although crewmen aboard the *Cedarville* felt only a moderate impact, the sharply raked bow of the Norwegian freighter had pierced the hull of their vessel amidship, slashing a hole through the side tanks and into the cargo hold. The *Topdalsfjord* remained imbedded in the side of Joppich's ship for a few moments, until the *Cedarville*'s forward motion pulled it clear of the Norwegian vessel. In the fog, the two ships drifted apart and soon lost sight of each other.

Eleven feet of the *Topdalsfjord*'s bow had been severely damaged by the collision, but flooding was limited to the forepeak area, which was separated from the rest of the ship by a watertight bulkhead. While the vessel was in no immediate danger of sinking, the captain had the ship's two lifeboats prepared for launching.

Aboard the *Cedarville*, tons of water were pouring into the breached cargo hold, causing the crippled ship to take on a deep list to port. Joppich ordered the ship's engine stopped, sounded the general alarm bells, broadcast a "mayday," and ordered the port anchor dropped. Crewmen put their life jackets on and mustered at the lifeboat stations on the *Cedarville*'s stern. They swung the two boats out ready for boarding should the captain give the order to abandon ship. There was no sign of panic or confusion among the crew.

As Captain Joppich and his officers assessed damage to the *Cedarville*, it became obvious to them that the uncontrolled flooding of the cargo hold would eventually sink the ship. About twenty-five minutes after the collision, at 10:10 A.M., Joppich decided to attempt to beach his ship. The anchor was raised

and the vessel came hard left at full speed to make a dash for shallow water. Third Mate Cook, still on the radar, gave the captain a courseline to the beach. Fifteen minutes later, while still two miles from the safety of shallow water, the *Cedarville* suddenly rolled over to starboard and sank. As the ship made its death roll, the crewmen gathered on the stern attempted to launch the two lifeboats. The starboard boat, with several crewmembers aboard, was released as the ship sank beneath it, but the portside lifeboat could not be freed from its falls, and it was carried under as the *Cedarville* sank. Both of the ship's life rafts floated free as the ship plunged to the bottom of the Straits. Most of the crew were thrown into the 36° water.

The *Weissenburg*, under the command of Captain Werner May, had followed the *Cedarville* through the thick fog as it made its run for the beach. At 10:30 A.M., the bow lookout on the *Weissenburg* reported that he could hear men crying out from the water ahead. May ordered his ship's lifeboats to be launched to pick up survivors from the frigid waters. The *Weissenburg*'s boats plucked six *Cedarville* crewmen from the Straits. Twenty-one other survivors were found aboard a lifeboat and life raft from the *Cedarville*. One crewman died before he could be taken aboard the *Weissenburg*, and a second crewman died about an hour later, despite efforts by the German crew to counteract the effects of shock and hypothermia that many of the crewmen suffered from. Third Mate Charlie Cook, last seen struggling to put his life jacket on as the *Cedarville* sank, went down with the ship. Captain Joppich was thrown clear and found clinging to his life jacket in the cold water. He had never put the life jacket on.

Among those who went down with the *Cedarville* were Chief Engineer Donald Lamp, First Assistant Engineer Reinhold Radtke, Stokerman Eugene Jones, and Oiler Hugh Wingo, all of whom had been on duty in the engine room. They had manned the *Cedarville*'s boilers and pumps during the desperate race for the beach and were apparently trapped in the engine room when the ship plunged to the bottom.

Captain Joppich, a quiet, mild-mannered family man, never sailed again. The Coast Guard investigation into the sinking concluded that he had violated the nautical rules of the road by failing to operate his ship at moderate speed in fog. During the inquiry, Joppich claimed that the *Cedarville* had been operating at slow ahead for a considerable period of time before the collision, as was the *Topdalsfjord.* Testimony by other crewmembers, however, combined with computations of the *Cedarville*'s average speed from entries made in the ship's log over several hours prior to the collision, refuted Joppich's testimony. In their report on the sinking, Coast Guard investigators stated: "The version . . . as related by Captain Joppich is considered self-serving and false and is accordingly rejected. Hence it is concluded that the *Cedarville* was operated at full speed almost up to the jaws of the collision." Based on that finding, the Coast Guard initiated action to revoke Joppich's master's license.

The greatest tragedy of the *Cedarville* sinking, however, lies not in the fact that the collision could have been avoided had Joppich exercised prudent seamanship, but that the resulting loss of life was unnecessary. While Captain Joppich's attempt to beach his ship was proper, the Coast Guard investigators concluded: "The Master . . . judged poorly the peril to his crew and vessel and the time remaining for him to beach his ship. He should have beached his vessel on the nearest shoal, or deciding against that, he should have steered the correct course for the nearest land. The beaching course furnished by the Third Mate was incorrect and the Master should have immediately realized this."

The Coast Guard investigators found that the location selected by the third mate for beaching the *Cedarville* was 4.3 miles from the site of the collision. Two other beaching sites— Graham Shoal and Old Mackinac Point—were only 1 mile and 2 miles away, respectively. Since the *Cedarville* travelled 2.3 miles before it sank, the ship could most certainly have been successfully beached had one of the closer sites been chosen. While the error was made by the third mate, Captain Joppich, himself an experienced Great Lakes pilot, should have caught the error and taken appropriate action.

Joppich was also criticized in the Coast Guard report for not minimizing the number of personnel in the engine room and for not having unessential crewmembers abandon ship before attempting to beach the boat. A captain's primary concern should always be for the safety of the crew. Given the fact that there was no way for Joppich to know that the crippled *Cedarville* would stay afloat long enough to be beached, he should have had all unneeded personnel off in the lifeboats before attempting the beaching. The crewmen standing by at the lifeboat stations, several of whom died as a result of the sinking, were relying on their captain's judgment, and he let them down.[7]

For the second time in less than eight years, the residents of Rogers City mourned the loss of family members and friends who had died at sea. In this instance, however, the mourning was often combined with anger over the unnecessary loss of life.

Missing on Lake Huron

The annals of Great Lakes shipping are replete with instances of ships sinking without ever broadcasting a distress signal. Before the advent of radio communications on the lakes in the early 1920s, it was quite common, in fact. The first knowledge of a sinking often came when the vessel failed to show up at its destination or when flotsam from the ships— or the bodies of crewmembers—would be found washed up on a beach. After radios came into wide use on the lakes, however, most stricken vessels were in contact with other ships or shore stations at the first sign of trouble, as was the case with both the *Bradley* and the *Cedarville.*

At about noon on November 30, 1966, however, the Coast Guard Rescue Coordination Center in Cleveland received a call from an official at Bethlehem Steel Corporation to report that one of their ships, the *Str. Daniel J. Morrell*, was overdue. The call came in the aftermath of a vicious storm that struck the lakes on the evening of November 28 and continued throughout the next day, with winds of 50–60 miles an hour and wave heights estimated at 25 feet. The strong winds and high seas were accompanied by rain and snow.

Coast Guard surface vessels and aircraft immediately launched a search for the missing vessel, and broadcasts were made to all commercial ships on the lakes, requesting that they maintain a lookout for the *Morrell.* An hour later, the *Str. G. G. Post* re-

The *Str. Daniel J. Morrell* before its sinking in November 1966 on Lake Huron. One of the original "standard 600-footers" launched in 1906, the *Morrell* broke up and sank before crewmembers could issue a distress call. A sistership, the *Edward Y. Townsend,* suffered a cracked deck in the same storm and never operated again. (Institute for Great Lakes Research, Bowling Green State University)

ported that it had sighted a body wearing a life jacket stencilled with the name of the *Morrell* about 8 miles off Harbor Beach on lower Lake Huron. During the afternoon hours, Coast Guard search vessels and aircraft recovered the bodies of eight *Morrell* crewmembers from the waters off Michigan's thumb. At about four o'clock in the afternoon, searchers found three bodies and one survivor in one of the *Morrell*'s life rafts, which had washed up on the beach below Huron City, Michigan, a few miles north of Harbor Beach. The survivor, twenty-six-year-old Dennis Hale of Ashtabula, Ohio, was barely clinging to life, and he was rushed immediately to the hospital in Harbor Beach.

The stocky watchman was to be the lone survivor from the *Morrell*. Hale's twenty-eight shipmates either went down with their ship or died in the frigid waters of lower Lake Huron in the long hours that passed between the time the *Morrell* sank, shortly after 2:00 A.M. on November 29, until the vessel was reported missing some thirty-four hours later. From his hospital bed, Hale told Coast Guard officials that he had been awakened about 2:00 A.M. by what he described as a loud bang. A second bang occurred a few minutes later, followed shortly by the sound of the ship's general alarm bells. Hale grabbed his life jacket and went out on deck, clad only in his underwear.

Looking aft, Hale had noticed that the center of the ship was higher than the stern. Aware for the first time that it might be necessary to abandon ship, Hale ran back to his cabin to get his pants. The lights weren't working in the bow section of the ship, and in the darkness he could find only his heavy wool peacoat. Slipping into the coat and his life jacket, Hale proceeded to the *Morrell*'s forward life raft, where the other deck personnel, including the master and mates, had gathered.

Hale said he could hear what he took to be metal tearing and working against itself in the midship area of the vessel. No attempt was made to get to the lifeboats on the stern because of the damage amidships. According to Hale, virtually all of the deck personnel sat on the raft to await the sinking of the ship, which they felt was inevitable. No attempt was made to throw the raft over the side, which would be normal practice in such a situation.

Watching the deck area amidships, Hale said he could see a crack develop at the starboard gunwale and spread across the deck, sparks flashing where the twisted metal rubbed together. The ship then broke into two sections, and Hale said it appeared that the stern was ramming and pushing the bow section and it eventually shoved the bow off to the side. Still perched on the life raft with the other deck crewmembers, Hale said the stern section appeared to be still under power, and it continued to bump into the port side of the bow section. The bow section gradually settled in the water and as it sank, the raft was thrown clear in a torrent of waves. Hale came to the surface about ten feet from the raft, which was empty, and he and three of his shipmates managed to climb aboard it. The only other crewmember he saw after entering the water was a lone figure still on the *Morrell*'s forecastle as the bow slipped beneath the water. When the bow section sank, Hale could still see the stern section about half a mile away. The stern lights were still on, and it appeared that the section was under power, steaming away from the men on the raft.

Hale fired several distress flares shortly after the sinking, aware that there were supposed to be other ships nearby. With the air temperature at 33°, Hale and the three other survivors huddled together on the raft in a futile effort to keep warm. Two of the survivors died at about six in the morning, and the third succumbed at about four in the afternoon, all victims of hypothermia. When found the next afternoon, Hale himself was suffering from acute hypothermia, and his hands and feet were badly frostbitten. He had survived by pulling the bodies of his dead shipmates on top of him, providing just enough warmth to endure the long ordeal on the raft.

The Coast Guard's investigation, which included taking samples of steel from the sunken stern section of the ship, attributed the casualty to structural failure resulting from a fracture of the hull's brittle steel. The steel used in many ships built before 1948 was subject to similar fractures, and a Coast Guard inspection of sixteen other pre-1948 ships in the aftermath of the *Morrell*'s loss turned up two other vessels with incipient fractures and other signs of structural weaknesses.

Coast Guard investigators recommended that Great Lakes ships be equipped with inflatable life rafts both fore and aft to provide shipwrecked sailors with some protection from the elements. Like the Coast Guard officers who had investigated the sinking of the *Bradley* eight years earlier, the four officers on the *Morrell* board concluded that "under the existing sea conditions, the lifeboats could not have been lowered and launched successfully." Like those on the *Bradley*, the *Morrell's* lifeboats were suspended from common boat hooks that would not even allow them to float free as the vessel sank.

The failure of the *Morrell's* captain to issue a distress call before the sinking was attributed to the loss of electrical power on the forward end of the ship as the result of power cables being severed amidships. There was no source of backup power for the two radio sets in the pilothouse, although a battery supplied emergency power for the ship's general alarm system. The Coast Guard investigators recommended that a backup power supply be provided on all Great Lakes ships to insure that radio units could be operated even if a vessel's primary power source was disabled.

The question was raised during the inquiry as to whether the *Morrell* should even have been out on Lake Huron in the storm. Most other ships on Lake Huron that night had sought refuge, several after having been unable to make headway in the high seas or after having broached, knocked off course by the power of the seas. Apparently only two other ships were out on Lake Huron that night, one only because the master feared that his vessel would roll over if he attempted to come about.

Like the *Bradley*, the *Morrell* had weathered many storms during its career on the lakes. As one of the original standard 600-footers built in 1906, the aging ship had been in service for sixty years. It had undergone a drydock inspection before the opening of the 1966 season, however, and was found fit for service. Given that, the board members concluded that there was no clear evidence to suggest that the master of the *Morrell* was negligent for taking his ship out into the storm.[8] The decision to push ahead or seek shelter is a judgment call for the captain. Captain Art Crawley had taken ships out into storms many times without ever encountering a serious problem, so there was nothing particularly unusual about the decision he made on the evening of November 28, 1966. Unfortunately, it was the wrong decision.

The Wreck of the Fitzgerald

Just two weeks short of nine years later, on November 10, 1975, the radio operator on duty at Coast Guard Group Headquarters in Sault Ste. Marie received a radio call from Captain Jesse Cooper, master of the *Str. Arthur M. Anderson*. As the captain talked, the radio operator wrote down his message in longhand on the station's radio log: "I am very concerned with the welfare of the *Steamer Edmund Fitzgerald*. He was right in front of us experiencing a little difficulty. He was taking a small amount of water and none of the upbound ships have passed him. I can see no lights as before and don't have him on radar. I just hope he didn't take a nose dive." After several unsuccessful attempts to make radio contact with the *Fitzgerald*, Coast Guard officials at the Soo notified the Rescue Coordination Center in Cleveland that there was an "uncertainty" concerning the ship. Within minutes, U.S. and Canadian Coast Guard air stations were ordered to deploy aircraft to search for the missing freighter. Coast Guard cutters stationed at the Soo and Duluth were also ordered to proceed to the scene as rapidly as possible.

At 9:00 P.M., the commanding officer of the Coast Guard Group Headquarters in the Soo contacted the *Anderson*, which had already reached Whitefish Bay, and asked them to reverse their course and assist in the search. At 10:30 P.M., a request also went out to three U.S. and four Canadian freighters anchored in or near Whitefish Bay to assist in the search. Because of the severity of the weather on Lake Superior, only two ships agreed to venture out of the protected waters of the bay, and one of those turned back after only twenty to thirty minutes. Masters of three saltwater vessels that were in or near the area where the *Fitzgerald* disappeared also were asked to join the search. All three replied that to do so would place their own ships in danger.

Throughout the night, the *Anderson*, the *Str. William Clay Ford*, and helicopters and fixed-wing aircraft of the U.S. and Canadian Coast Guards combed the east end of Lake Superior for evidence of the missing vessel. At about 8:00 A.M. on November 11, crewmen aboard the *Anderson* sighted a piece of the *Fitzgerald's* number one lifeboat about 9 miles east of where the *Fitzgerald* had last been seen. A second

The mysterious sinking of the *Str. Edmund Fitzgerald* with all hands during a November storm on Lake Superior in 1975 was immortalized in a popular song by Gordon Lightfoot. When it was launched in 1958, the 729-foot *"Fitz"* was the longest ship on the lakes. (Institute for Great Lakes Research, Bowling Green State University)

lifeboat, badly damaged, was sighted by the *Anderson*'s crew about an hour later. Both lifeboats were empty. The discovery of the lifeboats confirmed the suspicion that the *Anderson*'s captain had reported to the Coast Guard the previous evening: The *Str. Edmund Fitzgerald* had sunk in Lake Superior about sixteen miles from the sheltered waters of Whitefish Bay and the entrance to the St. Marys River. The twenty-nine crewmembers aboard the *Fitzgerald* apparently went down with their ship; no bodies were ever recovered.

The final voyage of the 729-foot straight-decker began at about 8:30 A.M. on November 9 when the ship finished taking on a load of 26,116 tons of taconite pellets at an ore dock in Superior, Wiscon-sin, and departed for Detroit, where the pellets were to be delivered to a steel mill. The trip down the lakes would normally have taken about two-and-a-half days, but a storm was brewing on the lakes, and Captain Ernest McSorley knew that he could be delayed by the weather.

The *Fitzgerald* was a classic ship, the epitome of a Great Lakes straight-decker. When launched in 1958, the *Fitz* was the first "maximum Seaway-size" ship built on the lakes, designed to match the size limits of the St. Lawrence Seaway, which was then nearing completion. The holder of many cargo records over the years, the *Fitzgerald* was owned by Northwestern Mutual Life Insurance Company, but operated by Columbia Transportation.

As Captain McSorley, a veteran of forty-four years on the lakes, departed the docks at Superior and nosed the big ship out onto Lake Superior, a major storm center was located over south-central Kansas, moving to the northeast. The National Weather Service, which termed it a "typical November storm," predicted that the storm's track would take it just south of Lake Superior by 7:00 P.M. on November 10. Because of the storm, McSorley chose a course that would take his ship east and north along the Canadian shore of the lake in order to stay in the lee of the north shore. Ahead of the *Fitzgerald* on the same course was the *Anderson*, which had loaded taconite at Two Harbors, Minnesota, for delivery to Gary, Indiana. As the weather continued to deteriorate, the two ships moved eastward, separated by 10 to 20 miles of white-capped waves.

At about 2:00 A.M. on November 10, Captain McSorley discussed the worsening weather conditions in a radiotelephone conversation with Captain Cooper of the *Anderson*. The gale warning for Lake Superior had just been replaced by a storm warning, and winds were expected to reach 50 miles per hour out of the northeast. The very fact that the two captains were on their ships' bridges attests to their concern over the weather. Normally, navigation duties are handled by a mate when the ship is on the lakes, particularly during the night.

The *Fitzgerald* overtook and passed the *Anderson* during the early morning hours as the two ships steamed into the teeth of the storm. With the *Fitz* gradually pulling ahead of the slower *Anderson*, the two ships closed on the Canadian shore at the east end of the lake at about 10:00 A.M. and turned southeastward on the leg of their voyage that would take them into Whitefish Bay. The center of the storm was passing just south of the lakes at the time, and winds had shifted from the northeast to southeast, blowing at just over 30 miles an hour. Aboard the *Anderson*, waves were recorded as being 10 to 12 feet high. As the storm moved on to the east, Cooper and McSorley knew that the wind would eventually shift to the northwest and probably intensify.

By midafternoon, the *Fitzgerald* and *Anderson* passed west of Michipicoten Island, and both ships set courses that would take them east of Caribou Island and safely clear of the shoals at its north end. The *Fitzgerald* was about 16 miles ahead of the *Anderson*. Both ships were being buffeted by winds

that had increased to about 45 miles an hour, now blowing out of the northwest. Seas had increased to 12 to 16 feet and it had started to snow. Because of the snow, the personnel in the *Anderson*'s pilothouse lost sight of the *Fitzgerald*, though they could still track the ship on their radar.

Shortly after his ship passed Caribou Island, around 3:30 in the afternoon, Captain McSorley called Captain Cooper on the radio. McSorley reported that he had a fence rail down, two vents had been lost or damaged, and his ship had taken on a list. Aboard the *Anderson*, Cooper and the two mates in the pilothouse with him at the time understood McSorley to be talking about damaged ballast tank vents and a "small list." None of them felt McSorley was expressing any real concern about the welfare of his ship, although the captain of the *Fitzgerald* did say that he was going to slow down to allow the *Anderson* to close the distance between them. Cooper asked McSorley if he had his pumps going. McSorley replied, "Yes, both of them." Before Cooper signed off, he told McSorley that he would keep an eye on the *Fitz*.

Between 4:10 and 4:15 P.M., the *Fitzgerald* again called the *Anderson*, reporting that its radars weren't working. With darkness rapidly settling over the lake, the *Fitzgerald* asked the *Anderson* to keep track of them on their radar and assist them in navigating. Personnel on the *Anderson* said they would oblige. Winds had climbed to over 60 miles an hour, and personnel aboard the *Anderson* estimated the height of the waves to be 12 to 18 feet. Both ships were taking a substantial amount of water over their decks, the waves striking them on their stern quarters on the starboard side.

During the next two hours, personnel on the *Anderson* estimated that some waves reached a height of 25 feet. With freeboard of less than 12 feet, the deck of the *Fitzgerald* would have been covered with water most of the time, sometimes to a depth of as much as 13 feet. Driven by the screeching winds, the waves would have hammered at the *Fitz*'s hull and superstructure with brutal force.

As the *Fitzgerald* approached the entrance to Whitefish Bay, personnel in the pilothouse were unable to pick up the radio beacon at Whitefish Point on their ship's radio direction-finder. In a radio call to the Coast Guard station at Grand Marais, Michigan, made at about 4:40 P.M., they were informed that there had been a power failure and the radio beacon was inoperative. Between 5:00 and 5:30 P.M., McSorley received a call from Captain Cedric Woodard, a Great Lakes pilot who was aboard the Swedish freighter *Avafors* in the vicinity of Whitefish Point. Woodard informed McSorley that the Whitefish Point light was on, but that the radio beacon was still not working. At one point in the conversation, Captain McSorley paused and, apparently in response to something that had been said in the *Fitzgerald*'s pilothouse, stated, "Don't allow nobody on deck," and then said something about a vent. Returning to his conversation with Woodard, he reported that his ship had a "bad list," had lost both radars, and was taking heavy seas over the deck. It was one of the worst seas he had ever been in, he said.

At 7:00 P.M., one of the mates on the *Anderson* called McSorley to tell him that radar showed the *Fitzgerald* to be about 10 miles ahead of the *Anderson* and about 15 miles from Crisp Point, west of Whitefish Point. A few minutes later, the Mate again called McSorley to let him know that there was a "radar target," another ship, about 9 miles ahead of the *Fitzgerald*. After assuring McSorley that the approaching ship would pass west of the *Fitzgerald*, the mate on the *Anderson* asked, "Oh, by the way, how are you making out with your problems?" "We're holding our own," came the reply.

Captain Cooper returned to the *Anderson*'s pilothouse at about 7:10 P.M., after having been in his cabin for about an hour. He checked the radar at that time and saw the *Fitzgerald* was about 9 miles ahead and approximately 16 miles north-northwest of Whitefish Point. In an hour or two, both the *Anderson* and the *Fitzgerald* would be in Whitefish Bay and sheltered from the wind and waves that had put both ships close to 10 hours behind schedule. A few minutes after Cooper returned to the pilothouse, the snow stopped and visibility improved considerably. The mate on watch could see the lights of three saltwater ships that were coming out of Whitefish Bay—the *Nanfri*, *Benfri*, and *Avafors*— about 17 or 18 miles ahead of the *Anderson*. He was surprised that he couldn't see the lights of the *Fitzgerald*, because it should have been closer than the three salties. Captain Cooper thought that the *Fitzgerald* might have had a blackout, and he asked everyone in the pilothouse to look for the ship's silhouette on

the horizon. Checking his radar, Cooper could see three distinct targets—the three salties that were upbound—but not the *Fitzgerald*.

The captain of the *Anderson* then attempted to call the *Fitzgerald* on the radio, but got no reply. He then called the *Str. William Clay Ford*, which was riding at anchor in Whitefish Bay, to make sure that his ship's radio set was working. Personnel on the *Ford* assured Cooper that his signal was strong. Cooper then called the *Nanfri*, one of the three saltwater ships, and talked with the pilot aboard. The pilot told Cooper that he had no contacts on his radar that could be the *Fitzgerald*. A few minutes later, at 8:32 P.M. on November 10, Cooper made his call to the Coast Guard radio operator at the Soo to express his concern about the *Fitzgerald*, setting in motion the search-and-rescue operation.

A four-member Coast Guard board conducted an exhaustive investigation into the sinking. Their report, issued fifteen months later, concluded:

> Because there were neither witnesses nor survivors and because of the complexity of the hull wreckage, the actual, final sequence of events culminating in the sinking of the *Fitzgerald* cannot be determined. Whatever the sequence, however, it is evident that the end was so rapid and catastrophic that there was no time to warn the crew, to attempt to launch lifeboats or liferafts, to don life jackets, or even to make a distress call.

The sunken hull of the *Fitzgerald* was located on November 14, 1975, by a U.S. Navy aircraft using magnetic anamoly detecting equipment. A slight oil slick covered the surface at the location, about 17 miles northwest of Whitefish Point, almost on the U.S.–Canadian border.

During the fall of 1975 and spring of 1976, side-scanning sonar equipment, a sort of underwater radar, was used to establish an accurate position for the wreck, which was found to be in two pieces in 530 feet of water. Between May 20 and 28, 1976, a Navy unmanned submarine was used to take photographs and videotape the wreck. During the twelve dives, totalling more than fifty-six hours on the bottom, the *CURV II* submersible recorded 43,255 feet of videotape and took 895 color slides of the wreck.

The bow section of the *Fitzgerald*, about 276 feet long, was found to be in an upright position on the bottom. The stern section, 253 feet long, was 170 feet from the bow and upside down. Between the two sections the bottom was covered with torn metal and taconite pellets that had spilled out of the ship's cargo hold. Photos of the bow and stern clearly showed the name of the vessel, confirming that it was, in fact, the *Fitzgerald*.

Based on their analysis of the condition of the wreck, the Coast Guard board concluded that massive flooding of the *Fitzgerald's* cargo hold had occurred before the sinking, causing the ship to progressively sink deeper in the water:

> Finally, as the storm reached its peak intensity, so much freeboard was lost that the bow pitched down and dove into a wall of water and the vessel was unable to recover. Within a matter of seconds, the cargo rushed forward, the bow plowed into the bottom of the lake, and the midships structure disintegrated, allowing the submerged section, now emptied of cargo, to roll over and override the other structure, finally coming to rest upside down atop the disintegrated middle portion of the ship.

While crewmembers on the *Fitzgerald* were clearly aware that their ship had taken on some water as a result of the topside damage that they had reported to the *Anderson* at 3:30 in the afternoon, the board members felt that it was unlikely that they were aware of the extent of the flooding. The damage they reported—two vents lost or damaged—could have resulted in the flooding of two of the ballast tanks located along the hull of the ship, or flooding of the tunnel that runs the length of the ship just above the ballast tanks. While such flooding would have caused the *Fitzgerald* to list, it would not have been serious enough to cause the ship to sink. That conclusion is supported by the fact that McSorley told Cooper that he had "both pumps" going, when, in fact, the *Fitz* was equipped with four pumps. According to the board, that suggests "that the flooding was evaluated by personnel on board *Fitzgerald* as not sufficiently serious to create a danger of loss of the vessel."[9]

On the other hand, McSorley's decision to slow down so that the *Anderson* would close with his ship might indicate that he either knew or sensed that his ship's problems were more serious than he let on in his conversation with Captain Cooper. Some hint of that might also have been revealed during his late afternoon radio contact with the pilot aboard the

Avafors, during which he was overhead telling someone not to let anyone out on deck.

Why a crewmember would consider going out on the deck of the *Fitzgerald* on the afternoon of November 10 is a total mystery to anyone who has been aboard a freighter in foul weather. Ships like the *Fitzgerald* are equipped with passageways, referred to as tunnels, that run the full length of the ship. The tunnels are located on each side of the ship, sandwiched between the ballast tanks and the main deck. By using the tunnels, crewmembers can move between the bow and stern without being exposed to the elements. In a storm like the one the *Fitzgerald* was in on November 10, crewmembers would certainly have used the tunnels. With the size of the waves that were rolling across the *Fitzgerald's* deck and smashing up against the after side of the forward deckhouse, venturing out on deck would have been not just foolhardy, but extremely dangerous. Why then would one or more crewmen aboard the ship have considered such an action? Perhaps out of desperation.

The Coast Guard board determined that the damage to the fence and vents reported by Captain McSorley could have resulted from some floating object, possibly a large log, that was brought aboard the *Fitzgerald's* deck in heavy seas, or by some heavy object breaking loose on the deck. They reasoned that the former was most likely, but their view was purely conjecture. Remember, however, that water entering the tunnel or ballast tanks through damaged vents would not have been sufficient to sink the *Fitzgerald*. Somehow, a large amount of water had to get into the cargo hold area of the ship.

The Coast Guard board members concluded that the cargo hold had flooded as a result of "ineffective hatch closures," a function of both the crew's failure to properly maintain the hatch covers, coamings, and gaskets that create a watertight seal between the covers and coamings, and their failure to properly secure the hatch clamps that hold the covers securely to the coamings. Each of the twenty-one hatches on the *Fitzgerald* was equipped with sixty-eight double-pivot clamps that locked the hatch covers to the coamings. Underwater photographs and videotapes showed clearly that many of the hatch clamps on the ship had not been damaged in the sinking. As the ship went down, however, the pressure of air in the cargo holds would have literally

Coast Guard investigators concluded that the failure to properly secure hatch clamps played a significant role in the sinking of the *Fitzgerald*. Here deck crewmembers aboard the *M/V Mesabi Miner* lower a hatch cover into place using the ship's hatch crane. Hatch clamps can be seen hanging down from the top edge of the hatch coaming. The crewmember on the left is holding one of the special tools used to put on the hatch clamps. (Author's Collection)

exploded the hatch covers off the coamings. That would normally break or bend any clamps that were securely dogged down, yet only a few clamps on the sunken hull of the *Fitz* were damaged.

That finding led investigators to conclude that sufficient water to sink the ship could have been taken in through gaps in the hatch covers, largely as a result of the failure of the crew to properly clamp down the hatch covers. A 1977 inspection of the *Str. Arthur B. Homer*, the *Fitzgerald*'s "sister ship," revealed that from inside the cargo hold light could be seen coming through between the hatch covers and coamings on 45 percent of the hatches. In some cases, the gap between the coaming and the gasket that was supposed to seal the opening was one-half inch wide. It is entirely possible that the *Fitzgerald* could have taken enough water in through gaps between its hatch coamings and hatch covers to gradually flood the cargo hold and cause it to sink as it did. On the other hand, that still doesn't explain why a crewmember or crewmembers wanted to go out on deck when 6 to 13 foot waves were rolling down it and crashing into the aft end of the superstructure.

What if, however, something had broken loose on deck and was battering the hatches and vents on the deck? The only objects on the deck heavy enough to do serious damage were the hatch crane and the spare propeller blade. The hatch crane would have been secured at the after end of the deck, while the spare propeller blade was bolted down in the midship area. Could the propeller blade have broken loose from its mounting and started battering up against the hatch coamings, smashing them in and allowing great quantities of water to cascade into the cargo hold? Given such a scenario, would crewmembers have considered going out on deck? And, if so, is there any action they could have taken to secure the heavy propeller blade? The answer to both questions is "possibly."

If something was happening out on deck that would eventually cause the ship to sink, a desperate crewmember might have been willing to risk the waves in an attempt to halt further damage. During a 1943 gale on Lake Superior, the *Str. Robert C. Stanley* began to break in two, a crack running across its deck and 12 to 14 feet down each side. In heavy seas and strong winds, crewmembers struggled on the rolling deck to pay out the cables from the fore and aft mooring winches. They ran the aft winch cables to bitts forward and the forward cables to bitts at the after end of the deck. When the powerful winches took a strain on the cables the crack closed up and the ship held together long enough to get to the Soo, where temporary repairs were made. Underwater photos and videotapes of the *Fitzgerald* reportedly show that a large amount of cable had been run off one of the ship's forward mooring winches. The cable had to have been intentionally run off; there is no other way it could have happened.

Could crewmembers on the *Fitzgerald* have been trying to secure a loose propeller blade by snagging on to it with a mooring cable? Possibly, but why wouldn't Captain McSorley have reported that sort of problem during his conversations with the *Anderson* and the *Avafors*? First, there was nothing that either of the two ships could have done to assist with such a problem. Second, by nature and tradition, Great Lakes captains are close-mouthed about problems aboard their ships. That's evident in the scanty information that McSorley gave to the *Anderson* regarding the problems aboard the *Fitz*. At the same time, even though McSorley was vague about the damage that had occurred, Captain Cooper didn't bother to press him for any further details, nor did the pilot aboard the *Avafors* when McSorley told him that the *Fitzgerald* had a bad list. The rule on the lakes is clearly: The less other people know about your ship's business, the better off you are.

McSorley might have been overly optimistic about his chances of making it to the safety of Whitefish Bay and didn't want to admit that *his* ship—the ship that *he* as captain was responsible for—was in trouble. If he did, and the ship made it to the safety of Whitefish Bay, as he undoubtedly thought it would, he knew he could expect to bear the brunt of a lot of razzing during the balance of his career. McSorley might not have wanted to announce that he had a spare propeller blade crashing around on his deck. Propeller blades don't just slip loose from the brackets that hold them to the deck. They are securely bolted down so they won't come loose even in the worst seas. If it comes loose, it is because it was not properly secured, and the captain is supposed to insure that things like that don't happen on his ship.

According to one member of the Coast Guard board, during their investigation they found that during the 1975 season, McSorley had "tipped ship" once when dockside so that his engineers could inspect the propeller for damage. Tipping ship involves filling the forward ballast tanks, and probably flooding the forward cargo hold, so that the stern of the vessel is raised far enough out of the water to see the propeller blades.

If McSorley or the engineers aboard the *Fitzgerald* suspected that they had damaged one of the propeller blades and would have to replace it before departing the dock, some enterprising sailor might have shown the foresight to loosen the bolts holding the spare blade to the deck. The bolts would probably have been rusty and the nuts hard to remove, so, to prevent any loss of time if they had to replace the blade, someone might have decided to get a head-start on the task. If so, did that person remember to tighten the bolts back up after the inspection showed that none of the blades on the *Fitz*'s propeller needed to be replaced? If not, the spare blade could easily have torn loose in the storm on November 10. If it did, McSorley was just as much at fault as the crewmember who loosened the bolts. He was, after all, responsible for everything that went on aboard his ship, particularly anything that might have jeopardized the safety of the vessel. He might not have wanted to announce over the radio that he had been negligent in discharging his duties as captain, and that his negligence was imperiling his ship.

Without any survivors and with the hull of the *Fitzgerald* badly damaged as a result of plowing nose first into the bottom, we may never know for sure what caused the ship to sink. That topic can still generate heated discussion among Great Lakes sailors, each of whom has a favored explanation for the disaster. A surprising few are willing to accept the Coast Guard's explanation that the ship took water through its hatch covers. Fewer still feel that something loose on deck was causing fatal damage.

To this day, most sailors on the lakes will argue that the *Fitzgerald* touched bottom when passing over the six-fathom (36-foot) shoal off Caribou Island, a position that was advocated by the Lake Carriers' Association throughout the investigation into the sinking. A hydrographic survey conducted by the Canadian government in 1976 showed that the shoal actually extended one mile farther to the east than was shown on the navigational charts used aboard ships like the *Fitzgerald*. While that made the grounding argument more plausible, the reconstruction of the *Fitzgerald*'s course line by Coast Guard investigators would still have put the doomed ship safely to the east of the shoal.

Even some members of the Coast Guard board reportedly favored the grounding explanation during their confidential deliberations. Grounding on an uncharted, or erroneously charted, shoal is a convenient explanation because it exonerates virtually everyone who could possibly be held culpable in the sinking, including Captain McSorley and the crew of the *Fitzgerald*, Columbia Transportation, the Coast Guard, and the industry as a whole.

If the ship tore a hole in its bottom when it crossed over the uncharted shoal in Canadian waters in a vicious storm, navigating without the aid of radar, it would be easy to write off the disaster as just another case of bad luck on the lakes. The members of the Coast Guard board knew that a conclusion of grounding would have allowed them to avoid opening the can of worms that would surely be associated with any alternative explanation for the sinking. Their investigation, however, the most exhaustive ever conducted into a sinking on the lakes, just wouldn't allow them to take the easy way out and attribute the casualty to grounding.

Regardless of what actually caused the *Fitzgerald* to sink, the Coast Guard investigation had uncovered what they felt was a ticking time bomb, a bomb that was not likely to be diffused if the loss of the ship was officially blamed on grounding. They found that it was common practice aboard many ships not to dog down securely all of the clamps that are intended to seal the hatch covers to the coamings. Also, hatch cover gaskets and coamings were often in poor repair, many incapable of keeping water out of the cargo hold even if all the hatch clamps were properly put on. The board's investigation revealed that it is virtually impossible for crewmembers to determine how much water has leaked into the cargo hold of a loaded ship, and the lack of watertight subdivision between the cargo holds would allow any water taken in to migrate throughout the entire hold area. What's more, many experienced sailors who testified at the board's hearings claimed that it was impossible to pump water out of the cargo hold when it is loaded. Water in the cargo hold must drain all the way to the aft end of the hold before it can be pumped.

Even though the pilothouse logs of the *Fitzgerald*

Crewmembers in life-jackets lower a lifeboat during a fire and boat drill aboard a laker. The lifeboats have proven to be difficult, if not impossible, to launch in heavy seas. (Institute for Great Lakes Research, Bowling Green State University)

included notations that the required weekly fire and lifeboat drills had been held, many former *Fitzgerald* crewmembers testified that drills were only held irregularly. Lifeboat drills were usually held only in good weather and, even then, the boats were not actually put into the water. The only time that crewmembers had any actual experience in launching, boarding, and rowing a lifeboat was during the pre-season Coast Guard inspections, which take place while the vessel is dockside and in sheltered waters.

Coast Guard regulations also required the *Fitzgerald* to carry inflatable life rafts, but there was no requirement for crewmembers to train in the launching and boarding of rafts. Columbia Transportation, like most other shipping companies on the lakes, had no training program in the use of life rafts, and most sailors who testified during the hearings said that they had never even seen a raft inflated. Most of the sailors said that the rafts would probably afford them the best chance of surviving a shipwreck. Almost to a man they doubted that lifeboats could be launched in heavy seas. One Great Lakes Pilot seemed to speak for many sailors when he told the board: "I have said that if the damn ship is going to go down, I would get in my bunk and pull the blankets over my head and say, 'Let her go,' because there was no way of launching the boats."[10]

Even if sailors managed to abandon ship by launching a lifeboat or life raft, or by going overboard with a life jacket on, they would face an imminent danger of dying from hypothermia. Over the years, more shipwrecked sailors have probably died from hypothermia than from drowning. That was clearly evidenced in the sinking of the *Morrell*; it was a factor in the deaths of some of the *Cedarville*'s crewmembers; and it probably accounted for much loss of life when the *Bradley* went down.

The four members of the *Fitzgerald* board urged the Coast Guard and the shipping industry to take prompt action to alleviate the many problems that had surfaced during their investigation. While concluding that they had found no negligence in the loss of the *Fitzgerald*, they painted a bleak picture of the industry's overall commitment to safe operations:

The nature of Great Lakes shipping, with short voyages, much of the time in very protected waters, frequently with the same routine from trip to trip, leads to complacency and an overly optimistic attitude concerning the extreme weather hazards which can and do exist. The Marine Board feels that this attitude reflects itself at times in deferral of maintenance and repairs, in failure to prepare properly for heavy weather, and in the conviction that since refuges are near, safety is possible by "running for it." While it is true that sailing conditions are good during the summer season, changes can occur abruptly, with conditions arising rapidly. This tragic accident points out the need for all persons involved in Great Lakes shipping to foster increased awareness of the hazards which exist.[11]

More than a decade has now passed since the Coast Guard issued their findings in the *Fitzgerald* case. How successful has the industry been in diffusing the ticking time bomb?

Hatches: While the Coast Guard concluded that the loss of the *Fitzgerald* was caused by flooding of the cargo hold as the result of ineffective hatch closures, few sailors on the lakes accept that explanation. Some ships still commonly operate without all of their hatch clamps on, even when loaded and even during periods of foul weather.

Subdivision: The transverse bulkheads that divide the cargo holds of most Great Lakes ships are not watertight, so water taken into the hold can spread throughout the entire area. The Coast Guard subsequently proposed rules that would have required Great Lakes shipping companies to subdivide the cargo holds of their vessels with watertight bulkheads, noting that "even a minimum degree of watertight subdivision within the [*Fitzgerald's*] cargo hold could have effected a great change in the ultimate fate of both the ship and her crew."

The same argument had been made a decade earlier in the Coast Guard report on the sinking of the *Morrell* and could also have been made with respect to the losses of the *Bradley* and the *Cedarville*. In every case, watertight subdivision of their cargo holds might have kept the ships, or even broken sections of the ships, afloat long enough to have reduced the number of fatalities. The *Fitzgerald* could have made it into Whitefish Bay; the *Cedarville* would have had time to beach itself; and the sections of the *Bradley* and *Morrell* might have floated long enough to either have received assistance from another ship or to allow crewmembers to abandon ship in an orderly fashion.

The Lake Carriers' Association, representing the Great Lakes fleet owners, argued that the level of watertight integrity aboard lake freighters was adequate and that a requirement to replace existing screen bulkheads with watertight bulkheads would create an economic hardship for vessel operators. Despite the obvious safety advantages of additional cargo hold subdivision, they successfully forestalled Coast Guard attempts to implement the new subdivision rules. A few vessel owners have opted for watertight subdivision in the cargo holds on vessels built since 1975. Most ships on the lakes, however, still have no way of preventing flooding of the entire cargo hold area.

In addition, Coast Guard investigators who studied the sinking of the *Bradley* concluded that the ship's engine room area flooded because a watertight door in the bulkhead that separates the engine room from the cargo hold was not securely dogged shut. Today, more than thirty years after the sinking of the *Bradley*, it is still common practice on lakers to use only one dog when closing the watertight doors located at each end of the tunnels that connect the bow and stern sections, or the doors are left completely open. While sailors are aware that use of one dog or an open door won't prevent water in the tunnels from entering either the engine room or the ship's forepeak, securely dogging the doors shut is, shall we say, "inconvenient."

Pumping: Many experienced sailors who testified during the *Fitzgerald* hearings said that it is impossible to detect water in a ship's cargo hold when the vessel is loaded, and it is virtually impossible to pump it out because the pumps are located at the far aft end of the cargo hold. The Coast Guard recommended that action be taken to correct both problems, but no changes have yet been made.

Lifeboats: After the sinkings in 1901 of the *Western Reserve* and the *Gilcher*, sailors and industry observers, like the editor of the *Marine Review* who is quoted at the beginning of this chapter, questioned whether lifeboats could be launched in heavy seas. Subsequent experience, including lessons learned in the sinkings of the *Bradley*, *Morrell*, and *Fitzgerald*, has provided ample testimony that the type of lifeboats and launching davits in use on the lakes are virtually worthless if a ship has to be abandoned in rough waters.

Enclosed, motorized lifeboats that can be boarded before they are launched have been developed and are in wide use on saltwater vessels and offshore oil platforms throughout the world. While they seem well suited to use on the lakes, only a couple of vessels in the U.S. fleet have been equipped with such systems. The first to have one was M. A. Hanna's thousand-footer, the *George A. Stinson*. Interestingly, the manager of the Hanna fleet at the time the *Stinson* was built was a World War II Navy veteran who had spent an extended period of time on a life raft after his ship was sunk in the Pacific.

Life rafts: Given the shortcomings of the lifeboats in use on the lakes, virtually everyone agrees that life rafts afford crewmembers the best chance for survival if they have to abandon ship in heavy seas. In their investigation of the sinking of the *Fitzgerald*, however, the Coast Guard Board members found that sailors have little, if any, training in the launching and boarding of life rafts. An intensive training program was recommended, but little has been done to implement that recommendation.

Some crewmembers have had an opportunity to see a life raft inflated and launched, but few have had a chance to actually practice launching or boarding. Launching a raft can be a tricky procedure, particularly in high winds, as can getting from the deck of the ship to a raft that is being tossed about by wind and waves. Many sailors feel that the best way to board a raft is to inflate it on the deck of the ship, climb inside, and wait for the ship to sink out from underneath the raft. Unfortunately, that strategy could easily lead to the raft's air chambers being punctured as it is buffeted around on the deck as the vessel sinks, trapping the occupants in a tangle of heavy, wet fabric that is being dragged to the bottom by the sinking hull.

Survival suits: To protect shipwrecked sailors from hypothermia, the *Fitzgerald* board recommended that ships carry exposure suits for crewmembers. Coast Guard regulations requiring sailors to be provided with survival suits went into effect on January 1, 1980, for the Great Lakes. The bright orange suits, made of neoprene rubber similar to that used in suits worn by scuba divers, provide flotation and protect the wearer against the loss of body heat.

Few crewmembers, however, have had an opportunity to actually test the suits in the water or to leap from the deck of a ship into the water with a suit on. One myth subscribed to by at least a few sailors is

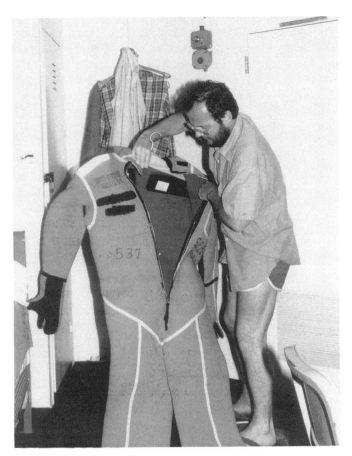

A crewmember inspects his survival suit prior to a fire and boat drill. Similar to the suits worn by Scuba divers during cold weather, they have been required equipment on lakers since shortly after the sinking of the *Fitzgerald*. (Author's collection)

that it would be possible to put a survival suit on in the water if you had to abandon ship in a hurry. Experiments conducted by strong swimmers in a flat, calm swimming pool have shown clearly that maneuver to be extremely dangerous, if not impossible.

Tests of the suits conducted in 3- to 5-foot waves by experienced swimmers also showed that some characteristics of the suits could cause the wearer to panic. Wearing a survival suit, a person generally floats flat on the water, instead of in the upright position that results when wearing a life jacket. In such a horizontal position, if you are floating face down you must lift your head to keep your face out of the water. That would be difficult to do for any extended period of time. Tests in waves also showed that it is difficult to roll over in a survival suit without some practice, because of the buoyancy characteristics of the suits, so a person floating face down is in serious risk of drowning.

The suits also have a face protector to protect the wearer's mouth and nostrils from water and cold air. During tests in waves, the face protectors on some suits were prone to fill with water when waves splashed the wearer in the face or when the face was submerged. In a suit that fits tight in the neck or chin area, the water trapped in the face protector didn't always drain out, creating a serious hazard of drowning if the wearer panicked and aspirated the water.

Survival suits are an excellent addition to the lifesaving equipment carried aboard ships, and they have the potential to save many lives in future marine disasters. Like most other equipment, however, the value of the suits is undermined by the amount of training and experience in their use afforded to sailors. Unfortunately, in a disaster situation, some shipwrecked sailors could actually die *as a result of* wearing survival suits that are intended to save their lives.

Inspections: After the loss of the *Fitzgerald*, the Coast Guard implemented the pre-November inspection program that had been recommended by the Board of Investigation. Coast Guard inspectors now board all U.S. ships during the fall to inspect hatch and vent closures and lifesaving equipment. The ridership program continues in effect and is a positive development, although the value of the program could be enhanced if vessel personnel were not forewarned that inspectors will be boarding their ship.

The time bomb ticks on. While the fall inspection program and the requirement for survival suits are both positive developments, few other changes have come about as a result of the sinking of the *Fitzgerald* or the other ships lost in the past three decades on the lakes. Since the loss of the *Fitz*, some captains may be more prone to go to anchor, rather than venturing out in a severe storm, but there are still too many who like to portray themselves as "heavy weather sailors." They take great delight in steaming past the anchored ships of their more conservative peers and out into the teeth of a full-blown storm. Since 1975, lady luck has ridden with those captains and their ships, though many industry observers feel it is only a matter of time before the practice results in another tragedy.

It is hard to understand why a captain would expose a ship and crew to such a risk. In the weeks before the sinking of the *Bradley*, for example, Captain Roland Bryan had written a letter to his girlfriend in which he said, "This boat is getting pretty ripe for too much weather. I'll be glad when they get her fixed up." In a letter to another friend, he wrote: "The hull is not good . . . have to nurse her along . . . 'take it easy' were my instructions."[12] Yet Bryan took his ship out in the face of severe storm warnings, and in the hours just before the sinking he chose to leave the lee of the Wisconsin shore and cut across the center of Lake Michigan in 65 mile an hour winds and waves that were often more than 20 feet high.

While the loss of the *Cedarville* is still etched deeply into the memories of most captains on the lakes, many still operate their ships at full speed when the lakes and rivers are blanketed in fog. Luck has ridden with them, too, although there have been a number of close calls.

Captain Jim Wilson, a retired Coast Guard inspection officer who now specializes in serving as an expert witness in marine casualty cases, says that most shipwrecks are the result of complacency. Wilson, one of four Coast Guard officers who served on the *Fitzgerald* board, feels that virtually all vessel casualties can be attributed to human error that arises out of the monotonous routine aboard most lake freighter. "The past is prologue," says Wilson. "If we don't learn from out past mistakes, we are destined to eventually repeat them." The routine on the lakes, he feels, lulls sailors into a false sense of security that borders on infallibility—the "Titanic syndrome." Unsafe practices are overlooked, and some even become accepted as part of the standard shipboard routine, such as not securing hatch covers properly or not dogging watertight doors shut. "If the ship ever gets into trouble," Wilson continues, "crewmembers find—too late, unfortunately—that their complacency has cost them whatever margin of safety they should have had."

In his book, *Our Seamen, An Appeal*, Samuel Plimsoll quotes a shipowner to the effect that "if a small number of well-known shipowners were put aboard one of their own vessels when she was ready for sea, we should, in the event of bad weather, see that with them had disappeared from our annals nine-tenths of the losses we deplore."[13] A more likely scenario is that the shipowners would see that all of the safety problems were corrected before the ship sailed. That may suggest an avenue for correcting the pervasive safety problems on Great Lakes ships: Require shipowners, top Coast Guard officials, hull insurance underwriters, and the loved ones of crewmembers to regularly ride the boats. We might then be astonished at how rapidly the problems could be dealt with.

In the interim, the time bomb continues to tick. Most sailors are fatalistic about the likely outcome. They seem to feel that it is not a question of whether another ship will be lost, but only when the tragedy will occur and to which ship.

Notes

1. J. B. Mansfield, *History of the Great Lakes*, vol. I (Chicago: J. H. Beers, 1899; reprint Cleveland: Freshwater Press, 1972), 507.
2. Mansfield, 507.
3. George J. Ryan, "Enhancing Weather Forecasting on the Great Lakes," *Seaway Review* (Sept. 1984): 99.
4. Harlan Hatcher and Erich A. Walter, *A Pictorial History of the Great Lakes* (New York: Bonanza Books, 1963), 277–81.
5. James A. Wilson, "A Critical Look at our Marine Transportation," *Seaway Review* (Sept. 1983): 11–13.

6. Factual information on the sinking of the *Bradley* was taken from *Marine Casualty Report: SS Carl D. Bradley* (Washington, DC: U.S. Coast Guard, 1959).

7. Details on the sinking of the *Cedarville* were extracted from *Marine Casualty Report: SS Cedarville* (Washington, DC: U.S. Coast Guard, 1967).

8. All information regarding the loss of the *Morrell* was drawn from *Marine Casualty Report: SS Daniel J. Morrell* (Washington, DC: U.S. Coast Guard, 1968).

9. Details regarding the sinking of the *Fitzgerald* are from *Marine Casualty Report: SS Edmund Fitzgerald* (Washington, DC: U.S. Coast Guard, 1977).

10. The statement was recounted in Frederick Stonehouse, *The Wreck of the Edmund Fitzgerald* (AuTrain, MI: Avery Color Studios, 1977), 18.

11. *Marine Casualty Report: SS Edmund Fitzgerald*, 103.

12. William Ratigan, *Shipwrecks and Survivors* (Grand Rapids, MI: Wm. B. Eerdmans Publishing, 1960), 18.

13. Harry Benford, "Samuel Plimsoll: His Book and His Mark," *Seaway Review* (Jan.–Mar. 1986): 79.

8

Support Services: Bum Boats, Mailboats, and Icebreakers

Ships bearing the colors of over 50 nations regularly ply the waters of the Great Lakes, making economists and geographers alike call the Great Lakes and their connecting waterways the most important inland water transportation system in the world.
—Jacques LesStrang, *The Great Lakes Ports of North America*, 1973

You've often heard me say that the St. Lawrence Seaway may well be the best kept secret in our hemisphere. I think now that it has been the best kept secret in the world.
—James L. Emery, U.S. Seaway Administrator, *Seaway Review*, 1985

In the quiet stillness of a summer night, the long freighter glides slowly under the Ambassador Bridge on its trip down the Detroit River. As the freighter clears the bridge, a 45-foot boat departs its dock just south of the bridge on the Detroit side of the river and steers toward the freighter, the throaty rhythm of its engine drowned out by the deep rumble of the big ship's powerful diesels. As it draws alongside the moving freighter, the speed of the small boat, the *J. W. Westcott II*, is matched to that of the massive ore boat, the distance between the two slowly diminishing until their hulls touch and they begin to move down the river together, the *Westcott* almost invisible in the shadow of the freighter.

From the deck of the freighter, the mate of the watch pays out on a rope to lower a plastic 5-gallon pail to the two figures on the deck of the *Westcott*, whose heads are 10 feet below the deck of the ore boat. One of the men grabs the pail, places an armload of newspapers and letters in it, and yanks twice on the rope. Feeling the rope jerk, the mate hoists the pail from the blackness below and swings it onto the steel deck of the freighter. Next to him, two crewmembers begin dropping bulky white laundry bags to the deck of the small boat.

When the last of the bags of dirty laundry has been stacked on the aft deck of the *Westcott*, its engine roars as it speeds up and turns away from the freighter to head back to its moorings. Its horn emits one long and two short toots, the salute piercing the quiet of the night. On the deck of the freighter, the mate tucks the bundle of newspapers and letters under his arm and waves at the two crewmen standing at the stern of the mailboat. Before the two figures on the *Westcott* can return the wave, the night is shattered by the deep roar of the freighter's own air horn as it growls out one long and two short blasts in reply to the salute from the mailboat.

This scene is repeated thousands of times during each shipping season as the *J. W. Westcott II* delivers mail to every ship that passes the Westcott Company's facility on the Detroit waterfront. The Marine Post Office at Detroit was established in 1895 as an adjunct to the Detroit Post Office and is today the only post office in the country that exists solely to deliver mail to ships. The *Westcott* has even been assigned its own zip code—48222—underscoring the importance of the Marine Post Office to the sailors who crew the big freighters.

When the Marine Post Office first began at Detroit, vessel traffic on the river was so heavy that the service's one steam launch could not manage to call on every passing ship. In those days, the launch towed a small fleet of rowboats with it. When a ship approached and called out its name, a carrier would grab the mail addressed to that vessel and row over to it in one of the rowboats. In that way, several passing ships could be served simultaneously by a single steam tug.

During the first year of service, 46,994 pieces of mail were handled by the Marine Post Office at Detroit. As people became familiar with the new service, use of the post office increased rapidly. During the second year of operation, the volume of mail handled increased by almost 400 percent with a total of 175,850 letters delivered to more than 19,000 ships that passed Detroit that season. In addition to delivering the mail, personnel of the Marine Post Office recorded the name of every vessel that passed Detroit upbound or downbound. Their traffic logs provided shipowners with vital information on the whereabouts of their ships in the days before ship-to-shore radio communications.

Today, the Westcott Company provides a variety of other services to personnel aboard the U.S., Canadian, and foreign-flag ships that pass Detroit. In addition to processing inbound and outbound mail, the firm operates a chandlery that supplies ships with groceries, cleaning supplies, navigational charts, and other things needed to keep the vessels operating between ports.

Crew changes are often made at the mailboat, a service that has grown in importance since many vessel personnel have been entitled to vacations every couple of months. It is not always convenient for sailors to get on or off their ships at loading or unloading ports because they are often located far from public transportation services.

Westcott Company personnel also handle laundry for many of the ships. Bags of dirty linens dropped off at the mailboat are sent out to a commercial laundry for cleaning and are returned to the ship on its return voyage.

The Marine Post Office is just one of many vital support services necessary to keep the big freighters moving up and down the lakes, part of an elaborate industry infrastructure that has developed over the past two centuries. In addition to the Westcott operation, the infrastructure includes a wide range of government agencies and private firms that provide important, often essential, services to the ships. While it is difficult to single out one support service as being more important than the others, there are a number of government agencies in both the U.S. and Canada that are responsible for maintaining the most essential element of the system—the waterway itself. Included are the U.S. Army Corps of Engineers, the U.S. and Canadian agencies that manage the St. Lawrence Seaway and Welland Canal, and the U.S. and Canadian Coast Guards.

The Corps of Engineers is responsible for maintaining the navigable waterways of the United States, including the Great Lakes. The agency's early involvement with the nation's waterways was in support of the U.S. Navy, but since the War of 1812, its emphasis has gradually shifted to support of the commercial maritime industry, which is considered to be essential to both the economic well-being and national defense of the country. The Corps' primary function is dredging. An ongoing program of dredging is necessary to maintain channels and harbors at the prescribed depths. Without regular dredging, many of the channels and harbors used by commercial vessels would eventually fill in with silt and sand to the extent that they would become unnavigable.

The Corps is also involved in an ongoing program of dredging that is intended not just to maintain, but to improve the waterways used by commercial vessels. Channel improvement programs include both the widening and deepening of channels. Widening

173

of channels is often intended to make them safer, to give ships more room to pass each other, and to eliminate hazardous turns that can cause problems for the personnel who navigate commercial vessels. Some of the Corps' widening and deepening operations, however, are designed to allow larger ships to utilize the waterways. In the Great Lakes system, each successive generation of longer, wider, and deeper freighters has led to extensive dredging of channels and harbors to allow the ships to operate safely and efficiently.

On the Great Lakes, pressure on the Corps to deepen harbors and river channels has declined somewhat during the past few years. This is a result of high water levels being experienced on the lakes because of an extended period of above average precipitation in the region. Lake levels 3 to 5 feet above the historic mean have allowed shipping companies to establish new iron ore cargo records that are almost 10,000 tons higher than those set five or six years ago. On a thousand-footer, each extra inch of water depth allows the ship to carry about 200 additional tons of iron ore; each additional foot of water depth, then, means 2,400 extra tons each trip. Spread over an entire season, the additional tonnage would total 120–150,000 tons and represent significant additional income for the shipping company.

As water levels in the lakes begin to recede, however, the Corps can expect shipping company executives to increase their lobbying for extensive dredging programs. While both the Poe and MacArthur Locks at the Soo can accommodate ships with drafts of up to 31 feet, channel depths in the St. Marys River and many of the harbors around the lakes are limited to a maximum of about 27 feet at normal water depths. Dredging harbors and channels to the 31-foot maximum draft of the locks would add substantial carrying capacity for most ships in the fleet. The 48 inches of additional draft the largest ships would gain would mean that they could carry an extra 10,000 tons each trip, 500–600,000 more tons each season.

Since 1881, the Corps has also been responsible for operation of the St. Marys Falls Canal, commonly referred to as the Soo Locks. Located on the St. Marys River at Sault Ste. Marie, Michigan, the locks raise or lower ships 21 feet to compensate for the difference in water levels between Lake Superior and the lower lakes. The rapids at the Soo caused by

The mailboat *J. W. Westcott II* delivers mail to each ship that passes its station on the Detroit River. Here crewmembers aboard a laker throw bags of dirty laundry down to the *Westcott*. The laundry will be sent out for cleaning and returned to the ship on its return voyage. (Author's collection)

the difference in elevation between Lake Superior and the lower lakes have always created an obstacle for commerce on the lakes. The first lock at the Soo was actually constructed by the Northwest Fur Company in 1797. Located on the Canadian side of the river, the 38-foot-long lock was designed for use by the large freight canoes used by fur trappers and traders. It eliminated the strenuous and time-consuming practice of portaging canoes and cargoes around the rapids.[1]

The Northwest Fur Company lock was destroyed during the War of 1812 and not replaced until 1855. During that forty-three-year period, the bottleneck at the Soo became an increasingly serious problem for commercial interests in the region. Lake Superior was literally cut off from the lower lakes. Vessels from the lower lakes could navigate only as far as the lower end of the rapids at Sault Ste. Marie. Conversely, ships on Lake Superior could operate only above the rapids. Cargo had to be portaged around the rapids using freight wagons. A tramway was eventually built around the rapids, along what is now known as Portage Avenue in the Soo. Designed primarily to speed up the movement of cargo, the tramway was even used to move some smaller ships around the rapids, eliminating the time-consuming task of unloading them.

With the discovery of copper and iron ore in the Lake Superior region, however, even the tramway proved inadequate to handle the growing commerce between Lake Superior and the lower lakes. In 1852, Congress passed legislation granting 750,000 acres of federal land to the state of Michigan to be used to compensate any company that would build a viable lock at the Soo.[2] Support for the legislation was not unanimous, however. Among the leaders of the opposition was the great orator Henry Clay. The distinguished senior senator from Kentucky opposed building a lock on the northern frontier of the U.S., arguing that "it is a work beyond the remotest settlement of the United States, if not the moon."[3]

Despite Clay's vehement objections, the legislation passed, and the franchise to build the lock was subsequently awarded to the Fairbanks Scale Company, a Vermont firm that had extensive mining interests in Michigan's Upper Peninsula. The task was of epic proportions for that time. Much of the two locks and more than a mile of approaching channels had to be hewn out of solid rock by gangs of laborers working with almost primitive tools. The success of the project was made even more astounding by the fact that the excavations and construction were managed by Charles T. Harvey.

Harvey was a young accountant who worked as western regional manager for Fairbanks. He had come to the Soo in 1852 to recuperate from a bout with typhoid, and he quickly grasped both the need for the lock and the potential economic gain in store for the company that would build it. Harvey convinced his employers to take on the venture and was designated their manager for the project. When construction began in June 1853, Harvey was only twenty-four years old. More significantly, the eager and energetic young man had no prior construction experience.

By the first winter, Harvey had two thousand workers employed on the project, primarily recent Irish and German immigrants who were recruited in Detroit and New York. Although numerous obstacles were encountered during construction, Harvey proved to be a brilliant manager. The project was completed in less than two years and at a cost of just under $1 million.

The first canal consisted of two locks, each 350 feet long and 70 feet wide. The upper lock raised or lowered vessels 8 feet, the downstream lock 10 feet. The depth over the lock sills was only 9 feet, meaning that when the locks were flooded to the level of the lower lakes they could accommodate only ships with drafts of less than 9 feet. The approach canal was more than a mile long, 100 feet wide, and 12 feet deep.[4]

The completed locks were turned over to the state of Michigan on May 31, 1855, and officially opened to commerce on June 18 in ceremonies presided over by numerous Michigan officials. The first vessel to transit the locks was the *Str. Illinois*, which was en route to Lake Superior. The first downbound vessel to use the locks was the *Str. Baltimore*. One month later, the two-masted brig *Columbia* carried the first load of iron ore through the locks. In only five years, the locks at the Soo were to play an important role in support of Union efforts in the Civil War by insuring a steady flow of iron to meet the nation's war needs. By then, a virtual river of red was flowing from the iron mines on the Lake Superior ranges to the smelters and mills in Ohio and Pennsylvania.

As payment for construction of the locks, the Fairbanks company was allowed to claim 750,000 acres of federal lands in Michigan. They chose approximately 40,000 acres of land in the iron ranges, 150,000 acres in the copper region of the Keweenaw Peninsula, and 560,000 acres of prime timberland in Michigan's Lower Peninsula.[5]

Boats that passed through the State Lock, as it was then known, were required to pay a toll of four cents per ton until 1877, when the toll was reduced to three cents per ton. By the time control of the locks was transferred to the federal government in 1881, virtually the full cost of building the locks had been recovered through the tolls. Since the locks have been under the jurisdiction of the Corps of Engineers, vessels have been able to transit the locks toll free.

Today there are four locks at the Soo, though only two are generally in use. The largest of the locks is the massive Poe Lock, the second lock named for the Corps of Engineers colonel who served as Detroit district engineer from 1870–73 and 1883–95. Opened in 1968, the Poe is 1,200 feet in length, 110 feet wide, and 32 feet deep. The lock could accommodate ships of up to 1,100 feet in length, although the longest vessel on the lakes at present is just over 1,000 feet long.

The second lock in operation at the Soo is the MacArthur, opened in 1943 and named for the popular World War II general. The "Mac," as it is commonly called, is 800 feet long, 80 feet wide, and 31 feet deep. It can handle ships of up to about 730 feet in length, with beams of up to 75 feet.

The other two U.S. locks at the Soo, the Davis and Sabin, were put into operation in 1914 and 1919, respectively. They are identical in size, both being 1,350 feet long, 80 feet wide, and 23 feet deep. While the length and width of the two locks is adequate to accommodate most ships operating on the lakes today, their limitation to a 23-foot draft makes them essentially obsolete.

The Corps and commercial interests on the lakes are awaiting final budgetary approval for the construction of a new lock at the Soo, to be built on the site of the present Sabin and Davis locks. The new lock will be a twin to the Poe, built primarily to handle thousand-footers. At present, if the Poe Lock were to be disabled for some reason, thousand-footers would not be able to operate between Lake Superior and the lower lakes. With the thirteen thousand-footers on the lakes accounting for a large share of the U.S. fleet's carrying capacity, closure of the Poe Lock would seriously impair the industry. Not only would the U.S. shipping companies suffer, however, so too would the U.S. steel industry which benefits from the lower transportation costs that result from use of the highly efficient thousand-footers.

As important as they are, the locks at Sault Ste. Marie were not the first locks built on the Great Lakes and St. Lawrence River system. In 1783, more than seventy years before the opening of the State Lock, Royal Engineers in Canada completed work on a series of four canals between Montreal and Lachine on the St. Lawrence River. The canals allowed freight canoes and bateaus to bypass rapids on the St. Lawrence River without portaging. The size of those first locks were eventually enlarged and, in 1825, the Lachine Canal at Montreal was opened for navigation. The Lachine Canal consisted of twelve locks, each 100 feet long and 25 feet wide, with a depth over the sills of 5 feet. They allowed vessels to bypass the turbulent Lachine Rapids on their travels between the upper St. Lawrence and Lake Ontario.[6]

While the route between the Atlantic and Lake Ontario was gradually being improved, vessel travel west of Lake Ontario was impossible because of Niagara Falls, which blocked the way to Lake Erie and the upper lakes. In the fall of 1829, that last barrier to travel on the Great Lakes and St. Lawrence System was finally broached with the opening of the first Welland Canal by a group of private entrepreneurs.

The original route around Niagara consisted of a series of canals and forty locks that connected several rivers between Lake Ontario and Lake Erie. The locks were built of wood and each was 110 feet long, 22 feet wide, and 8 feet deep. Boats were towed through the narrow canal by teams of horses. In 1842, the Ontario government purchased the canal and began a series of improvements. The forty original wooden locks were replaced by twenty-seven locks of cut stone, each being 150 feet long, 26 feet wide, and 10 feet deep. A canal was also dug between the towns of Welland and Port Colborne on Lake Erie, much of it through solid rock, which provided a more direct route than the original canal. In 1867, the canal was taken over by the new federal government of Canada. Major improvements were again made on the canal between 1881 and 1887, resulting in the enlargement of locks to 270 feet in length, 45

The *Str. Benson Ford* enters the lowest of three adjoining "flight locks" in the Welland Canal. The Monrovian-registered *Federal Saguenay* can be seen in the lock above the *Ford*. (Author's collection)

feet in width, and 12 feet in depth. The present Welland system was completed in 1932 at a cost of $132 million. The number of locks was reduced to eight, each of which is 820 feet long, 80 feet wide, and 30 feet deep.[7]

For the first time, the five Great Lakes were open to virtually unrestricted vessel traffic. Travel between Lake Ontario and the St. Lawrence River, however, continued to be limited to canallers, ships that were under 260 feet in length, with beams of about 44 feet and drafts under 12 feet, the maximum dimensions that could be accommodated by the St. Lawrence canals and locks.

Only the smallest saltwater vessels were able to enter the Great Lakes because of the restrictive size of the locks between Montreal and Lake Ontario. People around the lakes who were unfamiliar with the limitations of the St. Lawrence system often commented on how much smaller the saltwater ships were than the 600-foot lakers then a common sight on the lakes. They didn't realize that the larger saltwater vessels, every bit the equals of the bulk freighters that operated on the lakes, were forced to discharge their cargoes at Montreal and other deep-water ports on the upper St. Lawrence. Those cargoes were then either shipped overland or carried into the lakes by the canallers. For all intents and purposes, the Great Lakes were still cut off from the ocean, at least for normal marine commerce.

The irony of the lakes draining into the ocean by way of the St. Lawrence River, but that route not being open to full-sized ships, had not gone unnoticed. As early as 1892, a congressman representing the farm areas of Minnesota, Swedish immigrant John Lind, had sponsored a resolution calling for establishment of a joint U.S.–Canadian committee to study the possibilities of opening a water route from the head of Lake Superior to the sea. Two years later, the Deep Waterways Association was formed in Canada. They supported Lind's call for a binational group to study improving the St. Lawrence waterway. The study group that was subsequently formed took little time in reaching the conclusion that a viable route to the Atlantic—a "seaway"—could be established via the St. Lawrence River. The seaway proposal was endorsed by President Grover Cleveland. A series of engineering studies were conducted, but no further significant action occurred until after World War I when the Great

Lakes–St. Lawrence Tidewater Association was formed. The new association, the brainchild of a Duluth lawyer named Charles Craig, was made up of representatives of a number of the Great Lakes states. For sixteen years the group lobbied unsuccessfully for construction of a seaway, opposed by public and private utility companies that wanted to reserve the river for production of hydroelectric power.

In 1932, a treaty was signed by Canadian Prime Minister R. B. Bennett and U.S. President Herbert Hoover that committed the two nations to working together to construct a seaway to a draft of 27 feet. Under terms of the treaty, the two nations were to share in the costs of constructing the needed locks and channels in the International Rapids section of the river, bounded on the north by Quebec and on the south by the state of New York. There was immediate, strong opposition to the Hoover-Bennett Treaty by the railroads, privately owned utility companies, coal interests, and Eastern and Gulf Coast ports. A number of Great Lakes interests even objected to the seaway proposal, including the powerful Lake Carriers Association and port authorities in Chicago and Cleveland.

The most-often-cited argument against the seaway was cost. Those allied against the project argued that costs would total over $1 billion for the U.S. and Canada and that much of the U.S. share would have to be paid by taxpayers living outside the Great Lakes area who would not benefit from the seaway. Others objected to the possible diversion of business from U.S. ports and shipping companies. They even argued that construction of the seaway would open inland markets to unfair foreign competition by allowing tramp steamers to dump cheaply produced commodities on the Great Lakes market.

The Hoover-Bennett Treaty was finally brought up for a vote before the U.S. Senate in the spring of 1943, but failed to get the necessary two-thirds vote needed for ratification. At a White House press conference held the day of the vote, President Franklin Roosevelt, long an advocate of seaway construction, stated unequivocally: "Whether the thing goes through this afternoon or not makes no difference at all. The St. Lawrence Seaway is going to be built, just as sure as God made green apples." Roosevelt was right, of course, but he did not live to see positive action taken on the seaway proposal.

While U.S. officials again put the seaway on the

back burner, the Canadians grew impatient, announcing that they would proceed with the construction on an all-Canadian seaway. The Canadian St. Lawrence Seaway Authority was established and empowered to build the seaway from Montreal to Lake Erie with or without U.S. participation. As the Canadians proceeded unilaterally with their seaway plans, members of the U.S. Congress became alarmed. They realized that without U.S. participation, Canada would control access into the heart of North America, and they feared that American shippers would be charged exorbitant tolls to use the route. President Truman exhorted Congress to commit the U.S. to participation in the seaway's construction. It was no longer a question of whether the seaway would be built, he argued, but whether the U.S. would participate in the project and share in operation and control of the route. A seaway proposal sponsored by congressman John Blatnik of Duluth was put before the Congress, but it was defeated in the Senate during the 1952 session on a 43–40 vote. After Dwight Eisenhower assumed the presidency in 1953, new seaway legislation was introduced in the congress by Senator Alexander Wiley of Wisconsin and Representative George Dondero of Michigan. After another bitter battle, the legislation was finally enacted in the spring of 1954.

The massive construction project began in November of that year. Stretching for 190 miles, much of it through bedrock, the St. Lawrence Seaway presented a monumental challenge for builders. The scope of the project dwarfed the earlier construction of the 100-mile Suez Canal and the 50-mile Panama Canal. In Canada, eight thousand residents of seven communities were dislocated by the project, while over a thousand had to abandon their homes on the New York shore of the waterway. Three new communities were established in Ontario. Homes, churches, schools, factories, businesses, and even cemeteries were transplanted from the areas that would eventually be flooded by the new hydroelectric dams that were being built as part of the total seaway project.

Seven new locks were built to compensate for the 484-foot difference in elevation between Lake Ontario and the upper St. Lawrence River. Five of the locks are in Canada, built by the St. Lawrence Seaway Authority. The other two are in the U.S., constructed by the U.S. St. Lawrence Seaway Development Corporation.

To carve out the seaway, over twenty-two thousand workers moved 210 million cubic yards of rock and dirt and poured more than 6 million yards of concrete. Total costs for the project were just over $1 billion, including $600 million for U.S. and Canadian hydroelectric development, $322 million for the Canadian locks and channels, and $124 million for the U.S. locks and channels. The Canadian Seaway Authority went 80 percent over its budget; the U.S. Seaway Corporation 42 percent.

With President Eisenhower and Queen Elizabeth II presiding, the monumental link between the waters of the Great Lakes and the Atlantic Ocean was officially dedicated on June 26, 1959. Over 20 million tons of cargo moved through the system the first year it was in operation as the previously landlocked ports of the Great Lakes became international ports.[8] In 1970, the international character of the Great Lakes ports was officially recognized when President Richard Nixon signed legislation that gave the Great Lakes and St. Lawrence Seaway status as "America's Fourth Seacoast."

Costs of operating and maintaining the Seaway are paid for by tolls charged to vessels transiting the system. Seventy-one percent of the revenues go to the Canadian Seaway Authority, with the balance to the U.S. Seaway Corporation. For a maximum Seaway-size vessel, tolls for transiting the Montreal to Lake Ontario section of the Seaway total about $1,600 for a vessel in ballast to approximately $15–$56,000 for a loaded ship, depending on the type of cargo being carried. Tolls for the Welland Canal portion of the system would run from about $1,400 for an empty ship to $10–$15,000 for a laden vessel.

Supporters of the system have long claimed that the tolls are exorbitant and constitute an impediment to use of the system, primarily by foreign-flag shipping companies. They note that the U.S. portion of the St. Lawrence is the only navigational system in the country required to support itself from tolls collected on users. Of the 27,000 miles of navigable waters in North America, the only tolls in existence are on the 124 miles of the seaway and the 27 miles of the Welland Canal. The toll requirements for the seaway were written into the Wiley-Dondero legislation to help eliminate some opposition in the Congress, but other waterways constructed with federal funds have not been similarly burdened with toll

An aerial photo showing construction on the Eisenhower
Lock of the St. Lawrence Seaway in 1956. One of two U.S.
locks in the system, the Eisenhower is located at
Massena, New York. (St. Lawrence Seaway Development
Corporation)

In August 1957, the towering concrete walls of the Eisenhower lock are nearing completion. Like the other seven locks in the 190-mile system, the Eisenhower is capable of handling ships up to 730 feet long and 75 feet wide. (St. Lawrence Seaway Development Corporation)

requirements. That includes the extensive Mississippi River system and the newer Tennessee-Tombigbee Waterway, both of which are in competition with the Great Lakes–St. Lawrence system for cargo moving out of the U.S. Midwest.

In the closing days of 1986, legislation was pushed through just hours before the adjournment of the Ninety-ninth Congress to eliminate tolls on the U.S. portion of the seaway and authorize the spending of $39 million in general fund revenues for repair of the two aging U.S. locks. Enactment of that legislation was followed several months later by word from the Canadian Seaway Authority that it intended to hike tolls on its portion of the Seaway, significantly diminishing the value of the U.S. action to gain equitable treatment for the seaway and help encourage its use by international shippers. U.S. officials, along with many Canadian port and maritime officials, immediately began pressing for the reduction or elimination of Canadian tolls. That campaign is still raging. It has united industry leaders on both the U.S. and Canadian sides of the system in much the same way they worked together to build the seaway originally.

From its opening in 1959, tonnages moving through the seaway rose steadily, reaching a high of more than 57 million tons in 1973. Studies projected that the seaway would reach its maximum capacity by 1990. While the Corps of Engineers studied the possibility of building an all-American canal to bypass the anticipated bottleneck at the Welland, a project the Corps' budget analysts calculated would cost more than $2 billion, traffic began to slowly decline on the seaway. By the 1986 season, traffic had fallen to under 40 million tons, well below the maximum design capacity of the system.

While the potential problem of overcapacity on the system was averted, industry leaders began to fear that the system was rapidly becoming obsolete. The most modern and efficient ocean vessels are too large to fit into the seaway locks, so cargo that could move in and out of the lakes by water is being handled at ports on the upper St. Lawrence River and the east coasts of the U.S. and Canada. The major U.S. and Canadian railroads have established efficient systems to move cargo overland between the industrial and agricultural areas of the Great Lakes region to the coastal ports, what is referred to in the industry as the landbridge.

Ports east of the seaway locks on the St. Lawrence, including Montreal and Quebec City, have also experienced significant increases in traffic concurrent with the decline in traffic through the seaway system. Much of the container traffic originating at Great Lakes port cities, such as Detroit and Chicago, now moves overland to Montreal by rail. Incoming cargo often follows the same route, being offloaded at Montreal, Quebec City, or East Coast ports and railed to its final destination.

In evaluating the state of the seaway system in 1966, William O'Neil, president of the Seaway Authority said, "It is difficult to be optimistic about the prospects for significant improvement in seaway traffic but, at the same time, we should recognize that this present malaise is not something peculiar to the region. The shipping industry worldwide is going through a difficult period as a result of the effects that the recent recession had on international trade. Other transportation modes are also suffering."[9]

In an attempt to counter falling tonnages on the seaway system, U.S. and Canadian seaway officials, Great Lakes port administrators, executives of shipping companies, union officials, and heads of terminal and stevedoring firms have attempted to expand their program to market use of the system. Since 1985, they have visited annually key European cities on trade missions designed to familiarize European shipping executives with the seaway system and its advantages to firms shipping in or out of the Great Lakes region. Industry leaders who have participated in the trade missions have indicated that they were well received in Europe and their efforts may result in some additional cargo movements through the seaway. For the most part, however, shipping decisions are made largely on the basis of cost competitiveness. Shippers will choose the least expensive route and mode of transportation. In that respect, the seaway's size restrictions often mitigate against use of the St. Lawrence–Great Lakes route. As ocean vessels continue to increase in size, the seaway route will become even less competitive.

Another impediment to growth in the amount of traffic through the system is the fact that it is only in operation for about nine months of the year. Firms using the seaway must switch to a different route during the winter months when the system is shut down and vessels can only travel down the St. Lawrence River as far as Montreal. Like the international shipping business, the interlake bulk cargo trade is similarly adversely affected by the winter shutdown. Firms that rely on the bulk freighters to supply them with coal, iron ore, stone, or petroleum products are forced to stockpile large quantities of the materials before the close of the shipping season, an expensive proposition, or they must arrange to have the raw materials they need shipped overland by rail, also an expensive alternative.

The length of the season on the Great Lakes has always been dictated by "Mother Nature." Somewhere between the middle of December and first of January each year, a curtain of snow and ice descends on the lakes, bringing shipping to a halt. Over the years, the industry has learned to anticipate when the onset of bitter winter weather would bring the season to a close, and companies have managed to get their ships off the lakes before the rivers and harbors have been covered with their first patina of unyielding ice. There are many instances, however, when nature has surprised the industry by lowering that icy curtain earlier than industry officials anticipated.

In 1926, the early onset of winter took the industry completely by surprise, stranding 150 ships in the ice at Sault Ste. Marie. The *Chief Wawatam*, a large railroad ferry that normally operated between St. Ignace and Mackinaw City, and five tugs worked night and day for three weeks to free the ships from the ice. While the frantic icebreaking activity was successful in freeing most of the ships, twenty-six remained locked in the ice of the St. Marys River all winter.

The following year, another early winter storm descended on the upper lakes. As temperatures hovered at 40° below zero, more than twenty Canadian freighters were trapped in the St. Marys. The convoy carried more than 6 million bushels of grain destined for storage facilities in eastern Canada. The ships were not able to complete their voyages until they were freed from the ice the following April. A total of 247 ships and 5,000 sailors were trapped at the Soo by that early December freeze in 1927. It took ten days of icebreaking and a lull in the harsh weather to free the ships so they could finish the last voyage of the season. Those must have been exciting days for the residents of the Soo. Local farmers and shipkeepers used sleds to haul groceries and other provisions to the icebound ships, and many of the sailors walked ashore over the ice to buy tobacco.[10] Sailors being sailors, it's likely that the local saloons also did a land-office business before the ships were able to get underway.

Nature also controls the start of the season in the spring. Industry officials have learned that winter normally gives up its icy grip on the lakes by April 1, so that is when most of the fleets schedule their first ships to leave the lay-up docks, although some limited shipping activity often begins on the lower lakes in early March. It's common for ships to experience some ice problems in the rivers and harbors during the early part of the season, but the Coast Guard and private tug operators normally have their vessels standing by to lend assistance so that freighters don't experience serious delays. On occasion, however, nature also asserts its dominance in the spring.

Just after the navigation season opened in April 1984, several days of strong northerly winds pushed floating ice from Lake Huron down into the narrow St. Clair River, turning it into what one Great Lakes captain aptly described as a "giant Sno Cone." From the Blue Water Bridge at Port Huron to Lake St. Clair, the river was packed with broken chunks of ice that in some places extended all of the way from the surface to the riverbed. Traffic on the lakes was brought to a virtual standstill for a period of about ten days.

The Coast Guard closed the river to vessel traffic, forcing more than ninety ships to go to anchor, while U.S. and Canadian icebreakers worked to break through the ice jam. The largest concentration of ships was caught on the southside of the jam, including many freighters that had just left their lay-up docks on Lake Erie and a number of saltwater ships making their first trips of the season into the lakes. Ships waiting to go up the river filled every available anchorage in the Detroit River and along the north shore of Lake Erie, all the way to the Welland Canal. When the icebreakers finally broke the jam and the ice began to flow down into Lake St. Clair, the river flushed itself out in a matter of a few hours. Before that happened, though, the delays had cost shipping companies millions of dollars.

After succumbing to nature's limits on season length for a hundred years, Great Lakes shipping officials began in the late 1960s to argue that extending the navigational season was feasible from both the economic and engineering perspectives. While

Winter normally brings shipping to a halt on the Great Lakes around Christmas time. Here five self-unloaders of the USS Great Lakes Fleet are laid up at their home port of Rogers City, Michigan. (Author's collection)

there had been talk for decades of extending the season, the stage was finally set in the late sixties to do battle with the forces of nature. The 1967 shipping season was extended until January 3, 1968, ten days to two weeks longer than normal. It was a conservative beginning, but it launched a program that would become the central focus of the industry for the next decade, the most aggressive project ever undertaken by shipping interests on the lakes.

A number of factors converged to make the winter navigation project a reality: a healthy U.S. economy, the development of taconite, a belief that technology could overcome nature, a movement within the U.S. steel industry toward increased efficiency, and the emergence of a strong leader within the Great Lakes industry. While it is impossible to rank the factors in terms of their order of importance in bringing about winter navigation, it is safe to say that if any one of them had been absent the program would probably not have been implemented.

By 1967, the U.S. was deeply embroiled in Viet-

nam, and the war was stimulating the domestic economy. In addition to the high levels of military spending, billions were being poured into the economy each year by the extensive "Great Society" social programs that had emerged during the Kennedy and Johnson administrations. The budgets of government agencies swelled, including those of the Corps of Engineers and the Coast Guard. Government agencies, in fact, went looking for programs that would allow them to justify further staff and budget increases.

Buoyed by the war and record domestic auto sales, the steel industry was making a strong recovery from the slump it had experienced after the Korean War. Facing increasingly strong competition from foreign steel producers, however, the industry also began to search for opportunities to cut production costs. In the Great Lakes region, executives in the iron ore, steel, and shipping industries had long been aware of the costs that resulted from the lack of year-round shipping on the lakes. Expensive capital

The powerful Canadian icebreaker *DeGrosseliers* operates off Sarnia, Ontario, to clear an ice jam that brought vessel traffic to a virtual standstill in the St. Clair River in April 1984. (Author's collection)

equipment sat idle three to four months of the year, and companies incurred significant additional expense as the result of having to stockpile vital raw materials or ship by rail during the winter months.

Until 1955, it was virtually impossible to ship iron ore during the winter months because the moisture laden raw ore froze in stockpiles and couldn't be loaded into ships. If you could load it, you faced the prospect that it would freeze in the hold of the ship while in transit. With the development of benefication technology in 1955, however, more and more ore began to be shipped as taconite, marble-sized pellets of concentrated ore that were almost totally free of moisture. Unlike raw ore, taconite was relatively easy to handle during the winter months, eliminating one of the historic impediments to year-round operations on the lakes.

While the development of benefication technology in the 1950s eliminated one stumbling block to year-round shipping on the lakes, the 1960s saw the emergence of a national mindset that was based on a belief that we were technologically capable of solving any problem. That belief was most clearly evidenced in the U.S. space program and our national commitment to go to the moon by the early 1970s. Our national fascination with the seemingly infinite capabilities of our technology triggered high levels of spending on research and development in both the public and private sectors. Government and business leaders operated on the conviction that given enough resources, we could solve any problem with our technology. In addition to our investments in the space program, billions were poured into research and development projects intended to find solutions to a plethora of problems in fields like education, health care, unemployment, and poverty.

In that environment, the inherent difficulties of operating ships on the Great Lakes during the winter months became just one more example of a problem that could be solved through the application of our virtually unrestrained technological capability. What was needed, industry officials claimed, was a demonstration project that would allow us to identify the problems and develop solutions to them. Given the plentitude of federal resources, agencies like the Corps of Engineers and Coast Guard were very willing to get involved in projects that would allow them to dip deeper into the largess of the government coffers. New programs meant new personnel, more equipment, larger budgets, and greater prestige for the agencies involved, factors commonly associated with "success" within bureaucratic organizations.

What was needed was a strong leader to emerge within the Great Lakes maritime community—someone of vision who would realize that the unique circumstances of the time had set the stage for a program like winter navigation, someone who could muster the disparate resources available into a unified assault on the snow and ice that had for so long thwarted the industry on the lakes. That leader emerged during the 1960s in the person of Christian Beukema, vice president of U.S. Steel.

Beukema joined U.S. Steel in 1940 at its limestone quarry at Rogers City, Michigan. Moving steadily up through the management ranks, he became the giant steelmaker's vice president for ore, limestone and lake shipping in the early sixties. From his office at corporate headquarters in Pittsburgh, Beukema controlled U.S. Steel's iron ore and limestone mining operations and the U.S.S. Great Lakes Fleet, successor to the famous Pittsburgh fleet, at that time, the largest American fleet on the lakes.

Essentially, Beukema was responsible for insuring that adequate supplies of iron ore and stone were supplied to U.S. Steel's mills. With mounting pressure to reduce operating costs, he was also saddled with the responsibility to see that the raw materials were delivered at the lowest possible cost. In a 1971 article in *Seaway Review*, Beukema told why he became an advocate of winter navigation:

The U.S. Steel dedication to extended season navigation has been born out of the necessity that has marked all recent cost reduction efforts in the domestic steel industry. One does not need to belabor the extreme competition posture of the steel industry as it battles against the inroads made even in Great Lakes markets by foreign steels produced by low-cost foreign labor and floated to this country by low-cost foreign flag operators.

One thing has become abundantly clear to U.S. Steel—it must maximize utilization of its most efficient facilities to attain optimum costs. The transportation of iron units from Lake Superior became a likely area for increased performance when U.S. Steel commenced operating its first taconite pellet plant in Minnesota late in 1967. For the first time in history we had tonnage of iron ore to move that was of sufficiently low moisture content that frozen cargo was no threat.[11]

Although lakes' shipping companies were generally lukewarm about extending the navigation season, powerful U.S. Steel moved ahead unilaterally. Beukema and other U.S. Steel officials found both the Corps of Engineers and Coast Guard eager to participate in an extended-season demonstration project. Corps support was essential because the locks at Sault Ste. Marie would have to be kept open beyond the normal mid-December closing date, and the Coast Guard was needed to provide icebreaking support.

Following the modest extended-season success during the winter of 1967–68, ships were committed to winter operations at the end of the 1968 and 1969 seasons. The vessels operated until January 7 the first year and until around January 14 the second year with no significant problems.

In 1970, the Lake Carriers Association joined with U.S. Steel to lobby for federal funds that would allow the demonstration program to be continued and expanded. An amendment to the Rivers and Harbors Act of 1970 appropriated $6.5 million to fund a three-year program to determine whether it was feasible and economical to extend the shipping season on the lakes. The program was not without its opponents. Utility companies operating hydroelectric plants feared that icebreaking activities would cause flows of broken ice to clog the water intakes of their power-generating dams. Environmentalists around the lakes expressed concern that the fragile ecology of the shoreline areas would be damaged by ice flows and propeller wash concentrated under the shoreline ice cover. Labor unions representing personnel crewing the freighters, while not overtly opposing the demonstration project, had reservations based on safety considerations. They pointed out that the normal risks associated with vessel operations on the lakes were compounded during winter navigation.

Further concern about the program was expressed by residents of islands in the St. Marys River—Sugar, Lime, and Drummond—and of Harsens Island in the St. Clair River. During the normal navigational season, residents of the islands travel to and from the mainland by ferries. During the winter when ferries cannot operate, they drive to or from the mainland in cars or on snowmobiles, traveling across the solid ice cover of the rivers. Vessel operations in the rivers during the winter months would disrupt that ice cover. To allow island residents to get to and from the mainland while the extended-season operations were underway, a commitment was made to keep the ferries in service throughout the winter months. Significant problems were encountered, however, and there were many instances when the ferries could not operate or when they could not shuttle vehicles between the islands and the mainland. As a result, island residents were among the most vehement opponents of the winter navigation program.

Operation Taconite, as it was known, commenced at the end of the regular 1970 shipping season. The expanded project was under the control of a Winter Navigation Board, which consisted of officials of the Corps of Engineers, Coast Guard, St. Lawrence Seaway Development Corporation, National Oceanic and Atmospheric Administration, Maritime Administration, Department of the Interior, Environmental Protection Agency, Federal Power Commission, and the Great Lakes Commission. Some technical support was also provided by the National Aeronautics and Space Administration and the Atomic Energy Commission, while representatives of other interests, such as labor, were invited to participate in all board activities.

During the three years of the demonstration program authorized in the 1970 legislation, encompass-

ing the winter seasons of 1971–72, 1972–73, and 1973–74, the season on the upper lakes was extended into the month of February for the first time in history. Tonnages hauled after the normal close of the shipping season ranged from 4 million tons in 1971–72 to more than 10 million tons in 1973–74. Iron ore accounted for more than half of the total. The demonstration program was eventually extended through the winter of 1978–79. Congress appropriated a total of $13.7 million for the program, although $2.3 million authorized for activities on the St. Lawrence Seaway was never spent.

The program's greatest success came during the winter of 1974–75 when vessel operations never ceased on the upper lakes. For the first time in history, the lakes' industry could claim a twelve-month season. Industry officials began to shift from talking about *winter navigation* to using the terminology *year-round shipping*, subtle testimony to the industry's optimistic vision of the program's future. That optimism was reinforced during the 1975–76 season when, for the second year in a row, the system was kept open during the winter months, and ships participating in the program moved 15 million tons of cargo. A slight setback occurred during the 1976–77 season, however, when unusually severe weather forced the demonstration program to come to a halt during the month of February, resulting in only an eleven-month season. During the final two years of the program, the winters of 1977–78 and 1978–79, ships again operated continuously on the upper lakes, although tonnages failed to reach the record set during the 1975–76 season. The program was abandoned at the end of the 1978–79 season.

During the eight years of the congressionally authorized demonstration program, more than 4,000 winter transits were made through the Soo Locks. Extended season shipments through the locks totalled more than 41 million tons, averaging about 5 million tons a year. The program was also responsible for additional shipments on Lakes Michigan, Huron, and Erie, and some modest amounts of winter cargo moved through the Welland Canal, Lake Ontario, and the Lake Ontario-Montreal section of the St. Lawrence system. The Winter Navigation Board calculated that the additional cargo moved during the winter months had a market value of more than $2.5 billion.[12]

The icebreaker *Mackinaw* passing the U.S. Coast Guard
station at Sault Ste. Marie, Michigan. Buoys that have
been pulled from Lake Superior and the St. Marys River
before the onset of winter can be seen on the dock and in
the slip in the foreground. (Institute for Great Lakes Research, Bowling Green State University)

The end of year-round navigation came not because the program had proven to be unsuccessful, but as a result of a serious downturn in the U.S. economy. During 1980, the demand for iron ore, coal, grain, and stone declined dramatically. Total shipments of those commodities on the lakes fell by 32 million tons between 1979 and 1980. Iron ore tonnages dropped most precipitously, from 92 million tons in 1979 to 72 million tons in 1980. With many of the Great Lakes bulk freighters spending the 1980 season laid-up at docks around the lakes, the industry lost interest in operating ships beyond the normal close of the season.

Whether the program would have been continued if demand for raw materials had remained high, however, is questionable. Although the Winter Navigation Board labelled the program a success in their final report to Congress, it had come under increasing fire from critics. The loudest opposition to the winter navigation program came from residents of the islands in the St. Marys and St. Clair Rivers who experienced difficulty in getting to and from the mainland where they worked, shopped, or went to school; environmentalists who feared that the ecosystems of the rivers would be damaged as a result of winter operations; and some Great Lakes sailors who questioned the safety of operating vessels during the harsh winter months. In the final analysis, those groups of opponents banded together to challenge the program on economic grounds. The program, they charged, largely benefitted only the shipping and steel companies, while the costs were being borne by the American taxpayers.

Economic analyses of the winter navigation program done under contract for the Winter Navigation Board touted benefit-cost ratios of 6:1, meaning that six dollars in benefits resulted from each dollar spent on the program. Those claims were seriously challenged by opponents of the program, though, and in their final report to Congress, the Winter Navigation Board touched only briefly, and carefully, on the economic benefits of the program, preferring instead to tout the non-economic gains that resulted from the demonstration project—and there were many. For the first time ever, the shipping companies and government agencies involved in the project were able to demonstrate that cargo could be moved on the upper lakes on a year-round basis. We

now know that we could keep the system open if we had to, such as in time of war.

We also learned a great deal about the technology needed to operate ships in the ice. Most of the project funds were used to develop bubbler systems to keep harbors and locks from icing over, ice booms to keep channels from being clogged by floating ice, buoys and other navigational aids that could survive in the ice, systems for improved ice and weather forecasting, and improved icebreaking techniques. Many studies were also conducted, including tests of a variety of sophisticated navigational systems and explorations into the impact of winter navigation on the environment. We now know what to anticipate if we ever again feel compelled to operate our ships in the winter. The knowledge we gained seems to have justified the costs of the project. Just knowing that we can operate year-round if we have to is probably worth the $11.4 million spent over the eight years.

On the other hand, the project fell short of proving that year-round shipping is economically feasible under normal circumstances. Most of the program's benefits accrued to the shipping and steel industries. Fleets participating in the program were able to carry some additional tonnage during the winter period that would otherwise have been moved by rail or not moved at all. They were also able to avoid the expense of laying-up their ships in the winter and paying unemployment compensation to their crews. The steel companies, though, were the real winners. They avoided the expenses of stockpiling raw materials on their docks prior to the end of the normal navigation season or paying the higher costs of shipping them during the winter months by rail, which is considerably more costly than using water transportation.

Implementation of the winter navigation program on an ongoing basis would constitute taxpayer subsidy of the shipping and steel industries. The program could not function without support from government agencies, like the Corps of Engineers and Coast Guard. If the shipping companies, in particular, had to pay for those services, either from government agencies or private businesses, winter operations would clearly be a losing proposition for them.

In the end, however, the question of whether winter navigation—year-round navigation—could be economically justified was a moot issue. With tonnages on the lakes dropping to their lowest levels since the Great Depression of the 1930s, the shipping companies lost interest in the program. They had trouble just trying to find enough cargo to keep their ships operating during the normal April–December season.

While the Winter Navigation Board had been headed by the Corps of Engineers, no government agency was more involved in the program than the Coast Guard. The Coast Guard has a broad range of maritime responsibilities, and virtually all of them came into play during the extended shipping seasons. The Ninth Coast Guard District, headquartered in Cleveland, has responsibility for the entire Great Lakes area. The Ninth District was represented on the Winter Navigation Board by the district commander, who is always a rear admiral. During the eight years of the demontration project, several different persons commanded the Ninth District and represented the Coast Guard on the board.

One of the Coast Guard's primary areas of responsibility is marine inspection, which, in the case of the commercial shipping industry involves both the inspection of vessels and vessel personnel. Coast Guard personnel inspect all commercial vessels annually at the start of the shipping season to insure that they are seaworthy and in compliance with regulations. Every five years, they perform a more extensive inspection of commercial vessels, which requires that ships be drydocked so that a thorough hull examination can be performed.

Vessels selected for participation in the winter navigation program were given an additional Coast Guard inspection before the start of the winter season to make sure that they were prepared to face the rigors of ice navigation. Since the 1975 loss of the *Str. Edmund Fitzgerald*, Coast Guard inspectors have also performed pre-November checks on many vessels. To eliminate the need to delay the vessels during the busy fall sailing season, the pre-November inspections are conducted while the vessels are in operation by Coast Guard "riders." Their primary interest is to insure that required lifesaving equipment is in good working order.

All merchant marine personnel are certificated or licensed by the Coast Guard for the positions they are authorized to hold aboard ship. Entry-level certificates, or tickets, for unlicensed sailors are issued basically on request, but upgrading to Able Bodied Seaman, Oiler, Qualified Member of the Engine Department, or officer's status requires a combination of documented experience and passage of an exam administered by the Coast Guard. Officer's exams are particularly comprehensive and are normally scheduled over a three- to five-day period.

The Coast Guard also operates a number of search and rescue (SAR) stations around the lakes, serving both commercial shipping and recreational boaters. The SAR stations are staffed on a twenty-four-hour basis during the boating season, with personnel monitoring VHF channel 16, the international distress channel. They operate rescue vessels that can be dispatched to aid vessels experiencing problems. The SAR stations can also call for assistance from Coast Guard air stations that operate both helicopters and fixed-wing aircraft in support of search and rescue operations. In addition, the Coast Guard operates Soo Control, a vessel traffic center that controls ship movements in the St. Marys River. Located on the riverbank just below the locks at the Soo, the station personnel are responsible for coordination of vessel traffic in the river channels. Ships transitting the river must report their positions to the Coast Guard at a number of specified points on the river. The radio operators at Soo Control then keep navigational personnel aboard the ships informed of other vessel traffic in the narrow and winding river, reducing the likelihood of collisions.

If a vessel becomes disabled in the river, Soo Control personnel are authorized to restrict vessel movements until the hazard has been eliminated. They can also shut the river down to vessel traffic during periods of inclement weather, such as fog, high winds, or snow. With the St. Marys River representing the primary bottleneck during the winter navigation operations, personnel at Soo Control played a crucial role in coordinating vessel movements. They provided ships with detailed information on ice conditions in the river, the availability of icebreaker assistance, locations and progress of other ships transitting the system, and the status of aids to navigation, such as buoys and range lights.

Aids to navigation were a particular problem area during the winter navigation program. Maintained by the Coast Guard, the aids to navigation define the narrow channels of the rivers and harbors around the lakes. Most of the aids are buoys that are anchored along the sides of the channels, indicating the limits of the deep water. Some of the buoys are lighted so they are visible at night; others are equipped with radar beacons, or racons, so they show up on a ship's radar scopes.

The floating buoys are subject to being crushed and sunk or carried away by ice during the winter, so most of them are removed near the end of the sailing season and replaced in the early spring by Coast Guard buoy tenders stationed around the lakes. Because of the inherent danger of attempting to navigate the rivers without the assistance of buoys, however, one major aspect of the Coast Guard's involvement in the winter navigation program was to develop a system of aids to navigation that could function during the winter months. This was a major challenge for the Coast Guard and led to the development and testing of a variety of buoys and anchoring systems specially designed to withstand the onslaught of ice. Maintaining adequate buoyage in the rivers and channels was a problem throughout the winter navigation program and led to the construction of additional permanent aids to navigation: lights located atop concrete platforms built on the riverbed along the edges of the channel at key locations.

Ships participating in the winter navigation program also relied heavily on the system of range lights and leading lights that the Coast Guard maintains along the river systems, the most extensive of which is on the St. Marys River. A leading light is merely a light mounted on a shore tower in line with the course for a particular stretch of river. Navigational personnel on the ships can line up on the light to help them stay on course and in the middle of the river channel. Range lights are an even more effective aid to navigation. They consist of two lighted towers located at the end of the courseline for a section of river. The towers are spaced some distance apart, so that when the ship is properly lined up on the course the light farthest away appears right over the top of the closer light. If the ship strays to the left or right of the channel, the lights will appear to separate. If the front light appears to be to the right of the rear light, the navigator knows that the ship has strayed to the left side of the channel, and vice versa.

The range light system, in use worldwide, began on Lake Huron in 1860. Dewitt Brawn, the fifteen-year-old son of the keeper of the lighthouse located at the mouth of the Saginaw River, erected two towers in line with the channel of the river. At night, the young boy would hoist a lantern to the top of each tower so ship captains could line up with them when coming into the river. The idea caught on rapidly and soon spread throughout the world maritime community.

The U.S. and Canadian Coast Guards have also operated an extensive system of lighthouses around the lakes, the first of which was erected at the mouth of the Niagara River in 1804. More than 150 lighthouses were eventually put into operation along the coasts of the five lakes. Once manned by Coast Guard lighthouse keepers, all of the lights have now been converted to automatic operation.

Until 1971, the Coast Guard also operated lightships, or floating lighthouses, at key locations along the Great Lakes shipping channels. The last of the lightships, the *Huron*, was retired from service in 1971 after marking the approach to the St. Clair River at the southern end of Lake Huron for thirty-five years. The last of twenty-two such ships that once served Great Lakes mariners, the 97-foot ship is now permanently moored at Port Huron, a relic of bygone days of proud service to the ships and sailors on the lakes.

The most impressive vessel in the Coast Guard fleet on the lakes is the venerable icebreaker *Mackinaw*, launched in 1944. Stationed on the Cheboygan River, just south of the Straits of Mackinac, the 290-foot "Mac" was the only icebreaker assigned to the lakes for a period of thirty-five years, although many other Coast Guard vessels have ice-strengthened hulls and can perform some limited icebreaking. With a beam of 75 feet and 10,000 horsepower, the *Mackinaw* is capable of opening a track through several feet of solid ice wide enough for most Great Lakes freighters to pass through. During winter navigation, the *Mackinaw* was regularly assisted by polar-class icebreakers temporarily assigned to the lakes from the Coast Guard's saltwater fleet, including the *Edisto*, *Westwind*, and *Southwind*.

During the final year of the demonstration project, the Ninth District also acquired the first of five new bay-class icebreakers, which are now stationed around the lakes. The bay-class boats are really icebreaking tugs, only 140 feet long, 38 feet wide, and

The now-retired Coast Guard lightship *Huron* on-station at the lower end of Lake Huron, near the entrance to the St. Clair River. The *Huron,* officially Lightship 103, was the only U.S. lightship with a black hull. (Institute for Great Lakes Research, Bowling Green State University)

Shortly after its launching in 1945, the Coast Guard ice-breaker *Mackinaw* assists four ocean freighters making a passage from Duluth to Chicago through moderate ice. The *"Mac"* is capable of forcing a channel through solid ice up to three feet thick. (Institute for Great Lakes Research, Bowling Green State University)

powered by 2,500 horsepower diesel engines. While the new icebreakers can't tackle ice as thick as the *Mackinaw* can, they do represent state-of-the-art technology in small vessel icebreaking. Each of the bay-class vessels can break through 18 to 20 inches of hard ice. Their hulls are lubricated by air that is forced out of holes along their keels, reducing friction between their hulls and the ice they encounter.

While the new generation of icebreakers were a welcome addition to the Coast Guard arsenal on the lakes, they are dwarfed by the newest icebreakers added to the Canadian Coast Guard fleet on the lakes. The *Pierre Radisson*, launched in 1978, and the *Des Groseilliers*, built in 1982, are arctic-class III icebreakers, among the most powerful in the world. The two ships are 322 feet long, with beams of 65 feet. Each is powered by six 16-cylinder diesel engines that generate a total of 13,600 horsepower. The only ships on the lakes more powerful are 1,000-foot long freighters, and they are more than three times longer than the two icebreakers. For their size, then, the *Radisson* and *Des Groseilliers* are the most powerful ships on the lakes.

The two ships can cruise at more than 14 miles an hour and can move steadily through 3 feet of solid ice. They are equipped with the latest navigational equipment, and both carry helicopters on board for ice surveillance and search and rescue work. The two new vessels are part of a Canadian icebreaker fleet that includes a total of nine vessels. They range in size from 109 feet up to the 322 feet of the *Radisson* and *Des Groseilliers*.

Some icebreaking on the lakes is also done by private tug companies that operate out of the major ports, although their efforts are primarily restricted to work in private harbors and channels. Before the advent of bowthrusters, the harbor tug business flourished around the lakes, providing maneuvering assistance to ships in rivers and harbors. In recent years, however, U.S. and Canadian lakers seldom take tugs, so most of the tug companies are primarily involved in assisting saltwater vessels that have less maneuverability than their Great Lakes counterparts.

The largest of the U.S. tug companies include: the Great Lakes Towing Company, a Cleveland-based firm that dates to 1899 and operates forty-four tugs at ten Great Lakes ports; Republic Towing, with six tugs stationed at Chicago and Duluth; Gaelic Tug Boat Company, operating ten tugs at Detroit and Toledo; and Selvick Marine, with nine tugs serving Milwaukee, Sturgeon Bay, and Green Bay, Wisconsin. Several other U.S. tug firms, including Canonie at Muskegon, Michigan, and Hannah Marine in Chicago, are primarily engaged in towing cargo barges between Great Lakes ports.

In addition to the mailboat and the icebreakers and tugs that provide vital support services to the bulk industry on the lakes, one other category of vessels deserves to be mentioned— the *bum boats*. Once a common sight at virtually every major port on the lakes, only one of the floating general stores remains in service today, at the twin ports of Superior, Wisconsin, and Duluth, Minnesota. Bum boats are so named because off-watch sailors often "bum around" on them. They tie up alongside freighters at the loading and unloading docks. On board, sailors can purchase everything from cold beer to work clothes, magazines, snacks, jewelry, film, and toilet articles. With docks often located miles from shipping areas and crewmembers not always able to get away from their ship, the bum boats have provided a vital service to sailors for many years. The remaining bum boat operators are barely eking out a living, however, and they may soon disappear from the lakes altogether.

One final support service of vital importance to the shipping industry on the Great Lakes is provided by the shipyards that service the freighters. While there were once dozens of shipyards scattered around the lakes, only five yards currently serve the large ships. On the American side there are three shipyards. The largest is Bay Shipbuilding in Sturgeon Bay, Wisconsin, which is also the only yard on the lakes with a drydock large enough to handle thousand-footers. The last lakes' ships built at Bay were the thousand-foot *Columbia Star*, launched in 1981, and the tug-barge tanker built for Amoco's Great Lakes operations in 1982. Since then the firm has been involved in repair work on lakers, conversions of several straight-deckers to self-unloaders, and the construction of ships for ocean service. No new vessels have been launched at Bay since 1987. Other shipyards on the U.S. side of the lakes include Toledo Shipbuilding in Toledo, Ohio, and Fraser Shipyard in Superior, Wisconsin. Both yards are primarily involved in repair work on lakers, rather than new construction.

The "bumboat" *Kaner I* alongside the cement boat *S. T. Crapo* at LaFarge Corporation's terminal in Superior, Wisconsin. The bum boat is a floating general store that serves merchant seaman. (Author's collection)

Bay Shipbuilding at Sturgeon Bay, Wisconsin, during the winter of 1989–90. The ten ships undergoing repairs include, from left to right, the *Burns Harbor, Joseph L. Block, U.S.C.G.C. Mackinaw, Kiisla, John G. Munson, American Mariner, Sam Laud, Sparrows Point, Paul H. Townsend,* and *Herbert C. Jackson.* The *Sparrows Point* and the Finnish tanker *Kiisla* had both suffered serious bottom damage while operating in the ice late in the 1989 season. (Bay Shipbuilding)

Only two Canadian yards survive on the Great Lakes: Port Arthur Shipbuilding at Thunder Bay, Ontario, and Port Weller Dry Docks, located at St. Catherines, Ontario, on the Welland Canal. The last new Canadian laker, the *M/V Paterson*, was launched in 1985 at the now-defunct Collingwood Shipyard in Collingwood, Ontario.

With no new freighters on the drawing boards, and only limited repair and retrofit projects available each year because of the reduced number of ships in operation, the remaining Great Lakes shipyards are struggling to survive. The demise of the once strong shipbuilding industry on the lakes is beginning to cause problems for the U.S. and Canadian fleets, particularly those U.S. fleets operating thousand-footers, who are finding it increasingly difficult to schedule their ships for drydockings. Like the fleets on the lakes, the shipyards, bum boat operators, tug companies, and even the firm operating the mailboat are experiencing rough sailing because of the downturn in trade on the lakes. Even the Corps of Engineers and the Coast Guard have faced sizable budget cuts as a result of concern over the federal deficit and reduced demand for their services on the lakes.

In the heyday of the Great Lakes industry, thousands of persons made good livings, or even got wealthy, providing services to the freighters. Few of them remain in business today, and those who have weathered the decline in the industry are unsure about the future. Next year, they too may disappear from the scene.

Notes

1. Harlan Hatcher and Erich A. Walter, *A Pictorial History of the Great Lakes* (New York: Bonanza Books, 1963), 248.
2. Ibid., 263.
3. Ibid.
4. John W. Larson, *Essayons: A History of the Detroit District U.S. Army Corps of Engineers* (Detroit: U.S. Army Corps of Engineers, 1981), 55.
5. Jacques LesStrang, *Seaway* (Seattle: Salisbury Press, 1976), 80.
6. Hatcher, 257.
7. Jacqueline Rabe, "The Four Welland Canals," *Telescope* (Nov.-Dec. 1985): 147–51.
8. LesStrang, 19–77.
9. Jacques LesStrang, ed., "The Directions of Change," *Seaway Review* (Oct.–Dec. 1986): 96.
10. Hatcher, 112–13.
11. Christian Beukema, "The Demonstration," *Seaway Review* (Summer 1971): 11.
12. Details regarding the winter navigation program were drawn from the following publications: *Final Survey Report on Navigation Season Extension for the Great Lakes and St. Lawrence Seaway* (Fort Belvoir, VA: U.S. Army Corps of Engineers, 1981), and *Final Survey Study for Great Lakes and St. Lawrence Seaway Navigation Extension* (Detroit: U.S. Army Corps of Engineers, 1979).

9

A Guide for Boatwatchers
and Armchair Captains

Down through the ages, the fascination and romance of ships has captivated the thousands who have watched the leviathans plow through calm or troubled global waters.
—Rev. Peter J. Van der Linden,
Great Lakes Ships We Remember, 1979

It is often said that baseball is America's national pastime, but that isn't really true. Few of us actually play baseball; what we do is watch baseball being played by others. *Watching* is undoubtedly the favorite pursuit of people in the U.S. and Canada. We watch sporting events, theater, ballet, television, birds, and even boats. We derive great pleasure from being spectators, and the more we know about whatever it is we are watching, the more enjoyment we get from the time we spend in the pursuit. Baseball and hockey are thrilling spectator sports, but if you don't know the teams, the players, the rules of the games, the plays, or the jargon used in the sport it can be a meaningless, even boring, experience. The same is true of *boatwatching*, a popular pastime along the shores of the Great Lakes.

If you have enough patience or a good pair of binoculars, it is possible to see freighters passing from virtually anywhere along the shores of the five lakes and the rivers that connect them. Most of the upbound and downbound shipping lanes are located within sight of shore, although when seen from the beach the ships may appear as little more than silhouettes passing along the horizon. Fortunately, there are many places where you can get a close-up view of lakers or even walk the decks of ships that have been retired from service on the lakes. In addition, there are a number of excellent maritime museums filled to overflowing with marine memorabilia, and many excellent books that have been written about shipping on the lakes.

As you set about learning the "players" in the Great Lakes shipping industry, you will find that while most of the ships operating on the lakes are part of either the U.S. or Canadian bulk fleets, there are also many foreign vessels that call at ports around the lakes. The easiest way to identify a ship's nation of registry is by the flag, or ensign, that is flown at the vessel's stern. If the ship is not flying the familiar stars and stripes of the U.S. or the distinctive Canadian flag with its red maple leaf, the ship is of foreign registry and entered the lakes through the St. Lawrence Seaway. Don't be misled if you see a U.S. or Canadian flag being flown from a mast on the ship's bow or above the pilothouse. When operating in foreign waters, ships always fly the flag of the host nation as a sign of respect. On the lakes, U.S. ships will fly the Canadian flag at their bow, while Canadian ships will fly the American flag. Foreign vessels will generally fly the flag of the country in whose waters they are operating or the flag of the country at whose ports they will next be calling.

Several other flags may be flown on the forward mast of a U.S. or Canadian laker. The ships quite often fly their fleet flag, and it is also common for them to sport a triangular blue pennant with white numbers on it. This is the personal flag of the vessel's master, and the number is his or her membership number in the International Association of Shipmasters, an organization for licensed captains.

It used to be quite easy to pick out foreign ships on the lakes, because most of them had their pilothouses and all crew accommodations located at their sterns, while U.S. and Canadian bulk freighters traditionally had their pilothouses and crew accommodations at their bows. Since 1973, however, all of the new U.S. and Canadian freighters have been built in the typical saltwater configuration, making it more difficult to tell the ships apart. There are still a lot of pre-1973 lakers around, with the traditional pilothouse at the bow, and they are all either U.S. or Canadian.

Many of the saltwater ships that come into the system have cargo cranes mounted on their decks. The cranes are used to load and unload breakbulk cargo, such as pallets of bagged grain or coils of steel. Since the U.S. and Canadian ships on the lakes carry only bulk cargo, they are not equipped with cargo cranes.

Even the ship's name can be a clue to whether a ship is a laker or a "saltie." While ship names are generally written in English, the standard language for international marine commerce, ocean vessels often have "foreign sounding" names or the name will be written in both English and the language of the country the ship operates out of. Japanese ships, for example, will almost always have their names written out in both English and Japanese. The name of the ship will be painted on both sides of the bow, on the stern, and on nameboards located above the pilothouse.

Below the name on the stern will be the vessel's hailing port. The hailing port indicates where the ship has been registered with government maritime officials, such as the Coast Guard in the U.S. or Canada, but it doesn't necessarily mean that it is the vessel's home port or the port the ship actually operates out of. It is very common for ships to operate under "flags of convenience," such as those of Panama or Liberia, even though the vessels may be owned by firms in the U.S. or Europe. The ships may operate out of New York, Piraeus, or Hamburg, but they are registered in Third World countries to take advantage of their relaxed manning and safety requirements.

Even on the lakes, hailing ports can be misleading. Many U.S. lakers show Wilmington, Delaware, as their hailing port, because registry there allows shipowners to take advantage of the state's favorable tax climate and minimal regulations of business operations. One ship in the U.S. fleet, the *M/V Presque Isle*, shows Los Angeles as its hailing port, even though it is impossible for the thousand-footer to leave the lakes. Los Angeles is, however, the location of the headquarters of Litton Industries, owners of the *Presque Isle*.

Most U.S. and Canadian ships operating on the lakes will fall into one of two categories: they will either be straight-deckers or self-unloaders. Unless a straight-decker has the traditional pilothouse forward, it is easy to confuse it with the saltwater ships that come into the system. If you see a self-unloader, on the other hand, it is almost certainly a U.S. or Canadian ship, even if it doesn't have a forward pilothouse. While self-unloaders are becoming more common in the ocean trades, few foreign self-unloaders come into the lakes.

Most self-unloaders can easily be identified by the long, skeleton-like unloading booms on their decks. Some of the thousand-footers, however, were built with unloading booms that run from port to starboard within the ship's stern, and they are not as obvious to boatwatchers. Remember, all thousand-footers are self-unloaders. If you don't see a boom on deck, it has a transverse boom stowed at the stern just below the main deck level. With the exception of a few ships that are engaged in the grain trade, most U.S. lakers in operation today are self-unloaders, but straight-deckers are still the mainstay of many of the Canadian fleets. In the grain trade, straight-deckers are more efficient than self-unloaders because they have a significantly higher cubic carrying capacity, the critical factor in carrying lightweight commodities like grain.

In addition to the self-unloaders and straight-deckers, boatwatchers on the lakes will also see cement boats and tankers. Almost all cement boats have grey hulls, which mask the cement dust that settles on them when loading and unloading. In addition, they do not have the normal large, rectangular hatches lining their decks. They load through small, round hatches that match up with the spouts on the loading facilities at the cement plants so that the cement is not exposed to moisture.

Most U.S. and Canadian tankers are fairly small ships, among the smallest currently operating on the lakes. They can easily be identified because their decks are a tangle of piping used to load and unload liquid bulk products, and there are generally a lot of signs on their decks to the effect that they are carrying flammable products and that no smoking is allowed.

The easiest way to identify which of the fourteen U.S. and fifteen Canadian fleets a particular ships belongs to is by the vessel's stack markings. Each fleet has a distinctive painting scheme for the stacks on their ships. The stacks can also give you some clue as to the age of the ship. Most ships built before World War II have very simple round stacks that look like large stovepipes, sloped backward a bit to achieve a limited degree of streamlining. Ships built between World War II and the early 1970s have stacks that are more streamlined. They are much larger, more elliptical than round, and their aft ends taper toward the vessel's stern. The top edges of the stacks are also often rounded off gracefully, rather than being blunt like those on the older boats.

Since the 1972 launching of the *M/V Stewart J. Cort*, most ships have been built with square stacks. The forward end of the new type of stack slopes back,

but the after ends are generally perpendicular to the deck that it is located on. While less attractive than the streamlined stacks that preceded them, they are less expensive to build and fit well with the blocky appearance of the newest ships.

Locations for Boatwatching

For boatwatchers interested in getting a close-up view of lake freighters in operation, the locks in the St. Lawrence, Welland, and at Sault Ste. Marie provide unequalled opportunities for spectators. Agencies operating the locks have constructed numerous viewing areas that allow spectators to get very close to the ships locking though. All three systems also operate visitor's centers with exhibits and films that explain the operation of the locks and their role in the shipping industry on the Great Lakes and St. Lawrence.

While most of the loading and unloading docks around the lakes are inaccessible to the general public, viewing areas have been provided at a few of the docks. Two of the best places to watch ships loading are at the twin ports of Duluth, Minnesota, and Superior, Wisconsin. Duluth and Superior are the busiest of the U.S. ports, accounting for a large share of the iron ore and grain that is shipped on the lakes, and the heavy port activity increases the probability that visitors will have an opportunity to see ships loading. Both ocean vessels and lakers can be viewed at numerous locations around the two ports, including a special viewing area that has been provided adjacent to the massive ore docks in Duluth by the Duluth, Missabe and Iron Range Railroad.

The chute-type docks in Marquette, Michigan, located adjacent to beautiful Presque Isle Park, may provide an even better opportunity to watch boats loading, although ship traffic at Marquette is not as heavy as at Duluth or Superior. The 1,200-foot dock at Marquette extends out from a public beach, so boatwatchers can get within a hundred feet of vessels loading there.

The ore docks at Escanaba, Michigan, on Bay de Noc, are not readily accessible to boatwatchers, but

The USS Great Lakes Fleet's *Str. John G. Munson,* a typical U.S. self-unloader, downbound on the St. Marys River. (Author's collection)

local residents can advise you on how to get close enough to the docks to get a good view. Visitors to northeastern Michigan should visit the Calcite limestone plant at Rogers City, home port for the self-unloading stone boats of the USS Great Lakes Fleet. Special viewing areas have been provided at both the quarry and the harbor where ships are loaded.

On the Canadian side, the port of Thunder Bay, Ontario, is the equivalent of Duluth and Superior on the U.S. side. Canadian lakers and foreign ships can be seen loading at many locations along the city's busy waterfront, site of the greatest concentration of grain terminals and elevators on the lakes.

One of the best places to watch boats on the lower lakes is at the Lorain Pellet Terminal at the mouth of the Black River in Lorain, Ohio. Lorain is unique in that it is both a loading and unloading port. Operated by LTV, the country's second largest steel company, the terminal was built as a transshipment facility for taconite destined for LTV's mills on the Cuyahoga River at Cleveland. Pellets are delivered to the terminal by thousand-footers that are too

The massive, blocky stern of the 1,000-foot *M/V Indiana Harbor,* showing its hailing port. Moored at the old ore dock at Ashland, Wisconsin, during a slack period for the industry, the ship dwarfs a 30-foot sailboat tied up behind it. (Author's collection)

Spectators along the Welland Canal watching the transit
of the "salty-laker" *M/V Prairie Harvest*. (St. Lawrence
Seaway Development Corporation)

large to navigate the serpentine Cuyahoga. At Lorain, the pellets discharged by the thousand-footers are loaded aboard smaller river-class vessels for the final leg of their trip to the LTV mills. The pellet terminal is a busy operation, and boatwatchers can view loading and unloading operations from the Black River bridge or from the riverbank directly across from the terminal. In both cases, spectators can get within several hundred feet of the ships, providing an exceptional view of both loading and unloading operations.

Toledo, Ohio, is another busy Lake Erie port that provides outstanding opportunities for boatwatchers. Like Lorain, both loading and unloading operations can be seen along the banks of the Maumee River that bisects downtown Toledo. Toledo is a major coal and grain port. Visitors can get an excellent view of ships loading grain at the terminals south of the downtown area, best viewed from the east bank of the Maumee. The coal docks are located near the mouth of the river, as is Toledo's international terminal. Ocean vessels can be seen loading and unloading general cargo at the terminal, which is best viewed from the opposite side of the river.

On Lake Michigan, there are numerous opportunities to view ships unloading at the ports of Burns Harbor, Indiana, and South Chicago, Illinois. They serve giant steel mills owned by Bethlehem Steel and U.S. Steel, respectively. Harbor tours of the expansive Burns Harbor port complex can be arranged through the Port Authority, operated by the Indiana Port Commission. There are also numerous excellent vantage points along the Calumet River from which boats can be watched making their ways slowly up or down the narrow and twisting river.

The best place to watch lake freighters unloading at Detroit is along the Rouge River, which connects Ford Motor Company's Rouge Steel complex with the Detroit River. Marine terminals along the Rouge receive shipments of stone, salt, liquid bulk, and cement, and spectators can often get bird's-eye views of the vessels from the numerous bridges that span the winding river. Several terminals along the Rouge and the nearby Detroit River also serve ocean vessels. Detroit is a major port for incoming shipments of steel, while the primary outbound cargo is scrap steel.

Across the mile-wide Detroit River, in Windsor, Ontario, both lake freighters and saltwater ships can be seen loading and unloading at the many terminals that line the waterfront. Like Detroit, Windsor handles a full-range of products, both inbound and outbound. South of the downtown area is a terminal complex that includes a modern grain elevator where agricultural products grown in southern Ontario are loaded aboard foreign vessels for shipment to international markets. The Windsor Harbour Commission, located in the Holiday Inn in downtown Windsor, can provide visitors with information on where to go in the area to get a good view of loading and unloading operations.

The Detroit River is also one of the major arteries connecting the Great Lakes, and freighters can be seen passing from anywhere along the shore, including the many parks that have been developed along the waterfronts in both Detroit and Windsor. Most of the downbound U.S. freighters that pass through Detroit are carrying iron ore or limestone to steel mills at Detroit or on Lake Erie; downbound Canadian boats would most often be carrying grain to ports along the St. Lawrence River. Upbound vessels will either be carrying coal or, more likely, steaming north in ballast.

Vessel traffic can also be watched from numerous points along the Cuyahoga River that runs through downtown Cleveland; the Buffalo River in Buffalo, New York; the Chicago River and canals that weave their way through urban Chicago; and the Milwaukee River in Milwaukee, Wisconsin. Because of the heavy vessel traffic going up the Cuyahoga to the LTV steel mills and other industrial facilities, boatwatchers stand a better chance of seeing freighters passing there than at Buffalo, Chicago, or Milwaukee.

North of the urban centers, the St. Clair River and St. Marys River are virtual paradises for boatwatchers. The St. Clair River connects Lake Huron with Lake St. Clair and the Detroit River north of the city of Detroit; the St. Marys links Lake Superior with northern Lake Huron. The cities of Port Huron and St. Clair, Michigan, and Sarnia, Ontario, provide excellent vantage points from which to view the heavy vessel traffic on the St. Clair River. At Port Huron, boatwatchers can see freighters passing under the Blue Water Bridge from a park located under the span that connects Port Huron with Sarnia. The retired lightship *Huron* is also moored at the park and river pilots can often be seen being transported to or from saltwater ships by the pilotboat that operates out of the pilot station near the park.

The St. Marys River is the busiest of the three major rivers that connect the Great Lakes. It is the most important artery for iron ore shipments bound from the Lake Superior orefields to mills on Lake Michigan, Lake Erie, and the Detroit River. Some coal and stone also moves upbound on the river. At its north end, the river runs between Sault Ste. Marie, Michigan, and Sault Ste. Marie, Ontario. The commercial and residential areas of both cities stretch along the historic waterway, providing boatwatchers with unparalleled opportunities to watch the long ships passing. Tour boats are also available to take visitors on a three-hour narrated tour through the locks and the harbor at the nearby Algoma Steel mill, where freighters can often be seen unloading iron ore, coal, or limestone.

South of the twin Soos, the river winds through farm and forest land on its way to Lake Huron. Boat traffic can be watched from a number of small communities located along the banks of the river. The best vantage point is at Barbeau, Michigan, where a ferry connects the mainland of Michigan's Upper Peninsula with Neebish Island. The ferry landing, just south of the village, is situated at a point where the river makes a sharp turn into Rock Cut, the downbound channel around the west side of Neebish Island.

At the point where the St. Marys dumps into Lake Huron, the river runs between the village of DeTour and Drummond Island. Ships can be seen entering or leaving the river from DeTour, which is also the pilot station for pilots who take saltwater ships through the St. Marys. Across the river, on Drummond Island, is the loading dock for Drummond Dolomite, producers of a stone very similar to limestone. Freighters can occasionally be seen loading at the dock there.

Lights and Whistles

Boatwatchers will find that the big freighters have a language of their own. Through whistle signals and the arrangements of their running lights, the ships speak to each other in a language unintelligible to most people who watch them from the shore. At the locks or loading and unloading docks, boatwatchers will hear one short blast of a ship's whistle just before it departs the dock, an unexpected, ear-shattering blast that often startles onlookers. The blast is nothing more than a signal from the captain to personnel handling the ship's lines on the dock to cast off the lines. Because of the distances involved, the whistle signal is more effective than trying to holler a command to the linehandlers.

When ships approach or overtake each other on the lakes or rivers, they also use their whistles to indicate their passing intentions. The most commonly heard signal is one long blast, indicating that the ship intends to make a port-to-port passage with the approaching vessel. The approaching ship will then repeat the signal, indicating that its captain has understood the passing agreement. When overtaking a ship, two short blasts would normally be sounded by the overtaking ship, indicating an intent to pass on the port side of the slower vessel.

Another commonly heard signal is one long blast followed by two short blasts, or what is referred to as a "short salute." It is the time-honored way in which mariners exchange greetings as their ships pass. Occasionally the three long and two shorts of the "long salute" are also used.

During fog or limited visibility due to inclement weather conditions, you can also hear ships sounding fog signals. Vessels underway are required to sound one long blast every two minutes. Anchored ships sound one long blast every minute.

The freighters also sound their whistles when approaching bridges that have to be raised or lowered to allow them to pass through. The proper signal for any particular bridge is specified in the volume of the *United States Coast Pilot* covering the Great Lakes. On any given stretch of river, different signals are required for each bridge to avoid confusion on the part of the bridgetenders.

At night, the ships also "talk" to each other with their running lights. Coast Guard rules require the freighters to show a white light at the top of both their bow and stern masts, with the forward light at least fifteen feet lower than the aft light. By observing the relationships between the bow and stern lights of another vessel, a mariner can tell the direction that vessel is steering in. Each ship also carries a red light on its port side and a green light on its starboard side. The sidelights are located above the pilothouse and are boxed in, or shielded, so that you can only see an approaching ship's red light from dead ahead or when you are passing to its port side. Similarly, the approaching ship's green sidelight can only be seen if you are dead ahead or steering to its starboard side. Again, the arrangement of the sidelights aids in determining the direction an approaching ship is moving in. If, for example, you can see both red and green lights showing on an approaching ship it indicates that you are potentially on a collision course and appropriate action needs to be taken to reach a passing agreement with the other vessel.

At anchor, a freighter would show two red lights, one over the top of the other, in lieu of the white lights required when underway. That notifies approaching ships that the vessel is at anchor. It is the responsibility of the approaching ship to stand clear. While there are many other whistle signals and arrangements of lights, those cited here are the ones most often used on the Great Lakes. A knowledge of the signals can help boatwatchers to better understand the "language" of the ships.

Maritime Museums

Boatwatching is not a totally fulfilling experience for many boat buffs, however. It is somewhat analogous to trying to understand a baseball game from out in the parking lot of a stadium. To really understand and appreciate the boats that operate on the lakes, you have to walk the decks, see hatches closeup, look into the cavernous cargo hold, visit the galley, tour crew quarters, see the complexity of the engine room, and stand on the bridge amid the radars and radios and grip the spokes of the ship's wheel.

None of the Great Lakes ships carry paying passengers, so ardent boatwatchers can't just book passage on a freighter. Fortunately, however, there are a number of places around the Great Lakes where boat buffs can go aboard lakers that have been retired from service. At Sault Ste. Marie, Michigan, just downstream from the Soo Locks, visitors can tour the *Str. Valley Camp*, a 525-foot freighter converted into a museum ship by Le Sault de Sainte Marie Historical Sites. The *Valley Camp* was launched in 1917 as the *Louis W. Hill* for Producers Steamship Company. In 1955, the boat was acquired by Wilson Transit Company, which wanted a small vessel to haul ore and stone up the Cuyahoga River to the LTV mills, then owned by Republic Steel. In 1957, Republic Steel purchased the *Valley Camp* from Wilson and put it into service under their own colors. The aging ship was retired by Republic in 1967 and became a museum ship in 1968.

The *Valley Camp* is typical of the straight-deck bulk freighters built during the early part of this century, but visitors need to be aware that it has been out of service for more than two decades and, as a result, differs dramatically from ships in operation today. It is a relic, an antique, that gives visitors a view of what lakers were like during an earlier era in the industry's history. The *Valley Camp*'s cargo holds now house a marine museum, including a special exhibit on the 1975 sinking of the *Edmund Fitzgerald*. The *Fitzgerald* display includes a mangled lifeboat and other equipment recovered after the tragic sinking. Also on display is a magnificent scale model of the *M/V Belle River*, a thousand-foot coal collier operated on the lakes by American Steamship Company.

At Superior, Wisconsin, boat buffs can visit the *Str. Meteor*, the last surviving whaleback, built just before the turn of the century by Captain Alexander McDougall's American Steel Barge Company. Like the *Valley Camp*, the *Meteor* has been converted to a museum ship and houses many excellent exhibits.

In 1986, when many shipping companies were getting rid of older ships that they no longer had cargoes for, several other communities around the lakes acquired vessels for conversion to museum ships. Toledo residents acquired the *Str. Willis B. Boyer*, a 617-foot straight-decker that had been launched in 1911—one of the famous "standard 600-footers." It was the largest freighter on the lakes at that time and held cargo records for iron ore, coal, and rye for more than six years. The *Boyer* was last owned by Cleveland-Cliffs Iron Company and perma-

The museum ship *Valley Camp* at Sault Ste. Marie, Michigan. Launched in 1917, the 545-foot freighter has been at the Soo since 1968, to the delight of tens of thousands of tourists who have visited it over the years. (Author's collection)

nently retired from service in 1985 when Cliffs abandoned its fleet operations.

At Duluth, the *Str. William A. Irvin*, once the flagship of the giant Pittsburgh Steamship Company, is also now open for tours at its berth adjacent to the downtown area. Owned by U.S. Steel throughout its career on the lakes, the *Irvin* had been a regular visitor to the ore docks in Duluth over the years, and many former crewmembers live in the Duluth area, which is headquarters for the USS Great Lakes Fleet, successor to the Pittsburgh fleet. Built in 1938, the 610-foot freighter is the "youngest" of the museum ships and typical of many vessels still in operation today.

Visitors to Erie, Pennsylvania, can visit the restored *Str. Niagara*, which was the oldest operating vessel on the lakes when withdrawn from service in 1985. Built in 1897 at Bay City, Michigan, the 257-foot *Niagara* spent its last twenty-five years as a sandsucker for the Erie Steamship Company, suctioning sand from the bottom of the lake for sale to foundries and concrete manufacturers.

Cleveland, long the unofficial "headquarters" of the Great Lakes shipping industry, finally has a museum ship of its own. When Cleveland-Cliffs abandoned its vessel operation, the Great Lakes Historical Society obtained the *Str. William G. Mather* for use as a museum ship. The *Mather* is a 618-foot straight-decker built in 1925 for Cleveland-Cliffs and named in honor of the company's president. The classic ship was the flagship of the Cliffs fleet from 1925 until 1952. For many years, the *Mather* was engaged in hauling taconite up the Cuyahoga to Republic Steel's mills, so it is likely that it will be right at home in the new berth planned along Cleveland's busy waterfront.

In addition to the museum ships, there are many other maritime museums around the lakes. The largest of them are the Dossin Great Lakes Museum on Belle Isle at Detroit; the Great Lakes Historical Society Museum in Vermilion, Ohio, west of Cleveland; and the Corps of Engineers' Canal Park Museum in Duluth. All three contain extensive exhibits that help visitors understand the Great Lakes maritime industry and its heritage.

Many excellent books have been written about

The *Str. Meteor,* the last surviving whaleback. Built in 1896 by Captain Alexander McDougall's American Steel Barge Co., the unique "pigboat" is now a museum ship at Superior, Wisconsin. (Author's collection)

Built in 1938 as the flagship for the giant Pittsburgh Steamship fleet, the *Str. William A. Irvin* is now a museum ship at Duluth, Minnesota. (Author's collection)

the industry. They fall into three main categories: (1) general books about the industry, similar to *Steamboats and Sailors*, (2) collections of vignettes, primarily dealing with ships that have operated on the lakes, and (3) accounts of shipwrecks and other adventures. An extensive list of books about the Great Lakes shipping industry can be found in the bibliography at the end of this volume. All have contributed to some degree to this book, and they can provide many hours of pleasant entertainment for any "armchair captains" who are interested in furthering their knowledge about the industry. A directory of U.S. bulk fleets operating on the Great Lakes has been included as an appendix for use by boatwatchers. The directory contains a complete listing of the ships owned and operated by each fleet.

The ships that operate on the Great Lakes are marvels of technology. More than that, by virtue of their size alone they stimulate our imaginations and captivate us with the graceful way in which they glide through the water. To boatwatchers through the centuries, the natural beauty of the lakes and their connecting rivers have always been improved upon by the presence of ships on the blue waters. Children who enjoy watching the long ships grow up to be parents who pass on to their children a measure of their love for the beautiful boats.

The history of the shipping industry on the lakes is rich with stories that can spark the imagination of young and old alike: stories about proud ships, stories of adventures upon the Inland Seas, stories of men and women whose lives were intertwined with the constant procession of ships, tales of sailors, storms, and shipwrecks. In the maritime museums and books about the industry, people who cherish the ships and sailors have preserved for posterity the saga of the industry's bygone days, documenting for present and future generations the important role Great Lakes shipping has played in the economic and social history of North America.

Few boatwatchers or armchair captains will ever have the marvelous adventure of making a trip aboard a lake freighter, but today they can capture at least part of the thrill of being a crewmember aboard a laker by visiting one of the growing number of museum ships that have been preserved by groups around the lakes. With the aid of just an average imagination, visitors to the museum ships can experience vicariously what it is like to be "in the window," piloting a ship the length of two football fields through the winding St. Marys River. They can make the long trek down the deck, imagining what it would be like for a wheelsman going aft for a cup of coffee during a night watch on Lake Superior. They can smell the ever-present aroma of hot oil in the engine room and reflect on what it must have been like to be standing the engine watch on the *Fitzgerald* on the evening of November 10, 1975. And they can marvel at the simple, functional beauty of the ships and wonder what marvelous stories they would tell if cold steel could speak.

Epilogue

Sailing Uncharted Waters

And when we see an American flag fluttering on the stern of a laker, we shouldn't think of that ship as a survivor, but a front runner.

—George J. Ryan, President, Lake Carriers' Association, *1988 Annual Report*

A hundred years ago, the Great Lakes maritime industry was in the midst of an unparalleled boom period. In virtually every respect, the final decade of the nineteenth century was quite literally the Golden Age of the maritime industry on the expansive inland seas of North America. During the 1890s, there were between 2,700 and 3,000 ships operating on the lakes, a fleet of record size. That record stands yet today, and in all likelihood it shall stand for eternity.

Not only was the fleet of the 1890s the largest ever, it was also the most diverse. While the economic successes of the early steamboats had sounded the death knell of the age of sail, from one-third to one-half of the fleet of the 1890s was still made up of sailing vessels. They ranged from small, often crudely built lumber hookers to majestic three-

masted schooners like the *J. I. Case*. One of the largest three masters built on the Great Lakes, the wood-hulled *Case* was 208 feet long, with spars towering nearly 200 feet above the water. Built in 1874 for the Case Plow Works of Racine, Wisconsin, the *Case* remained in service until 1933, although its final years were spent as a tow barge.

While there was considerable diversity in the types of sailing vessels operating in the 1890s, there was an even wider range of steamboats on the lakes. The stalwart little *R. J. Hackett*, the prototype for the distinctive Great Lakes bulk freighter that dominated the industry for a century, was still in service, as were many wood-hulled bulkers built along its lines. They had already been overshadowed, however, by iron-hulled and steel-hulled freighters that were twice as long as the 212-foot

Hackett and had five times the carrying capacity of ships of its generation.

In 1898, the "Queen of the Lakes" was the *Str. Samuel F. B. Morse*, a 476-foot goliath built for John D. Rockefeller's Bessemer Steamship Company. Rated at 4,936 gross tons, the *Morse* dwarfed the 921 gross ton *Hackett* and represented the state of the art in shipbuilding on the Great Lakes as the turn of the century neared. Its reign as the largest ship on the lakes would be short-lived, however.

As the decade and the century drew to a close, shipwrights at the American Ship Building yard in Lorain, Ohio, were preparing to launch the *Str. John W. Gates*, the first of the 500-footers. At 5,946 gross tons, the *Gates* and its "sisters" were large enough to carry four ships the size of the *Hackett* in their cargo holds, with room to spare.

Sharing the bulk trade of the 1890s with conventional bulk freighters like the *Hackett* and *Victory* were Captain Alexander McDougall's unusual whaleback freighters that were then at the peak of their popularity with the industry. McDougall's crowning glory, however, was the whaleback passenger steamer *Christopher Columbus*, launched in 1893 for the Chicago World's Fair. During its first year in operation, the ship carried more than two million passengers on day trips from the Chicago waterfront. The *Christopher Columbus* was just one of hundreds of passenger vessels operating on the Great Lakes in the 1890s. With railroads still in their infancy and the days of mass produced automobiles yet to come, the steamers were the primary means of transportation between the port cities dotting the shoreline of the inland seas.

The *Christopher Columbus* was propeller driven, like the bulk freighters, but many of the passenger vessels of the 1890s still used sidewheels for propulsion. Typical of the many sidewheelers in service at the time were the *America*, a 165-foot vessel built primarily for the lower Lake Michigan excursion trade, and the *City of Erie*, a resplendent 316-foot ship built for the overnight Cleveland-to-Buffalo route. Passengers aboard those early steamers were treated to a bird's-eye view of the largest and most diverse commercial fleet ever to operate on the Great Lakes or anywhere else for that matter. In those last years of the nineteenth century, only the ocean fleets of England and Germany were larger than the U.S. fleet on the lakes,[1] and nowhere could you find greater variety in propulsion systems, hull materials, ship design or vessel sizes. It was truly the Golden Age of the Great Lakes maritime industry. Or was it?

Many industry observers would argue that while the 1890s were certainly a special period in the history of the industry, the real Golden Age occurred much more recently. The true gauge of any transportation system is its efficiency, and the giant fleet of the 1890s could not begin to compare in efficiency to the fleet that has operated on the lakes in the second half of the twentieth century.

During the 1890s, the 2,700 to 3,000 commercial vessels operating on the lakes totalled only 1.3 million gross tons, and no ship could carry even 10,000 tons of cargo in a single trip. Iron ore was the predominant cargo on the lakes then, as it is now, but total shipments in any year amounted to less than 14 million tons. By comparison, in 1979 the U.S. fleet on the lakes numbered just over 130 vessels, totalling just over 2 million gross tons, but they moved more than 92 million tons of iron ore. The largest ships—the thousand-footers—were capable of carrying in excess of 60,000 tons per trip. During the decade of the 1970s, the total cargo carried by the industry each year—iron ore, coal, grain, and stone—ranged from a low of 177 million tons in 1977 to a high of almost 215 million tons in both 1973 and 1979. Average annual shipments totalled in excess of 199 million tons for each year of the decade.

If the hallmark of a transportation industry is its efficiency, then the true Golden Age of the shipping industry on the Great Lakes may have been the 1970s. The industry of the 1970s certainly operated at a level of efficiency that could not even have been dreamt of during the 1890s. The industry wasn't as large, nor were the ships as diverse; it was simply more efficient.

Yes, the 1970s were a Golden Age for the industry on the lakes, but that period, too, is now relegated to the history books. Since 1979, the Great Lakes shipping industry has undergone a radical change. After the boom years of the 1970s, few people in the industry were prepared for the staggering events that would begin to unfold with the 1980 shipping season. During 1980, total cargo shipped on the lakes dropped by more than 32 million tons, with iron ore shipments falling by 19 million tons from the previous year. The downward trend continued during the 1981 season, with total shipments falling by another 7 million tons, but with ore shipments holding virtually steady. Then came the 1982 season and total tonnage plummeted by more than 50 million tons, with iron ore dropping by 37 million tons. Between 1979 and 1982, total tonnages shipped on the lakes declined by more than 90 million tons, a drop of 42 percent. Iron ore shipments fell from 92 million tons in 1979 to only 38 million tons during the 1982 season, representing a staggering 59 percent drop.[2]

Only about 70 U.S. ships out of a total fleet of about 120 fitted out at the start of the 1982 season, and many of those were laid-up by July.[3] Around the lakes, more than two thousand sailors found themselves without jobs. Many of them would never sail again. Many wondered whether their fleets, or their industry, would survive.

Few, if any, of the sailors had been around the industry long enough to remember a downturn of comparable severity. A few had experienced the recession of the late 1950s, but more cargo moved in those years than during 1982. In fact, the Great Lakes shipping industry had not experienced such low levels of tonnages since the Great Depression of the 1930s when iron ore shipments fell to as little as 4 million tons one season and total cargo moved amounted to less than 42 million tons.[4] While tonnages increased modestly during the 1983 and 1984 seasons, shipping companies still struggled to find cargoes for their ships. Even the ships that were operating weren't always operating profitably, since some companies dropped their shipping rates in an effort to secure more contracts for their vessels.

The depressed state of the industry was taking its toll on the shipping companies. A number of fleets were rumored to be experiencing serious financial difficulties. Two companies, Cleveland-Cliffs and M. A. Hanna, decided to abandon their marine operations and concentrate on more profitable ventures. Not every company was struggling, however. The fleet operated by the Rouge Steel subsidiary of Ford Motor Company actually prospered during the period. The three Ford straight-deckers, the *William Clay Ford*, *Benson Ford*, and *Ernest R. Breech*, were kept busy hauling iron ore to supply Ford's Detroit steel mill, while the self-unloader *Henry Ford II* brought in coal and stone. Rouge Steel marine officials were even able to land several lucrative con-

tracts for the *Breech* to move grain from Duluth and Superior to Buffalo.

When Cleveland-Cliffs decided to get out of the shipping business, Ford bought the two largest of the Cliffs' vessels, the self-unloaders *Walter A. Sterling* and *Edward B. Greene*, renaming them the *William Clay Ford* and *Benson Ford*, respectively. The former *William Clay* and *Benson* were scrapped. The addition of the two self-unloaders allowed Ford to improve the efficiency of its operations by eliminating the need to maintain and operate expensive bridge cranes that had been used to unload straight-deckers at the Rouge mill. At the same time, the self-unloaders gave Ford the opportunity to compete for cargoes bound for ports without shoreside unloading equipment.

The success of the Ford fleet during the difficult days of the early 1980s was due largely to the fact that the Ford ships were primarily engaged in hauling Ford cargoes. Ford's demand for iron ore, stone, and coal to feed its mills was sufficient to keep the vessels operating. At the same time, they did not have to compete with other fleets, so they were insulated from the price competition that had driven prices down within the Great Lakes industry. Or so most observers thought. During the first season that Ford operated its revitalized fleet, tonnages again dropped off. In 1985 total cargo on the lakes amounted to only 145 million tons, a drop of 19 million tons from the prior season. This dashed industry spirits, which had been buoyed by a brief surge in performance registered in 1984.

At the annual joint conference of the U.S. Lake Carriers' Association and the Canadian Dominion Marine Association, held just before the start of the 1986 shipping season, an international expert on bulk cargo movements told industry officials that it was highly unlikely they would ever again be called upon to move the tonnages they had grown used to during the 1940–1980 period. Roger M. Jones, president of the international bulk shipping consulting firm of Jones, Bardelmeier & Co., told the gathered industry leaders: "Barring a conventional war, there is very little likelihood that lakes shipping will ever make a full recovery from the current slump."[5] Jones based his ominous projections on the changed nature of the American steel industry. The nation's open hearth steel production capacity had dropped from 102 million tons in 1979 to less than 50 million tons

The foreign-flag *Anna* unloads coils of foreign steel at Detroit Marine Terminal. The influx of cheap foreign steel is partially blamed for the recession that staggered the Great Lakes shipping industry during the early 1980s. (Author's collection)

Cleveland-Cliffs's *Willis G. Boyer* and *William P. Snyder, Jr.* in lay-up at Toledo, Ohio, during the shipping recession in the early 1980s. Neither ship would operate again. (Authors' collection)

by 1986 as steel producers dismantled their aging and unprofitable mills. Most analysts anticipated even further reductions. "The shipping situation on the lakes is different than anything we have seen in the past," said Jones. "It's not cyclical. It's structural. The lakes industry is suffering from the same problem that is plaguing the ocean industry— overcapacity." In order to survive, according to Jones, the shipping industry on the lakes needed to act to reduce overcapacity and establish realistic rates. "The size of the fleet needs to be cut by 30 percent by scrapping older vessels," said Jones. "It will be 'survival of the fittest' during the coming years, and it is only the strongest, most imaginative, most innovative companies who will survive."[6]

Jones's predictions proved accurate as the downward trend continued during the 1986 season. A total of only 140 million tons moved on the lakes that season, a decline of 5 million tons from 1985 levels. Iron ore shipments dropped to the 45–46 million ton range, less than half of what had been carried during the record 1979 season, the second

lowest total since the depression years of the 1930s. The industry had begun to act, however. The American shipping companies were sending large numbers of their idle ships to the shipbreakers. Fleet size was cut from about 135 vessels in 1980 to 88 at the close of the 1986 season, a loss of 47 ships. Between 1976 and 1986, 62 U.S. vessels had been scrapped.

Just as significantly, the last new ship added to the U.S. fleet had been launched in 1985, and none of the shipping companies were even discussing the possibility that they would have any new vessels built in the foreseeable future. For the first time since the Great Depression, U.S. shipyards on the Great Lakes were idle.

George Ryan, president of the Lake Carriers' Association, acknowledged that the industry was struggling, but countered by pointing out that the U.S. fleet was "shrinking on paper only." Ryan noted that the sixty-two U.S. ships scrapped during the 1976– 86 period had an average age of sixty, old even by freshwater standards. The sixty-two vessels had an average per trip carrying capacity of only 13,419

The straight-decker *William Clay Ford* upbound light on Lake St. Clair. The last of the AAA-boats launched during the Korean War, in 1984 the 767-foot flagship of the Ford Motor Company fleet had the dubious distinction of being the first of its class to go to the shipbreakers. (Author's collection)

tons, half that of the newest generation of river-class lakers and less than one-fifth the capacity of the massive thousand-footers. Fifty-seven of the sixty-two ships were straight-deckers, which lacked the sophisticated self-unloading systems that had become the standard for the industry. The scrapped vessels had become excess to the industry not just as a result of the reduced tonnages being shipped, according to Ryan, but because they had largely been made obsolete by the newest generation of self-unloading freighters.[7] Between 1971 and 1982, the U.S. companies had commissioned twenty-eight new ships, thirteen of which were thousand-footers.

All of the new ships were self-unloaders, capable of discharging cargo at virtually any port on the lakes without the need for expensive shoreside unloading equipment that was needed by the traditional straight-deckers. Further, the 88 ships operated by the industry in 1985 had a combined per trip carrying capacity of 2.2 million tons, almost equal to the single trip carrying capacity of the 1938 fleet that numbered 305 ships, and greater than the capacity of the 3,000 ship fleets of the 1890s. The 13 thousand-footers alone had a combined carrying capacity of about 800,000 tons, while the 62 vessels sent to the shipbreakers during the ten-year period ending in 1986 could together carry only 832,000 tons. From the standpoint of efficiency, each thousand-footer was the equivalent of four or five of the older, smaller bulk freighters.

When Great Lakes fleets stopped building new ships in the early 1980s, Bay Shipbuilding of Sturgeon Bay, Wisconsin, landed a contract to build three container ships for Sea-Land's operations in the Pacific, including the *Sea-Land Kodiak,* shown here on sea trials on Lake Michigan. Since the *Kodiak* was launched, no new vessels have been built at Bay, the only shipyard left on the lakes with a drydock large enough to accommodate the thousand-footers. (Bay Shipbuilding)

A Coast Guard patrol boat on an emergency run passes Bethlehem Steel's 1,000-foot *M/V Burns Harbor* in the St. Marys River. Many Great Lakes boatwatchers dislike the blocky design of this latest generation of ships. (Author's collection)

Ryan, too, mourned the passing of the older freighters, many of which had colorful histories on the lakes, but he was quick to point out that "sentimentality cannot take precedence over economic realities. In order to survive in this super-competitive world, only the most efficient vessels have a future on the lakes. And by using the most efficient vessels, we help insure that Great Lakes shipping has a future."[8]

As if in response to the industry's severe streamlining, tonnages rose during both the 1987 and 1988 seasons. Overall tonnages rose by almost 30 million to more than 169 million, while iron ore shipments were up over 15 million tons by the end of the two seasons, totalling almost 61 million tons. Both iron ore and total cargo shipments reached their highest level since the 1981 season.

Further scrappings had reduced the fleet to less than seventy ships, but the shipping companies had 95 percent of their available carrying capacity in operation by the peak of the 1988 season. Even more importantly, sixty-two of those ships were still in operation on December 15, and fifty continued to operate into January as the shipping companies struggled to meet demands for cargo movements. With an unusually mild winter on the upper lakes, several ships continued to operate throughout much of the winter. The season didn't officially close until mid-March ice made further operations impossible.[9]

Lake Carriers' officials attributed much of the success of the 1988 season to the effectiveness of the Voluntary Restraint Arrangement (VRA) program implemented by the Reagan administration in 1984. This was an effort to reduce steel imports to no more than 20 percent of the total U.S. consumption and allow U.S. producers to modernize in order to compete better with foreign manufacturers. In 1984, imported steel accounted for a staggering 26.4 percent of total U.S. consumption, an all-time high. The VRA program was successful in gradually reducing imports after 1984, with the total falling to 20.3 percent of U.S. consumption in 1988. The reductions in imports allowed the domestic steel industry to operate at more than 90 percent of its total capacity throughout most of 1988, thereby increasing the demand for iron ore, stone, and coal movements on the lakes.

The VRA program expired in September 1989, however, and LCA officials are concerned that increases in steel imports could again stagger their industry. "To believe that foreign steelmakers will not again inundate the U.S. market with subsidized steel is naive," said an industry spokesperson. "President Bush has pledged his support for an extension of the VRA program. Congress should follow suit, and quickly, so further modernization of the American steel industry can proceed on schedule."[10]

The threat of increases in imports of foreign steel is only one of several issues that could have an impact on the future of the shipping industry on the Great Lakes. For example, both U.S. and Canadian fleets have taken strong positions against "user fee" legislation under consideration by their respective governments. With Ottawa and Washington struggling to reduce massive budget deficits, they have moved toward implementation of programs that would require users to pay for services they get from the federal governments. In the case of the shipping industry, user fee legislation could include services the industry receives from agencies like the Coast Guard and Corps of Engineers. This might include the costs of icebreaking, dredging of harbors and channels and construction and operation of locks. Costs of those programs would be allocated among the various users, including commercial shipping companies and recreational boaters. For the commercial fleets, user fees could add dramatically to their operating costs and potentially damage their competitive position within the transportation industry.

While the U.S. and Canadian fleets are united in their opposition to the proposed user fees, there are also issues over which they are at odds. The Canadian fleets, for example, would like U.S. law changed so that they can participate in U.S. intercoastal cargo movements. The U.S. intercoastal trade, involving shipments from one U.S. port to another, including ports on the Great Lakes, has been reserved for American-flag vessels since passage of the Jones Act in 1920. In recent years, the Canadian fleets have on several occasions attempted to have provisions of the Jones Act waived so that their ships could compete in iron ore, coal, and stone movements between U.S. ports. Having already lost most of the cross-lakes trade to the Canadian shipping companies, U.S. fleet officials have been vehement in their opposition to allowing their neighbors across the border to compete in the coastwise trade.

U.S. fleets on the lakes just cannot compete with

A foreign-flag vessel unloading cargo at an Algoma Steel dock in Sault Ste. Marie, Ontario. The salty is moored to the retired Great Lakes freighter *Sewell Avery*, which was sunk to form the face for the dock. Launched in 1943 as the Maritime Class freighter *Lancashire*, the *Avery* spent its entire career operating for U.S. Steel's famous "tin-stacker" fleet. (Author's collection)

Columbia Transportation's *Str. Crispin Oglebay* was laid up from 1981 until 1989 as the result of the downturn in shipping business on the Great Lakes. Shown here near the end of the successful 1989 season, the *Oglebay* is decorated for the holiday season with a lighted Christmas tree at the end of its self-unloading boom. (Institute for Great Lakes Research, Bowling Green State University)

foreign-flag operators. That is clearly evident in the pattern of trade between the U.S. and Canada on the Great Lakes, where virtually all of the cargo is now carried aboard Canadian ships at rates well below those that would be charged by the U.S. fleets. To a large extent, the U.S. operators are responsible for their own competitive disadvantages. Over the years, they have agreed to labor contracts that force them to carry more crewmembers on their ships than foreign competitors do, to pay higher salaries, and to provide more extravagant fringe benefit packages. On the lakes, U.S. ships normally operate with 3 to 10 more crewmembers than similar Canadian vessels, at an annual added cost of from $200,000 to $750,000 per ship. That added crew cost gets translated into higher costs per ton for the American fleets, putting them at a competitive disadvantage.

Another issue that troubles Great Lakes shipping officials is the extent to which their industry is dependent on the Poe Lock at Sault Ste. Marie. Fully two-thirds of the ships in today's U.S. fleet are too large to use the other locks available at the Soo. This creates a potentially disastrous situation for both the shipping and steel industries should the Poe be out of commission for any reason. Construction of another Poe-size lock at the Soo was authorized by Congress in 1986, but the latest Corps of Engineers projections suggest that construction of the new lock cannot begin until 1992 at the earliest, with completion no earlier than 2001. Disputes over funding the $240 million lock could delay construction even further.

The industry has also been plagued by sporadic shortages of qualified personnel at peak periods during the past several seasons. Though not as severe as the shortages experienced during the 1978 and 1979 seasons, they create serious problems for an industry that is prohibited by Coast Guard regulations from operating a vessel without a full crew. Some relief has been provided by the Great Lakes Maritime Academy, but it, too, has been seriously affected by the depression that ravaged the industry during the 1980s. When the academy was expanded after the record seasons at the end of the 1970s, it was intended that the school would eventually be able to admit 150 students a year to the three-year program, for a total of 450 students in residence at a time. During the 1988–89 academic year, however, only 53 cadets were enrolled in the deck and engine

programs at the academy. With employment prospects in the downsized shipping industry still far from certain, the school has been experiencing difficulty in attracting new students.

The downsized industry still has an important role to play, however. The modest 169 million tons of bulk cargoes moved by the industry during the 1988 season were transported at rates from 20 to 50 percent less than would have been charged by railroads, the next most efficient mode of moving bulk cargo. Rates aren't the only issue, though. The simple fact is that neither railroads nor trucking companies have the capacity to handle the tonnages carried each year by lake freighters. In 1988, for example, it would have taken 150,000 trains, each made up of 100 rail cars, or more than 2 million large trucks to replace the small fleet that operated on the lakes that year. To paraphrase Mark Twain, himself an old steamboat pilot: Reports of the industry's demise are clearly premature. In reality, the industry has never been more efficient than it is today, and it continues to be essential to the economic well-being of both the U.S. and Canada. "Great Lakes shipping is here to stay," LCA President George Ryan stated emphatically in 1986. "We've held our own against a recession and a barrage of steel imports, and we'll continue to do so."[11]

It is, however, an industry that has changed in some fundamental ways, and more changes can be expected in the future. It is an industry operating on uncharted, unfamiliar waters, where the unexpected has become commonplace. The pervasive uncertainties that confront the industry were borne out in the spring of 1989 when it was announced that Ford Motor Company had decided to sell its fleet to the Interlake Steamship Company. After surviving the shipping depression of the 1980s almost unscathed, Ford officials concluded that the bulk materials they needed to supply their River Rouge steelmaking operations could be moved more efficiently by other companies.

The Ford vessels were renamed and entered the 1989 season painted in the colors of the Interlake fleet. Thus ended Ford's sixty-five-year tradition in Great Lakes shipping, dating back to the 1924 launching of the *Henry Ford II*, the first of the Ford fleet. As if to insure the new industry's link to its past, however, Interlake officials rechristened the *Henry Ford II* as the *Samuel Mather*. It sails into the

When Cleveland-Cliffs abandoned its marine operations in the fall of 1984, Ford Motor Company purchased the *Walter A. Sterling* and renamed it the *William Clay Ford*. When Ford went out of the shipping business in 1989, the 826-foot self-unloader was purchased by the Interlake Steamship Company and rechristened as the *Lee A. Tregurtha*. (Author's collection)

uncertain future bearing the name of one of the industry's most respected pioneers.

The industry has changed greatly since Sam Mather joined with Colonel James Pickands and Jay Morse to form Pickands, Mather & Company in 1883. The waterway has changed, the people have changed, the ships have changed, and even the cargoes have changed. Many in the industry, and a lot of boat buffs around the lakes, would cry out as Henry Arthur Jones did in *Silver King*: "Oh God! Put back Thy universe and give me yesterday."

But the past is now merely prologue, the logbook into which the successes and failures of today and tomorrow will be entered. For the shipping industry on North America's great inland seas, the log is thick, recording a saga of epic proportions. It is upon those dog-eared pages that the continuing story of the steamboats and sailors of the Great Lakes will be entered.

Notes

1. James Barry, *Ships of the Great Lakes* (Berkeley: Howell-North Books, 1973), 145.
2. *1982 Annual Report* (Cleveland: Lake Carriers' Association, 1983), 18.
3. George J. Ryan, "Great Lakes Shipping at the Mid-Decade," *Seaway Review* (Jan.–Mar. 1986): 67.
4. Jacques LesStrang, *Cargo Carriers of the Great Lakes* (New York: American Legacy Press, 1977), 15.
5. Roger M. Jones, "The Challenge of Survival," *Seaway Review* (July–Sept. 1986): 25.
6. Ibid.
7. George J. Ryan, "Changing of the Guard," *Seaway Review* (Oct.–Dec. 1986): 71.
8. Ibid., 72.
9. *1988 Annual Report* (Cleveland: Lake Carriers' Association, 1989), 56.
10. Ibid., 27.
11. Ryan, "Great Lakes Shipping at Mid-Decade," 69.

Appendix:
Directory of U.S. Great Lakes Fleets and Ships

Abbreviations Used

M/V = Diesel powered
Str. = Steam powered
(S) = Self-unloader
(SC) = Self-unloading cement carrier

American Steamship Company
3200 Marine Midland Center
Buffalo, New York 14203

Vessel	Year Built	Length	Beam	Mid-Summer Capacity
M/V Indiana Harbor (S)	1979	1,000	105	61,390
M/V Walter J. MacCarthy, Jr. (S)	1977	1,000	105	61,390
M/V St. Clair (S)	1976	770	92	39,560
M/V Adam E. Cornelius (S)	1973	680	78	27,340
M/V American Mariner (S)	1980	730	78	31,770
M/V H. Lee White (S)	1974	704	78	30,577
M/V Charles E. Wilson (S)	1973	680	78	29,260
M/V American Republic (S)	1981	635	68	24,270
M/V Buffalo (S)	1978	635	68	23,407
M/V Sam Laud (S)	1975	635	68	23,407
M/V Nicolet (S)	1905	535	60	11,536
Total:	11 vessels			363,907

Bethlehem Steel Corporation
Great Lakes Steamship Division
Rock Run South
5700 Lombardo Centre, Suite 135
Seven Hills, Ohio 44131

M/V Burns Harbor (S)	1980	1,000	105	61,000
M/V Stewart J. Cort (S)	1972	1,000	105	58,000
Total:	2 vessels			119,000

Cement Transit Company
(Subsidiary of Medusa Cement)
P.O. Box 5668
Cleveland, Ohio 44101

Str. Medusa Challenger (SC)	1906	552	56	11,300
Medusa Conquest (Barge) (SC)	1987	410	55	5,443
Total:	2 vessels			16,743

Cleveland Tankers
55 Public Square
Cleveland, Ohio 44101

M/V Gemini (Tankship)	1978	433	65	7,860
M/V Jupiter (Tankship)	1976	391	60	6,350
M/V Saturn (Tankship)	1974	384	55	5,550
Total:	2 vessels			13,410

Coastwise Trading Company
(A subsidiary of Amoco Oil Company)
Riley Road/Indiana Harbor
East Chicago, Indiana 46312

Vessel	Year Built	Length	Beam	Mid-Summer Capacity
M/V Michigan (Tug)	1982	115	34	N/A
Great Lakes (Tank barge)	1982	414	60	10,150
	Total:	1 vessel		10,150

Erie Sand Steamship Company
P.O. Box 153
Erie, Pennsylvania 16512

M/V Richard J. Reiss (S)	1943	621	60	15,173
	Total:	1 vessel		15,173

Inland Lakes Management
P.O. Box 646
Alpena, Michigan 49707

Str. J. A. W. Iglehart (SC)	1936	502	68	12,300
Str. S. T. Crapo (SC)	1927	403	60	8,900
Str. Emory M. Ford (SC)	1898	428	50	7,100
Str. J. B. Ford (SC)	1904	440	50	7,400
M/V Paul H. Townsend (SC)	1945	447	50	8,400
M/V Lewis G. Harriman (SC)	1923	350	55	6,300
Str. Alpena (SC)	1942	520	67	12,000
	Total:	7 vessels		62,300

Inland Steel Company
3210 Watling Street
East Chicago, Indiana 46312

M/V Joseph L. Block (S)	1976	728	78	37,200
Str. Edward L. Ryerson	1960	730	75	27,500
Str. Wilfred Sykes (S)	1949	678	70	21,500
	Total:	3 vessels		86,200

Interlake Steamship Company
629 Euclid Avenue
400 National City Bank Building
Cleveland, Ohio 44114

M/V Paul R. Tregurtha (S)	1981	1,014	105	62,200
M/V James R. Barker (S)	1976	1,000	105	60,500
M/V Mesabi Miner (S)	1977	1,000	105	60,500
Str. Charles M. Beeghly (S)	1959	806	75	31,000
Str. John Sherwin (S)	1958	806	75	31,500
Str. Herbert C. Jackson (S)	1959	690	75	24,800
Str. J. L. Mauthe	1953	647	70	21,400
Str. Elton Hoyt 2nd (S)	1952	698	70	22,300
Str. Lee A. Tregurtha (S)	1942	826	75	29,100
Str. Kaye E. Barker (S)	1952	767	70	25,360
M/V Samuel Mather (S)	1924	611	62	13,300
	Total:	11 vessels		346,260

Kinsman Lines
20325 Center Ridge Road
Cleveland, Ohio 44116

Str. Kinsman Enterprise	1927	631	65	16,000
Str. Kinsman Independent	1952	642	67	18,800
	Total:	2 vessels		34,800

Litton Great Lakes Corporation
P.O. Box 6241
Erie, Pennsylvania 16512

M/V Presque Isle (S) (Intergrated Tug-Barge)	1973	1,000	105	52,000
	Total:	1 vessel		52,000

M. A. Hanna Company
100 Erieview Plaza
Cleveland, Ohio 44114

M/V George A. Stinson (S)	1978	1,000	105	59,000
	Total:	1 vessel		59,000

Oglebay Norton Company
Columbia Transportation Division
P.O. Box 6508
Cleveland, Ohio 44101

Vessel	Year Built	Length	Beam	Mid-Summer Capacity
M/V Columbia Star (S)	1981	1,000	105	61,500
M/V Oglebay Norton (S)	1978	1,000	105	78,850
Str. Middletown (S)	1943	730	75	25,320
Str. Armco (S)	1953	767	70	25,000
Str. Reserve (S)	1953	767	70	27,400
M/V Fred R. White, Jr. (S)	1978	635	68	24,100
Str. Buckeye (S)	1952	699	70	23,200
Str. Courtney Burton (S)	1953	690	70	22,425
M/V Wolverine (S)	1974	630	68	19,700
M/V Joseph H. Frantz (S)	1925	618	62	13,600
Str. J. Burton Ayers (S)	1943	620	60	15,670
Str. Robert C. Norton (S)	1943	621	60	15,600
Str Crispin Oglebay (S)	1943	621	60	15,600

Pringle Transit Company
(Owned and operated by Oglebay Norton)

Vessel	Year Built	Length	Beam	Capacity
M/V William R. Roesch (S)	1973	630	68	19,700
M/V Paul Thayer (S)	1973	630	68	19,700

Total: 15 vessels 468,365

USS Great Lakes Fleet, Inc.
400 Missabe Building
Duluth, Minnesota 55802

Vessel	Year Built	Length	Beam	Capacity
M/V Edwin H. Gott (S)	1978	1,004	105	62,200
M/V Edgar B. Speer (S)	1980	1,004	105	62,200
M/V Roger Blough (S)	1972	858	105	43,900
Str. John G. Munson (S)	1952	768	72	25,550
Str. Arthur M. Anderson (S)	1952	767	70	25,360
Str. Philip R. Clarke (S)	1952	767	70	25,360
Str. Cason J. Calloway (S)	1952	767	70	25,300
M/V George A. Sloan (S)	1943	621	60	15,800
M/V Myron C. Taylor (S)	1929	604	60	12,450
M/V Calcite II (S)	1929	605	60	12,650
Str. Irvin L. Clymer (S)	1917	552	60	11,850

Total: 11 vessels 322,620

Bibliography

Barcus, Frank. *Freshwater Fury*. Detroit: Wayne State Univ. Press, 1960.

Barry, James P. *The Fate of the Lakes*. Grand Rapids, MI: Baker Book House, 1972.

———. *Ships of the Great Lakes*. Berkeley: Howell—North Books, 1973.

———. *Wrecks and Rescues of the Great Lakes: A Photographic History*. San Diego: Howell-North Books, 1981.

Beasley, Norman. *Freighters of Fortune*. New York: Harper & Brothers, 1930.

Benford, Harry. "Samuel Plimsoll: His Book and His Mark." *Seaway Review*, (Jan.-Mar. 1986): 79.

———. "Sixty Years of Shipbuilding." paper presented at the meeting of the Great Lakes Section of the Society of Naval Architects & Marine Engineers, October 5, 1956.

———. "Tight Corners: The Innovative American Republic." *Seaway Review* (Autumn 1981): 33–46.

Beukema, Christian. "The Demonstration: U.S. Steel, Winter 1970—71." *Seaway Review* (Summer 1971): 11–15.

Bowen, Dana Thomas. *Lore of the Lakes*. Daytona Beach: Dana Thomas Bowen, 1940.

———. *Memories of the Lakes*. Cleveland: Freshwater Press, 1969.

Boyer, Dwight. *Ghost Ships of the Great Lakes*. New York: Dodd, Mead & Company, 1968.

———, *Great Stories of the Great Lakes*. New York: Dodd, Mead & Company, 1966.

Brough, Lawrence A. *Autos on the Water*. Columbus: Chatham Communicators, 1987.

Channing, Edward, and Marion F. Lansing. *The Story of the Great Lakes*. New York: Macmillan Co., 1909.

Characteristics and Index of Maritime Administration Ship Designs. Washington, DC: U.S. Department of Transportation, 1987.

Clary, James. *Ladies of the Lakes*. Lansing: Michigan Department of Natural Resources, 1981.

Clowes, Ernest S. *Shipways to the Sea*. Baltimore: Williams and Wilkins Company, 1929.

Conrad, Joseph. "Heart of Darkness." In *Tales of Land and Sea*, 33–104. Garden City, NY: Hanover House, 1953.

Curwood, James Oliver. *The Great Lakes*. 1909.

Cuthbertson, George A. *Freshwater*. New York: Macmillan Co., 1931.

Deck and Engine Officers Supply and Demand, 1981–1990. Cleveland: Great Lakes Region Office, U.S. Maritime Administration, 1981.

Dewar, Gary S. "A Forgotten Class." *Telescope* (Mar.–Apr. 1989): 31–39.

"The Directions of Change." *Seaway Review* (Oct.–Dec. 1986): 9–104.

Dominion Marine Association Annual Report, 1986. Ottawa: Dominion Marine Association, 1986.

Doner, Mary Francis. *The Salvager: The Life of Captain Tom Reid on the Great Lakes*. Minneapolis: Ross and Haines, 1958.

Dorin, Patrick C. *The Lake Superior Iron Ore Railroads*. Seattle: Superior Publishing Co., 1969.

Dowling, Rev. Edward J., S.J. *The Lakers of World War I*. Detroit: Univ. of Detroit Press, 1967.

Ela, Jonathon. *The Faces of the Great Lakes*. San Francisco: Sierra Club Books, 1977.

Ellis, William Donohue. *The Cuyahoga*. New York: Holt, Rinehart and Winston, 1966.

Final Survey Report on Navigation Season Extension for the Great Lakes and St. Lawrence Seaway. Fort Belvoir, VA: U.S. Army Corps of Engineers, 1981.

Final Survey Study for Great Lakes and St. Lawrence Seaway Navigation Extension. Detroit: U.S. Army Corps of Engineers, 1979.

Glick, David T., ed. *Lake Log Chips*. Perrysburg, OH:

Institute for Great Lakes Research, Bowling Green State University, 1986–88.

Graham, R. D. "Benny and the Boom." *Telescope*. (Nov.-Dec. 1980): 154–56.

The Great Lakes/Seaway: Setting a Course for the '80s. Ottawa: Ontario Provincial Great Lakes/Seaway Task Force, 1981.

Greenwood, John O. *Greenwood's Guide to Great Lakes Shipping*. Cleveland: Freshwater Press, 1967–85.

———. *Namesakes of the Lakes*. Cleveland: Freshwater Press, 1970.

———. *Namesakes II*. Cleveland: Freshwater Press, 1973.

———. *Namesakes, 1900–1909*. Cleveland: Freshwater Press, 1987.

———. *Namesakes, 1910–1919*. Cleveland: Freshwater Press, 1986.

———. *Namesakes, 1920–1929*. Cleveland: Freshwater Press, 1984.

———. *Namesakes, 1930–1955*. Cleveland: Freshwater Press, 1978.

———. *Namesakes, 1956–1980*. Cleveland: Freshwater Press, 1981.

Gross, Harriet Engle, Marie Van Gemert, and Christine Thomas. "A Distance Between Worlds." *Seaway Review* (Winter 1983): 83–87.

———. "The Limitations They Cannot Ignore." *Seaway Review* (Summer 1984): 49–53.

———. "The Ongoing Dilemma." *Seaway Review* (Spring 1984): 53–58.

Hatcher, Harlan. *A Century of Iron and Men*. New York: Bobbs—Merrill Co., 1950.

———. *The Great Lakes*. New York: Oxford Univ. Press, 1944.

———and Erich A. Walter. *A Pictorial History of the Great Lakes*. New York: Bonanza Books, 1963.

Havighurst, Walter, ed. *The Great Lakes Reader*. New York: Macmillan Co., 1969.

———. *The Long Ships Passing*. New York: Macmillan Co., 1942.

———. *Vein of Iron*. New York: World Publishing Company, 1958.

Inches, H. C. *The Great Lakes Wooden Shipbuilding Era*. Cleveland: H. C. Inches, 1962.

Kelley, John J. "An Historic Thirty-Six Hours of Superior Seamanship." *Inland Seas* (Summer, 1984): 82–88.

Knight, David, ed. *Lake Log Chips*. Boyne City, MI: Harbor House Publishers, 1989.

Kuttruf, Karl, Robert E. Lee, and David T. Glick. *Ships of the Great Lakes: A Pictorial History*. Detroit: Wayne State Univ. Press, 1976.

Lake Carriers' Association Annual Report. Cleveland: Lake Carriers' Association, 1981–88.

Larson, John W. *Essayons: A History of the Detroit District, U.S. Army Corps of Engineers*. Detroit: U.S. Army Corps of Engineers, 1981.

LesStrang, Jacques. *Cargo Carriers of the Great Lakes*. New York: American Legacy Press, 1981.

———, ed. *The Great Lakes Ports of North America*. Ann Arbor: LesStrang Publishing Corporation, 1973.

———, ed. *The Great Lakes/St. Lawrence System*. Maple City, MI: Harbor House Publishers, 1984.

———. *Seaway*. Seattle: Salisbury Press, 1976.

———, ed. *Seaway Review*. Boyne City, MI: Harbor House Publishers, 1979–88.

Mabee, Carleton. *The Seaway Story*. New York: Macmillan Co., 1961.

McCormick, Jay. *November Storm*. Garden City, NY: Doubleday, Doran and Co., 1943.

Manse, Thomas. *Know Your Ships*. Sault Ste. Marie, MI: Thomas Manse, 1985.

Mansfield, J. B., ed. *History of the Great Lakes*. Chicago: J. H. Beers and Co., 1899. Reprint. Cleveland: Freshwater Press, 1972.

Marine Casualty Report: SS Carl D. Bradley. Washington, DC: U.S. Coast Guard, 1959.

Marine Casualty Report: SS Cedarville. Washington, DC: U.S. Coast Guard, 1967.

Marine Casualty Report: SS Daniel J. Morrell. Washington, DC: U.S. Coast Guard, 1968.

Marine Casualty Report: SS Edmund Fitzgerald. Washington, DC: U.S. Coast Guard, 1977.

Meakin, Alexander C. *G: The Story of The Great Lakes Towing Co.*. Vermilion, OH: Great Lakes Historical Society, 1984.

Mills, James Cook. *Our Inland Seas*. Chicago: A. C. McClurg and Co., 1910. Reprint. Cleveland: Freshwater Press, 1976.

Monson, Terry D. *The Role of Lakes Shipping in the Great Lakes Economy*. Houghton, MI: Michigan Technological Univ., 1980.

M/V James R. Barker. Cleveland: Pickands Mather and Co., 1976.

Myers, Harry F. "Remembering the 504's." *Inland Seas* 44, no. 2 (Summer 1988): 76–93.

Norrby, Ralph A., and Donald E. Ridley. "Notes on Thrusters for Ship Maneuvering and Dynamic Positioning." Paper presented at the annual meeting of the American Society of Naval Architects and Marine Engineers, November 1980.

Nute, Grace Lee. *Lake Superior*. New York: Bobbs-Merrill Co., 1944.

Parker, Jack. *Shipwrecks of Lake Huron*. AuTrain, MI: Avery Color Studios, 1986.

Plimsoll, Samuel. *Our Seamen, An Appeal*. London: Virtue and Co., 1873.

Quaife, Milo M. *Lake Michigan*. New York: Bobbs-Merrill, 1944.

Rabe, Jacqueline. "The Four Welland Canals." *Telescope* (Nov.-Dec. 1985): 147–51.

Ratigan, William. *Great Lakes Shipwrecks & Survivals*. Grand Rapids, MI: Wm. B. Eerdmans Publishing Co., 1960.

Rondot, Peter T., ed. *Great Lakes Red Book*. St. Clair Shores, MI: Fourth Seacoast Publishing Co., 1971.

Ryan, George J. "A Changing of the Guard." *Seaway Review* (Oct.–Dec. 1986): 71–72.

———. "Enhancing Weather Forecasting on the Great Lakes." *Seaway Review* (Sept. 1984): 99.

———, "Great Lakes Shipping at Mid-Decade" *Seaway Review* (Jan.–Mar. 1986): 67–69.

The St. Lawrence Seaway. Washington, DC: U.S. Department of Transportation, 1984.

"Stmr. McKee Sons Cited for Outstanding Seamanship." *The Bulletin of the Lake Carriers' Association* (July–Sept. 1974): 3–6.

Stonehouse, Frederick. *The Wreck of the Edmund Fitzgerald*. AuTrain, MI: Avery Color Studios, 1977.

Stories of the Great Lakes. New York: Century Co., 1893.

Telescope. Detroit: Great Lakes Maritime Institute, 1980–88.

Tripp, C. E., and G. H. Plude. "One Thousand Foot Great Lakes Self-Unloader—Erie Marine Hull 101." Paper presented to the Great Lakes and Great Rivers Section, Society of Naval Architects and Marine Engineers, January 21, 1971.

True, Dwight. "Sixty Years of Shipbuilding." Paper presented to the Great Lakes Section of the Society of Naval Architects and Marine Engineers, October 1956.

Turpin, Edward A., and William A. MacEwen. *Merchant Marine Officers Handbook*. Cambridge, MD: Cornell Maritime Press, 1965.

United States Coast Pilot, Vol. 6 (Washington, DC: U.S. Department of Commerce, 1988.

"U.S.–Canadian Cargo Disparities." *Seaway Review* (Jan.–Mar. 1986): 59–61.

Van Der Linden, Rev. Peter, ed. *Great Lakes Ships We Remember*. Cleveland: Freshwater Press, 1979.

———. *Great Lakes Ships We Remember II*. Cleveland: Freshwater Press, 1984.

Whitlark, Frederick Louis. *Introduction to the Lakes*. New York: Greenwich Book Publishers, 1959.

Williams, E. B., Kent C. Thornton, W. R. Douglas, and Paul Miedlich. "Design and Construction of Great Lakes Bulk Freighter Wilfred Sykes." *Marine Engineering and Shipping Review*, June 1950.

Wilson, James A. "A Critical Look at our Marine Transportation." *Seaway Review* (Sept. 1983): 11–13.

Wilterding, John H., Jr. *McDougall's Dream: The American Whaleback*. Duluth: Lakeside Printing, 1969.

Wright, Richard. *Freshwater Whales*. Kent, OH: Kent State Univ. Press, 1969.

Index

Titles in the Great Lakes Book Series